MARK WAID

TOM PEYER

WILFREDO TORRES

CAPTAIN KID™

VOLUME
1

SUPER-PEOPLE PROBLEMS

KELLY FITZPATRICK

A LARGER WORLD

AFTERSHOCK™

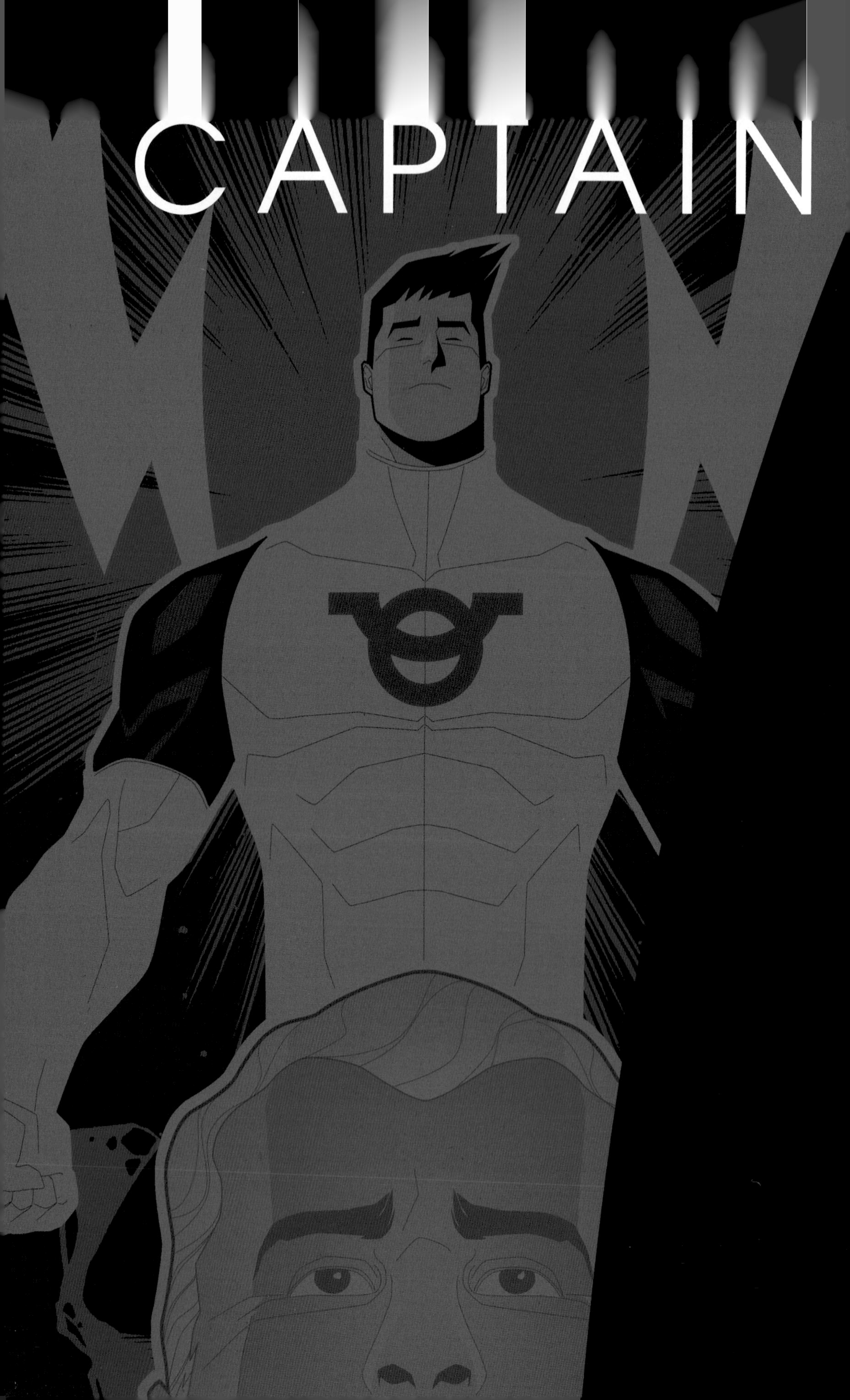
CAPTAIN

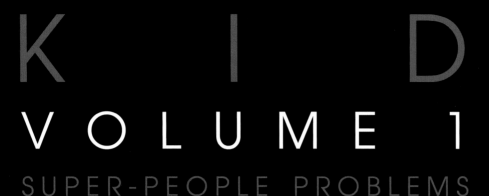

KID VOLUME 1

SUPER-PEOPLE PROBLEMS

MARK WAID &
TOM PEYER co-creators & co-writers

WILFREDO TORRES artist

issue #4 artwork by
BRENT PEEPLES & **ERIC GAPSTUR**

KELLY FITZPATRICK colorist

A LARGER WORLD letterers

WILFREDO TORRES & **KELLY FITZPATRICK** front & original series covers

JUAN DOE variant cover

JOHN J. HILL book & logo designer

MIKE MARTS editor

AFTERSHOCK™

MIKE MARTS - Editor-in-Chief • JOE PRUETT - Publisher/ Chief Creative Officer • LEE KRAMER - President
JAWAD QURESHI - SVP, Investor Relations • JON KRAMER - Chief Executive Officer • MIKE ZAGARI - SVP Digital/Creative
JAY BEHLING - Chief Financial Officer • STEPHAN NILSON - Publishing Operations Manager
LISA Y. WU - Retailer/Fan Relations Manager • ASHLEY WYATT - Publishing Assistant

AfterShock Trade Dress and Interior Design by JOHN J. HILL • AfterShock Logo Design by COMICRAFT
Original series production (issues 3-5) by CHARLES PRITCHETT • Proofreading by J. HARBORE & DOCTOR Z.
Publicity: contact AARON MARION (aaron@fifteenminutes.com) & RYAN CROY (ryan@fifteenminutes.com) at 15 MINUTES

PRINTED IN KOREA. First Printing: May 2017. 10 9 8 7 6 5 4 3 2 1

AFTERSHOCKCOMICS.COM Follow us on social media

INTRODUCTION

MARK WAID: CAPTAIN KID is the story of a middle-aged man who can become a super-powered teenager.

TOM PEYER: And he's not tortured by it.

WAID: Right. He really likes becoming this super-kid whose joints don't hurt and whose job isn't going away. But there are problems. His life isn't rejuvenated along with his body. His friends are still getting older, his job is less relevant. He gets to taste this fantasy, but his world stays real.

PEYER: That was something we didn't want to lose sight of, making his life believable. A panel in CAPTAIN KID #2 — chapter two of this book (shown on the right) — really caught my eye.

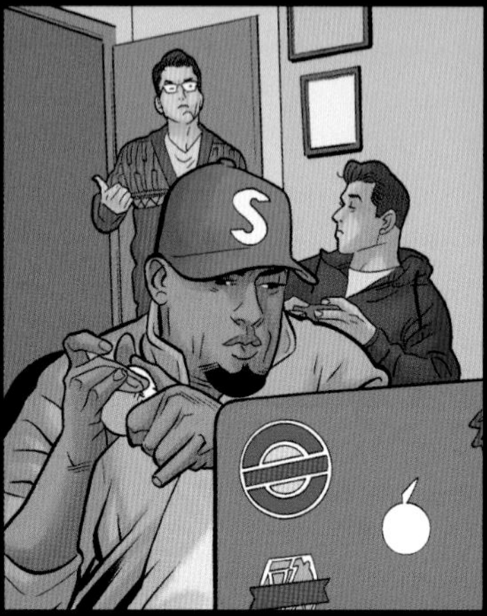

I loved that Bill-Bill, a pretty minor character, was fiddling with a baseball while sitting at his laptop. It made him so real and alive to me. When I paid Wilfredo the compliment, he said that the artist Brian Stelfreeze once told him, "no one is ever just sitting in a chair — they're always doing something else."

WAID: I call bullshit. I happen to know that you sit in a chair and do absolutely nothing.

PEYER: That was only for thirteen years!

WAID: What was so important that you couldn't write CAPTAIN KID the same decade you got the idea?

PEYER: I guess I needed a push.

WAID: A push? I harangued you for thirteen years.

PEYER: I guess I needed you to write it for me.

WAID: Fine. It's probably for the best that you waited. We need an optimistic comic for adults now more than ever —

PEYER: Don't get started on Trump again.

WAID: That's not what I mean. I mean, the easiest way to make a story seem "adult" is to heap it high with gratuitous misery. We see it everywhere, not just in comics. But that approach is as shallow and phony as it would be to make everything constantly happy. Adult life is about nuance.

PEYER: Right. Why can't adult comics offer some wish fulfillment along with all the dystopian wallow? We can let Captain Kid be happy about his powers. That's real. More real than having him find the bloodied corpse of a loved one in the next panel because the story needed a charge.

WAID: When you say it, it sounds geriatric.

PEYER: It has nothing to do with age. I choose to smell like urine.

WAID: This is what I have to look forward to. If I could rewind my age like Captain Kid, I'd keep it there. No changing back for me.

PEYER: You'd give up your whole life — your career, your relationships — to stay young?

WAID: To never be you.

PEYER: Okay, that I have sympathy for.

MARK WAID & TOM PEYER
March 2017

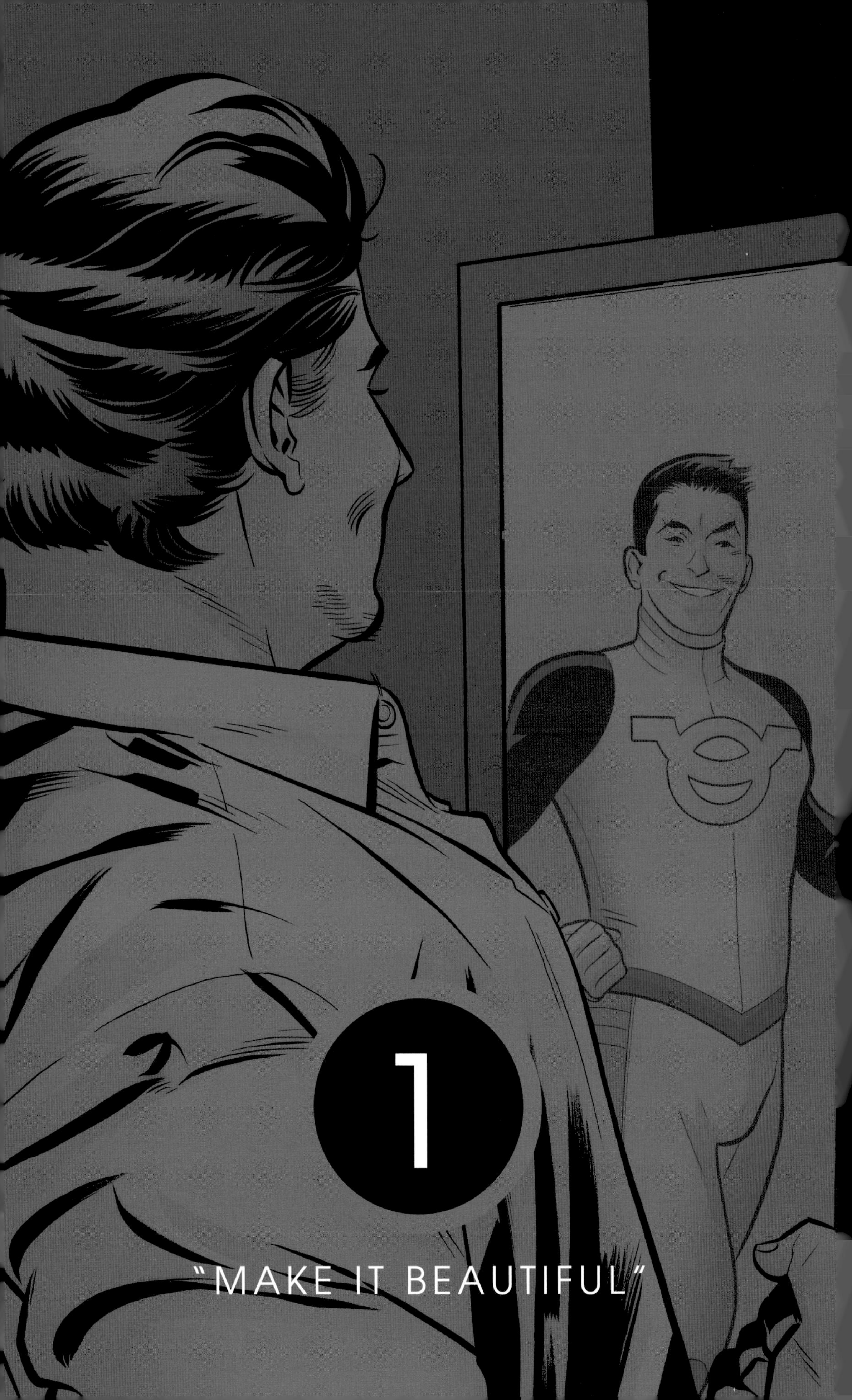
1
"MAKE IT BEAUTIFUL"

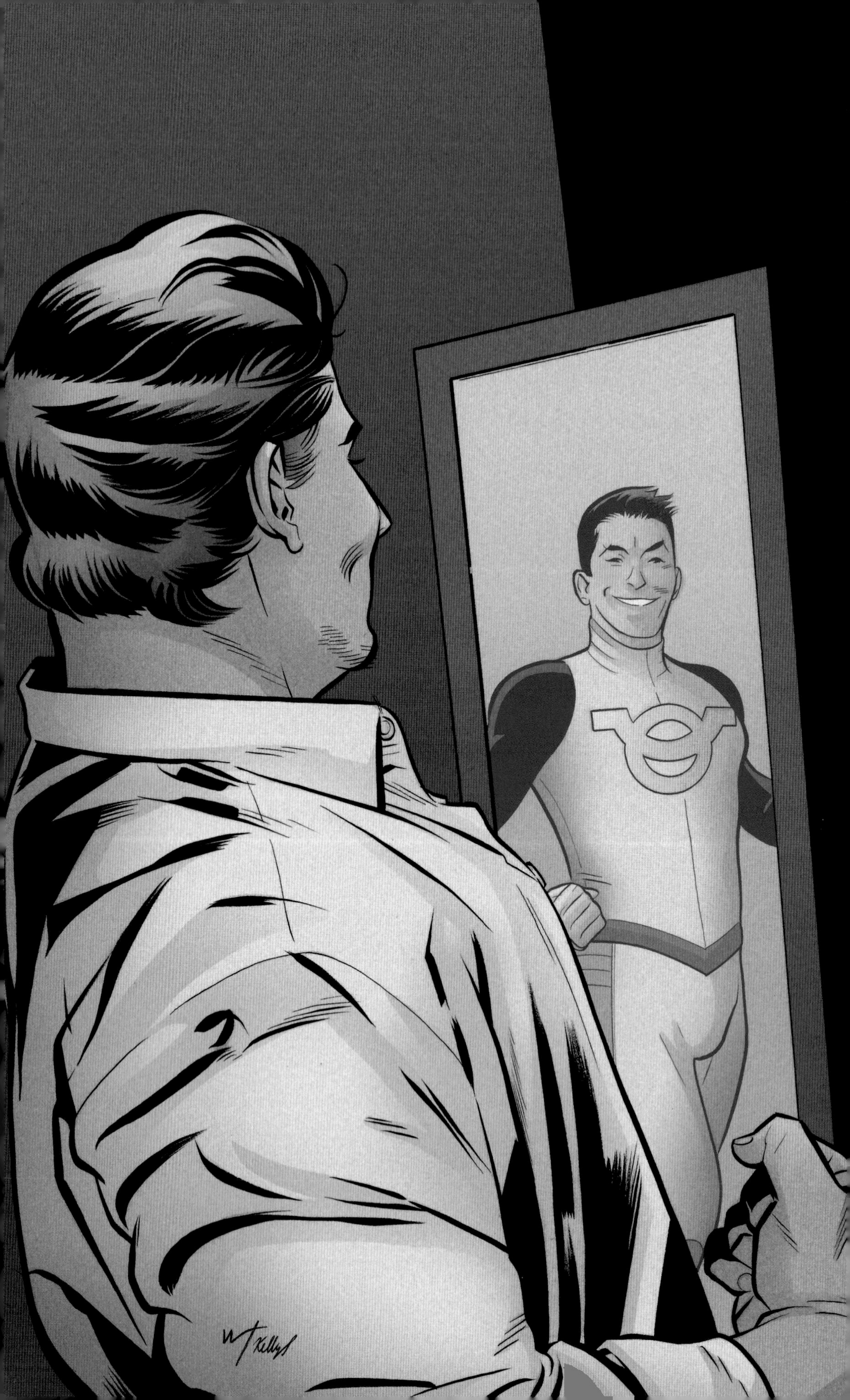

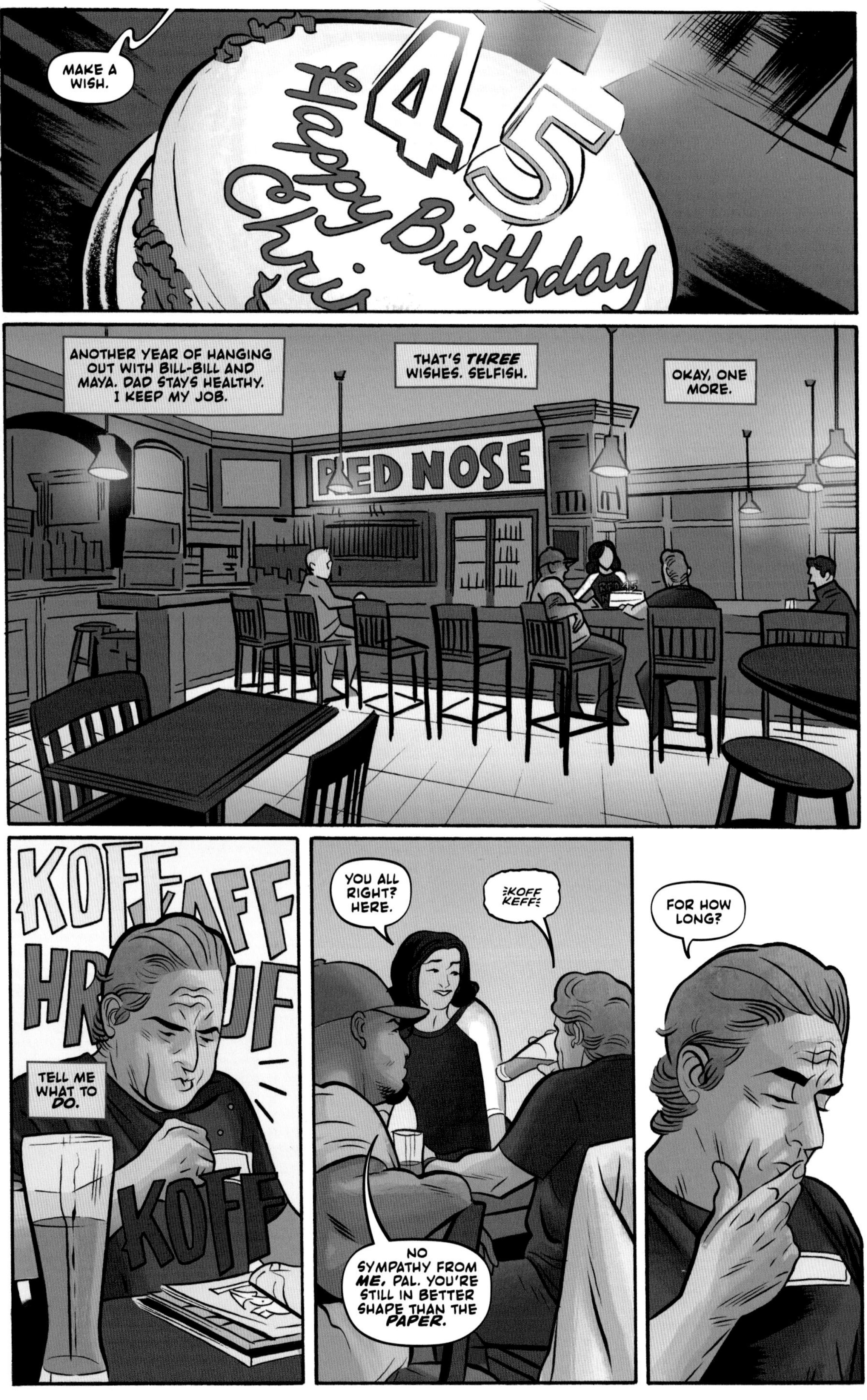
MAKE A WISH.
45
Happy Birthday Chri
ANOTHER YEAR OF HANGING OUT WITH BILL-BILL AND MAYA. DAD STAYS HEALTHY. I KEEP MY JOB.
THAT'S THREE WISHES. SELFISH.
OKAY, ONE MORE.
RED NOSE
KOFF KAFF
HRUF
TELL ME WHAT TO DO.
KOFF
YOU ALL RIGHT? HERE.
KOFF KEFF
NO SYMPATHY FROM ME, PAL. YOU'RE STILL IN BETTER SHAPE THAN THE PAPER.
FOR HOW LONG?

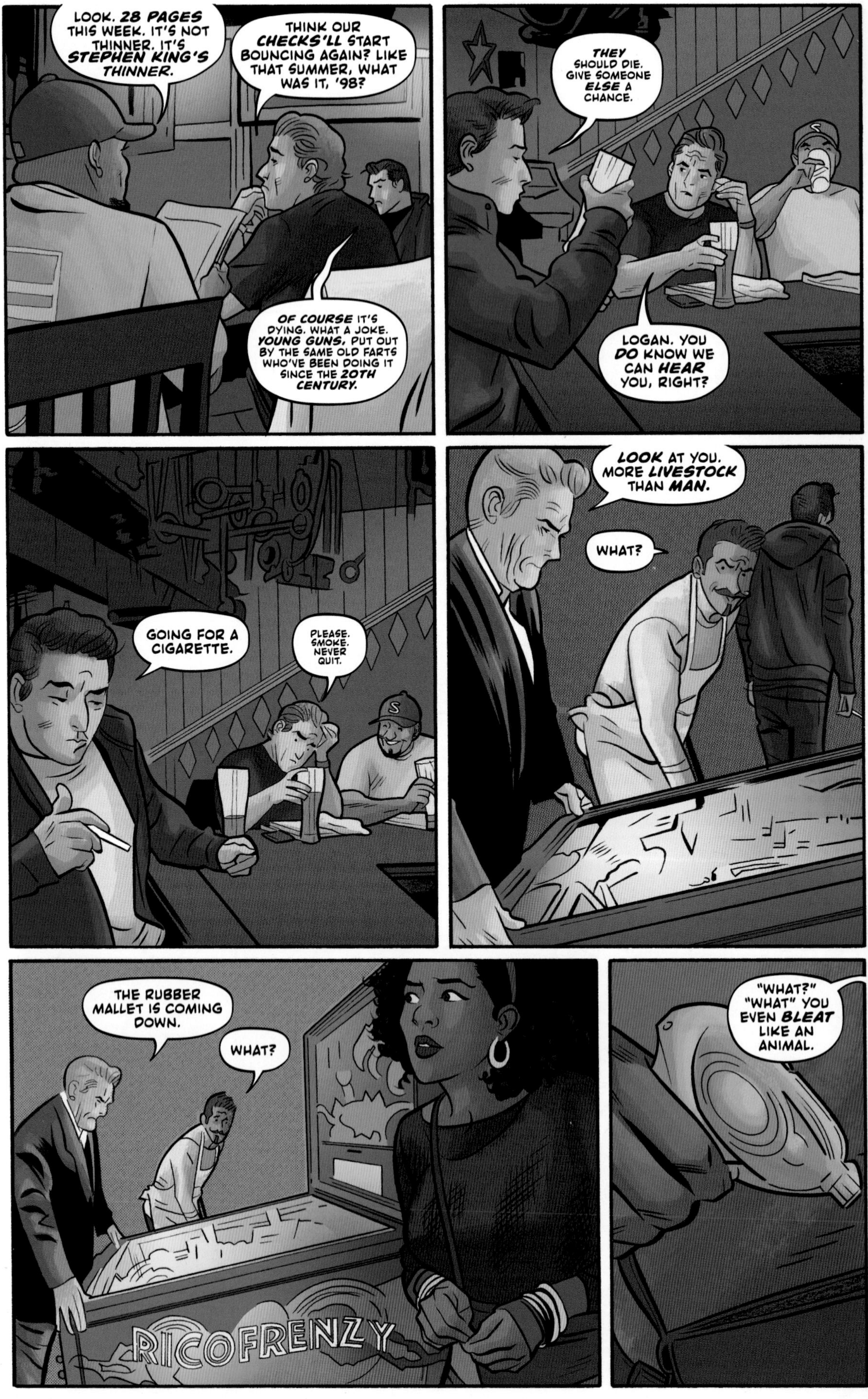
LOOK. 28 PAGES THIS WEEK. IT'S NOT THINNER. IT'S STEPHEN KING'S THINNER.
THINK OUR CHECKS'LL START BOUNCING AGAIN? LIKE THAT SUMMER, WHAT WAS IT, '98?
OF COURSE IT'S DYING. WHAT A JOKE. YOUNG GUNS, PUT OUT BY THE SAME OLD FARTS WHO'VE BEEN DOING IT SINCE THE 20TH CENTURY.
THEY SHOULD DIE. GIVE SOMEONE ELSE A CHANCE.
LOGAN. YOU DO KNOW WE CAN HEAR YOU, RIGHT?
GOING FOR A CIGARETTE.
PLEASE. SMOKE. NEVER QUIT.
LOOK AT YOU. MORE LIVESTOCK THAN MAN.
WHAT?
THE RUBBER MALLET IS COMING DOWN.
WHAT?
RICOFRENZY
"WHAT?" "WHAT" YOU EVEN BLEAT LIKE AN ANIMAL.

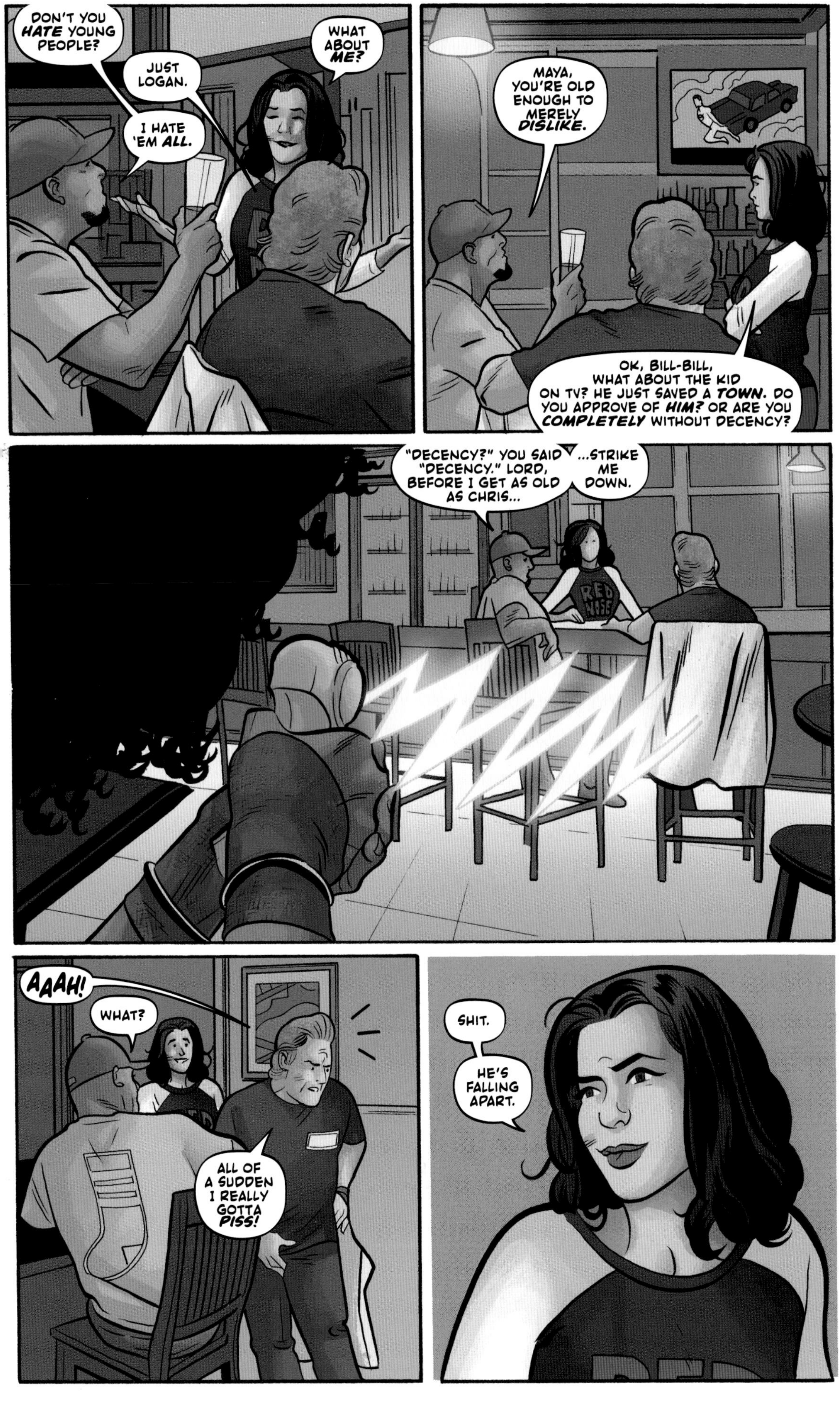
DON'T YOU HATE YOUNG PEOPLE?
JUST LOGAN.
WHAT ABOUT ME?
I HATE 'EM ALL.
MAYA, YOU'RE OLD ENOUGH TO MERELY DISLIKE.
OK, BILL-BILL, WHAT ABOUT THE KID ON TV? HE JUST SAVED A TOWN. DO YOU APPROVE OF HIM? OR ARE YOU COMPLETELY WITHOUT DECENCY?
"DECENCY?" YOU SAID "DECENCY." LORD, BEFORE I GET AS OLD AS CHRIS...
...STRIKE ME DOWN.
RED NOSE
AAAH!
WHAT?
ALL OF A SUDDEN I REALLY GOTTA PISS!
SHIT.
HE'S FALLING APART.

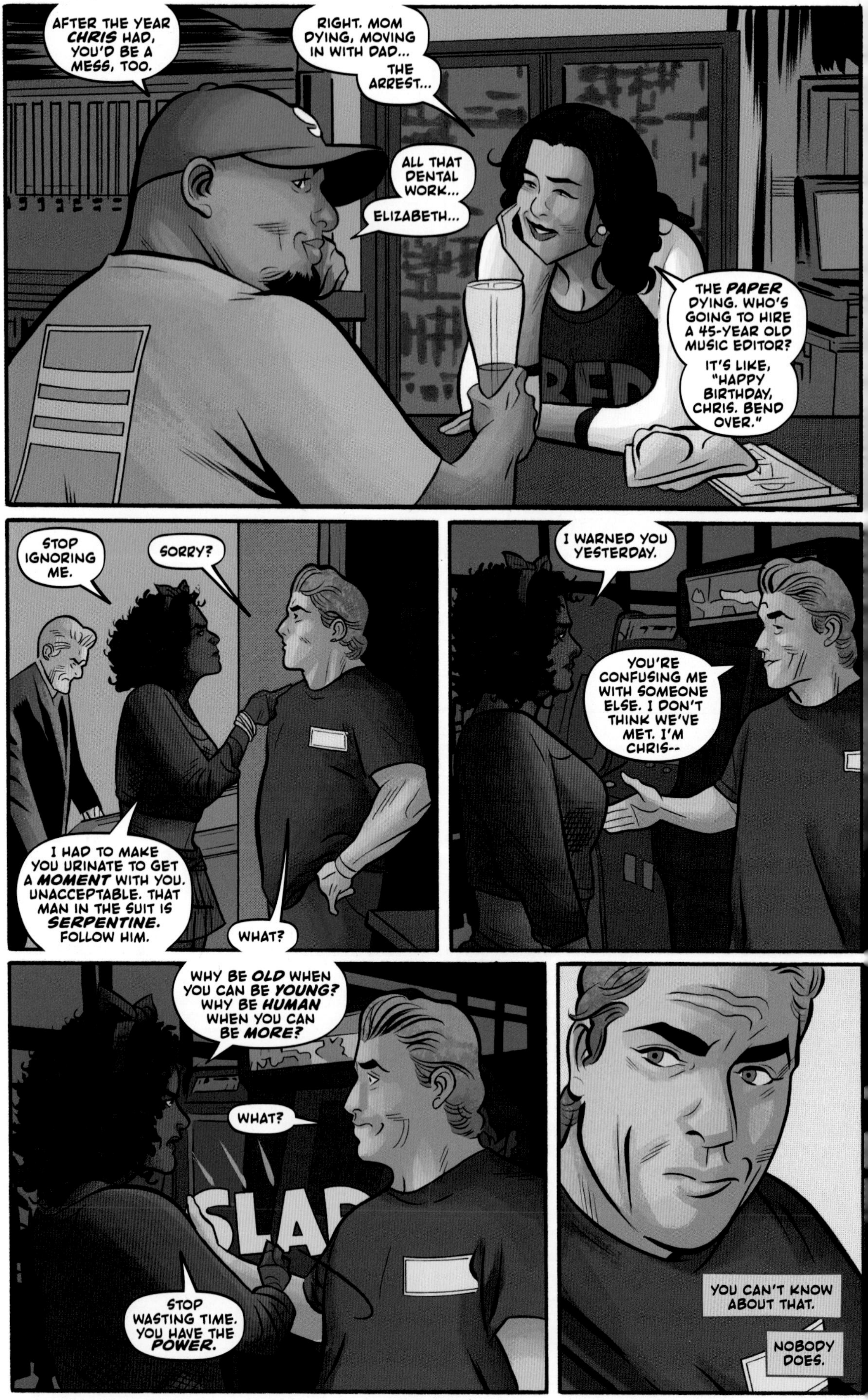
AFTER THE YEAR CHRIS HAD, YOU'D BE A MESS, TOO.
RIGHT. MOM DYING, MOVING IN WITH DAD...
THE ARREST...
ALL THAT DENTAL WORK...
ELIZABETH...
THE PAPER DYING. WHO'S GOING TO HIRE A 45-YEAR OLD MUSIC EDITOR?
IT'S LIKE, "HAPPY BIRTHDAY, CHRIS. BEND OVER."
STOP IGNORING ME.
SORRY?
I HAD TO MAKE YOU URINATE TO GET A MOMENT WITH YOU. UNACCEPTABLE. THAT MAN IN THE SUIT IS SERPENTINE. FOLLOW HIM.
WHAT?
I WARNED YOU YESTERDAY.
YOU'RE CONFUSING ME WITH SOMEONE ELSE. I DON'T THINK WE'VE MET. I'M CHRIS--
WHY BE OLD WHEN YOU CAN BE YOUNG? WHY BE HUMAN WHEN YOU CAN BE MORE?
WHAT?
STOP WASTING TIME. YOU HAVE THE POWER.
YOU CAN'T KNOW ABOUT THAT.
NOBODY DOES.

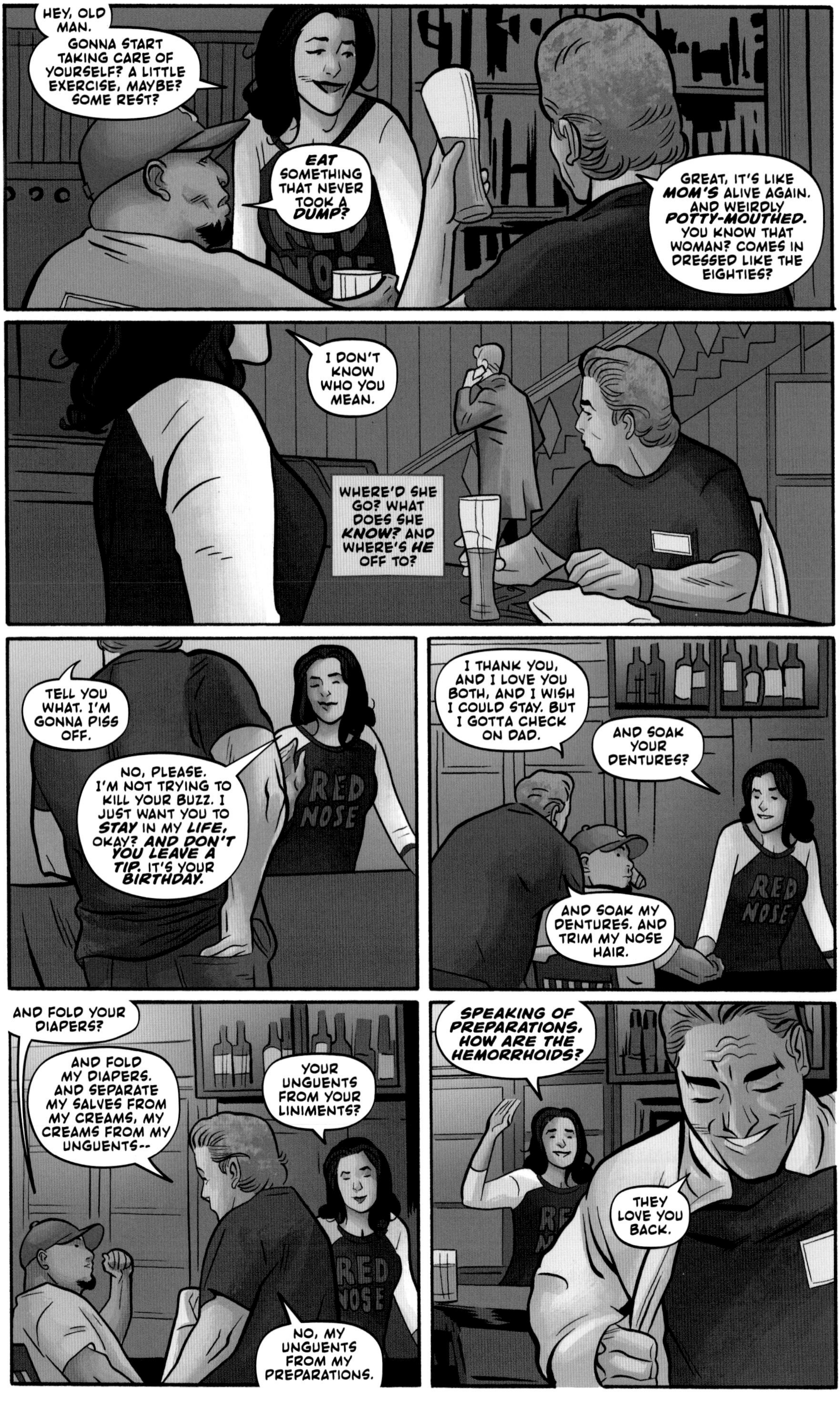
HEY, OLD MAN.
GONNA START TAKING CARE OF YOURSELF? A LITTLE EXERCISE, MAYBE? SOME REST?
EAT SOMETHING THAT NEVER TOOK A DUMP?
GREAT, IT'S LIKE MOM'S ALIVE AGAIN. AND WEIRDLY POTTY-MOUTHED. YOU KNOW THAT WOMAN? COMES IN DRESSED LIKE THE EIGHTIES?
I DON'T KNOW WHO YOU MEAN.
WHERE'D SHE GO? WHAT DOES SHE KNOW? AND WHERE'S HE OFF TO?
TELL YOU WHAT. I'M GONNA PISS OFF.
NO, PLEASE. I'M NOT TRYING TO KILL YOUR BUZZ. I JUST WANT YOU TO STAY IN MY LIFE, OKAY? AND DON'T YOU LEAVE A TIP. IT'S YOUR BIRTHDAY.
I THANK YOU, AND I LOVE YOU BOTH, AND I WISH I COULD STAY. BUT I GOTTA CHECK ON DAD.
AND SOAK YOUR DENTURES?
AND SOAK MY DENTURES. AND TRIM MY NOSE HAIR.
AND FOLD YOUR DIAPERS?
AND FOLD MY DIAPERS. AND SEPARATE MY SALVES FROM MY CREAMS, MY CREAMS FROM MY UNGUENTS--
YOUR UNGUENTS FROM YOUR LINIMENTS?
NO, MY UNGUENTS FROM MY PREPARATIONS.
SPEAKING OF PREPARATIONS, HOW ARE THE HEMORRHOIDS?
THEY LOVE YOU BACK.

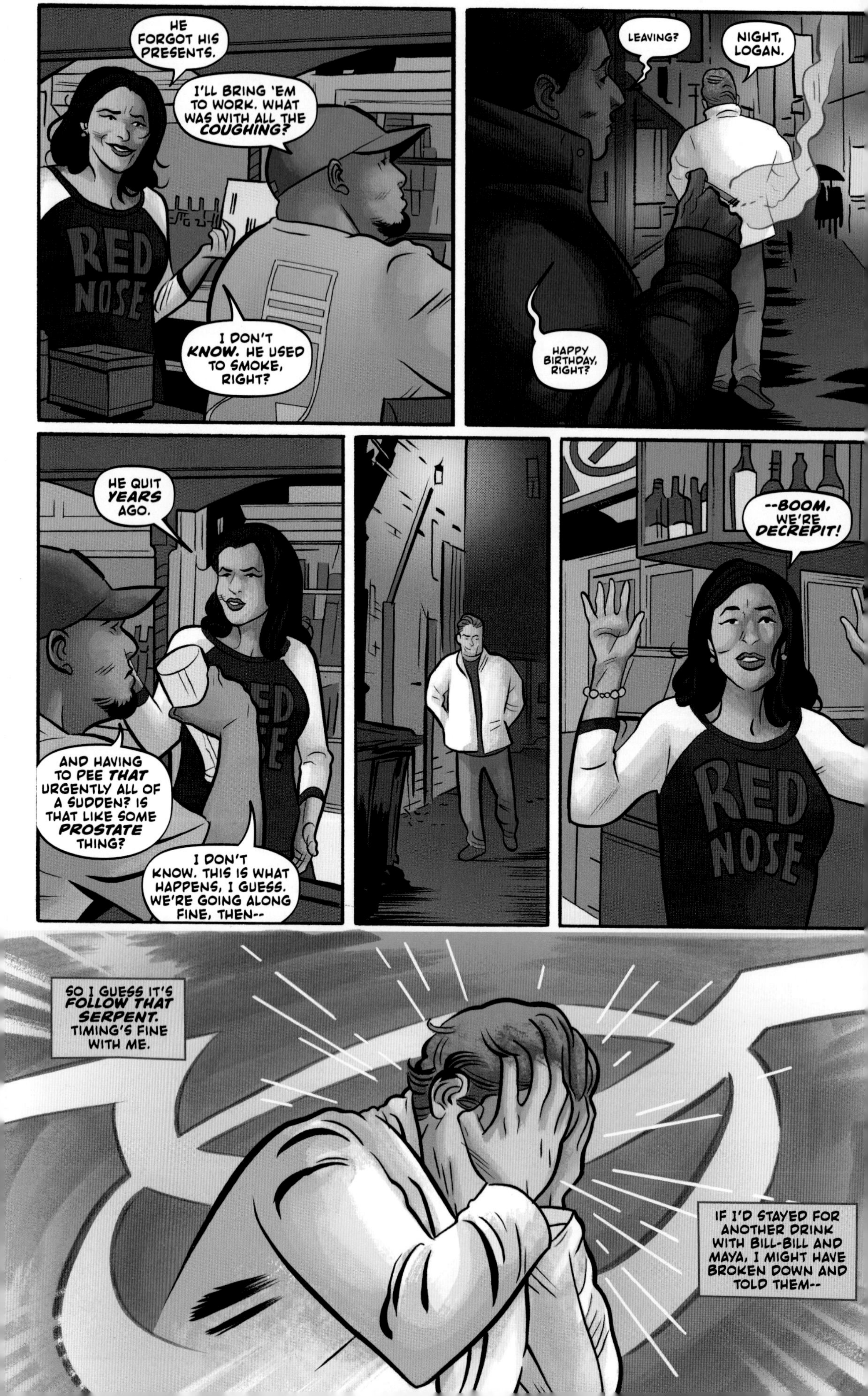

HE FORGOT HIS PRESENTS.
I'LL BRING 'EM TO WORK. WHAT WAS WITH ALL THE COUGHING?
I DON'T KNOW. HE USED TO SMOKE, RIGHT?
RED NOSE
LEAVING?
NIGHT, LOGAN.
HAPPY BIRTHDAY, RIGHT?
HE QUIT YEARS AGO.
AND HAVING TO PEE THAT URGENTLY ALL OF A SUDDEN? IS THAT LIKE SOME PROSTATE THING?
I DON'T KNOW. THIS IS WHAT HAPPENS, I GUESS. WE'RE GOING ALONG FINE, THEN--
--BOOM. WE'RE DECREPIT!
RED NOSE
SO I GUESS IT'S FOLLOW THAT SERPENT. TIMING'S FINE WITH ME.
IF I'D STAYED FOR ANOTHER DRINK WITH BILL-BILL AND MAYA, I MIGHT HAVE BROKEN DOWN AND TOLD THEM--

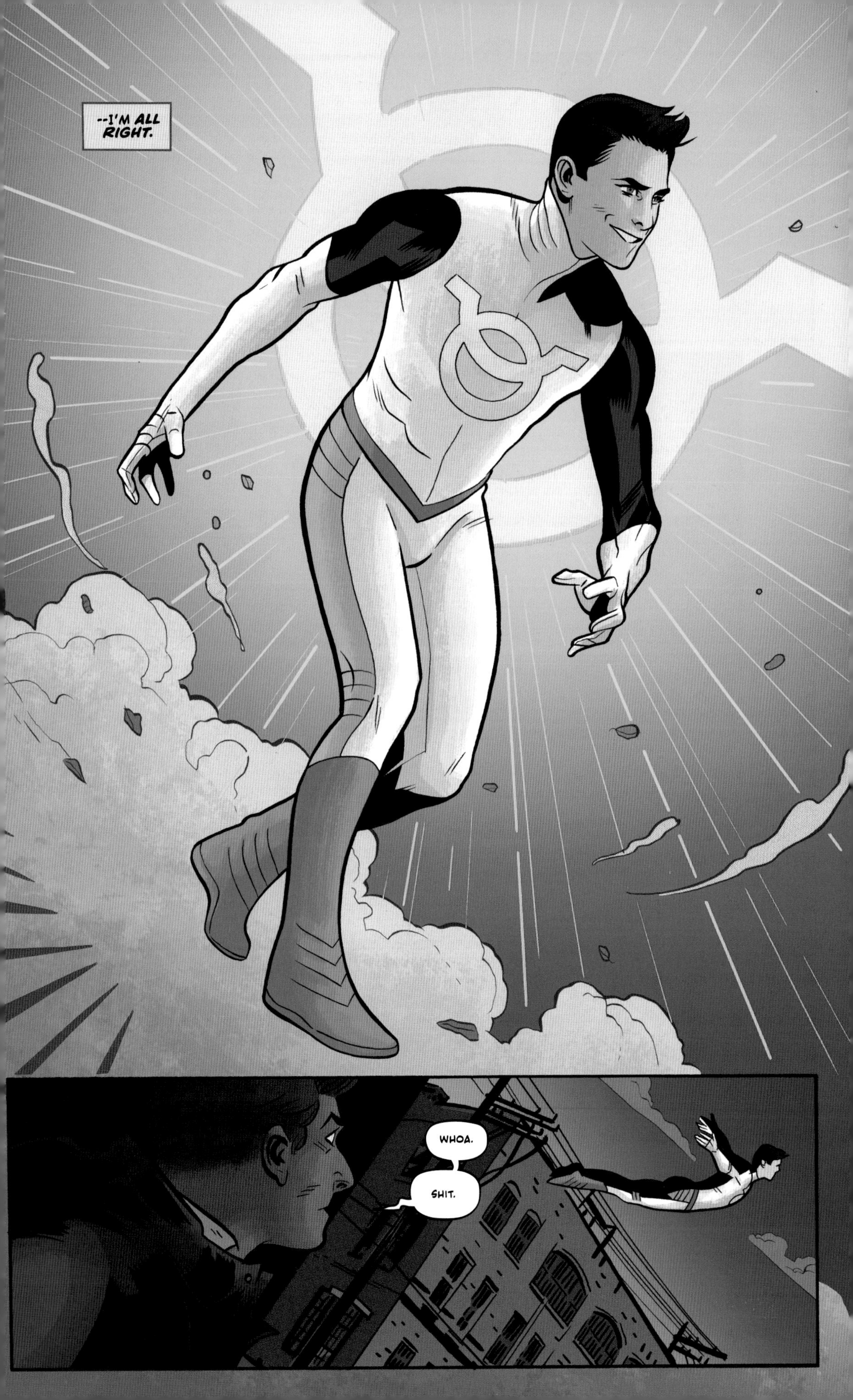
--I'M ALL RIGHT.
WHOA.
SHIT.

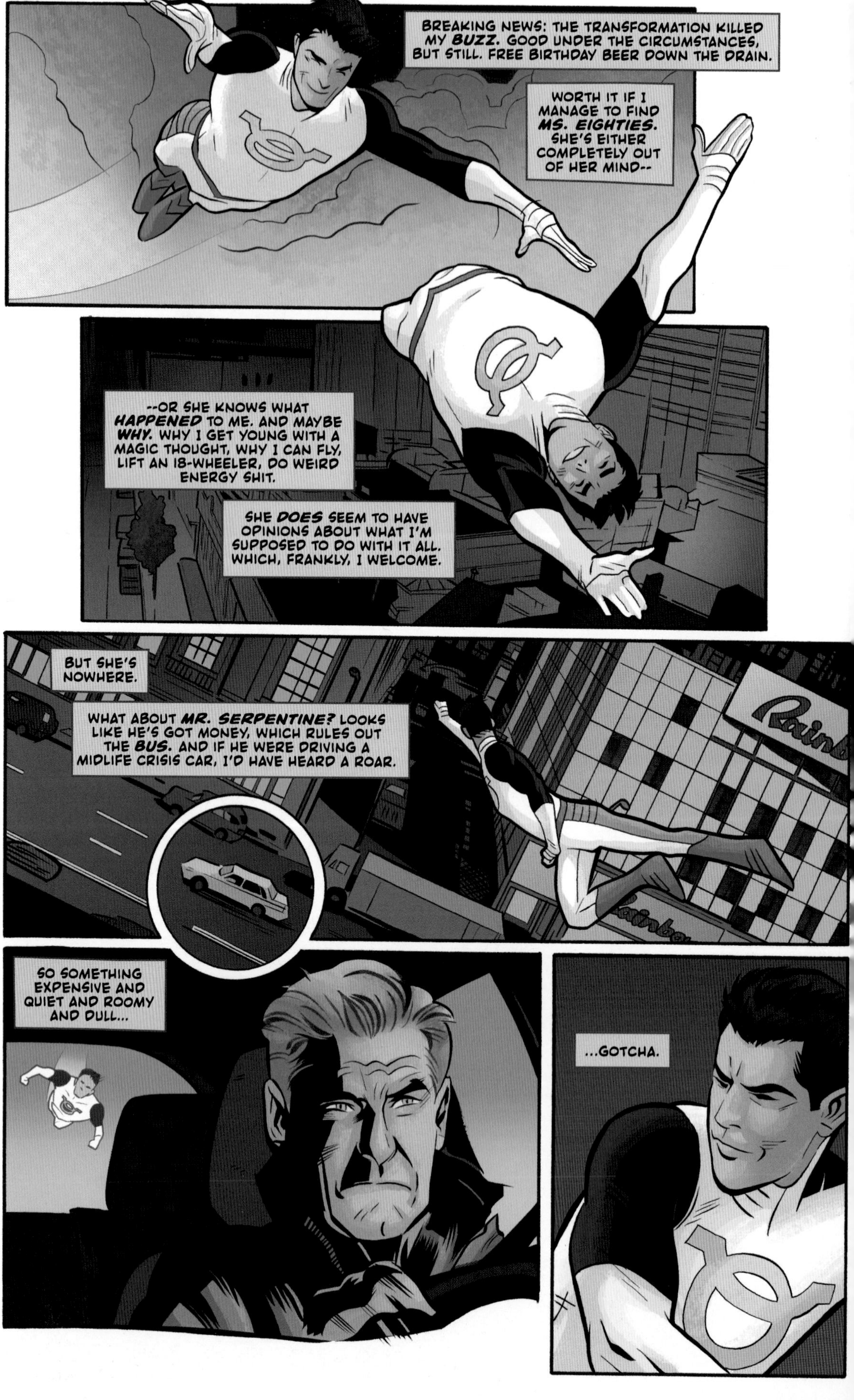
BREAKING NEWS: THE TRANSFORMATION KILLED MY BUZZ. GOOD UNDER THE CIRCUMSTANCES, BUT STILL. FREE BIRTHDAY BEER DOWN THE DRAIN.
WORTH IT IF I MANAGE TO FIND MS. EIGHTIES. SHE'S EITHER COMPLETELY OUT OF HER MIND--
--OR SHE KNOWS WHAT HAPPENED TO ME. AND MAYBE WHY. WHY I GET YOUNG WITH A MAGIC THOUGHT, WHY I CAN FLY, LIFT AN 18-WHEELER, DO WEIRD ENERGY SHIT.
SHE DOES SEEM TO HAVE OPINIONS ABOUT WHAT I'M SUPPOSED TO DO WITH IT ALL. WHICH, FRANKLY, I WELCOME.
BUT SHE'S NOWHERE.
WHAT ABOUT MR. SERPENTINE? LOOKS LIKE HE'S GOT MONEY, WHICH RULES OUT THE BUS. AND IF HE WERE DRIVING A MIDLIFE CRISIS CAR, I'D HAVE HEARD A ROAR.
SO SOMETHING EXPENSIVE AND QUIET AND ROOMY AND DULL...
...GOTCHA.

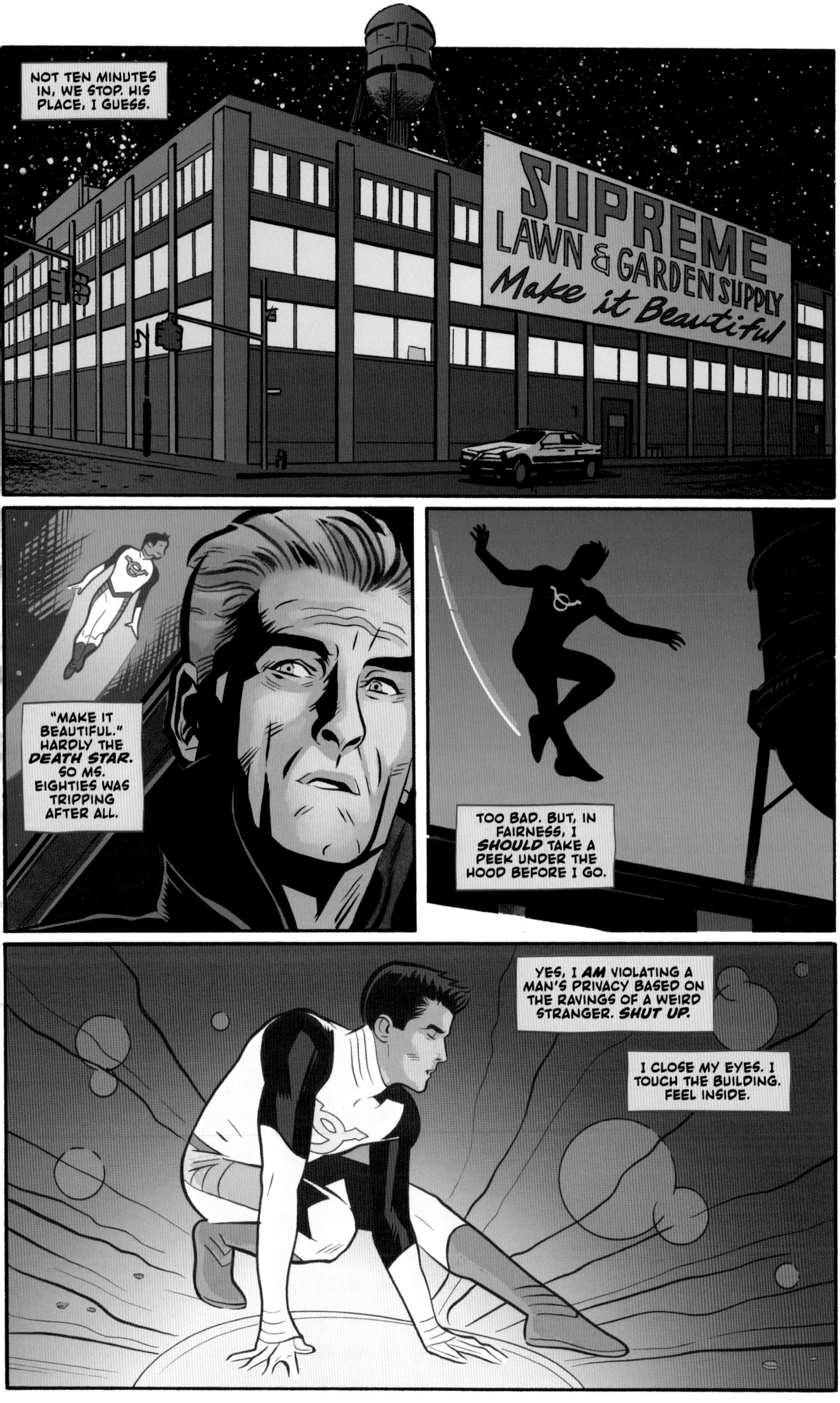
NOT TEN MINUTES IN, WE STOP. HIS PLACE, I GUESS.
SUPREME LAWN & GARDEN SUPPLY
Make it Beautiful
"MAKE IT BEAUTIFUL." HARDLY THE DEATH STAR. SO MS. EIGHTIES WAS TRIPPING AFTER ALL.
TOO BAD. BUT, IN FAIRNESS, I SHOULD TAKE A PEEK UNDER THE HOOD BEFORE I GO.
YES, I AM VIOLATING A MAN'S PRIVACY BASED ON THE RAVINGS OF A WEIRD STRANGER. SHUT UP.
I CLOSE MY EYES. I TOUCH THE BUILDING. FEEL INSIDE.

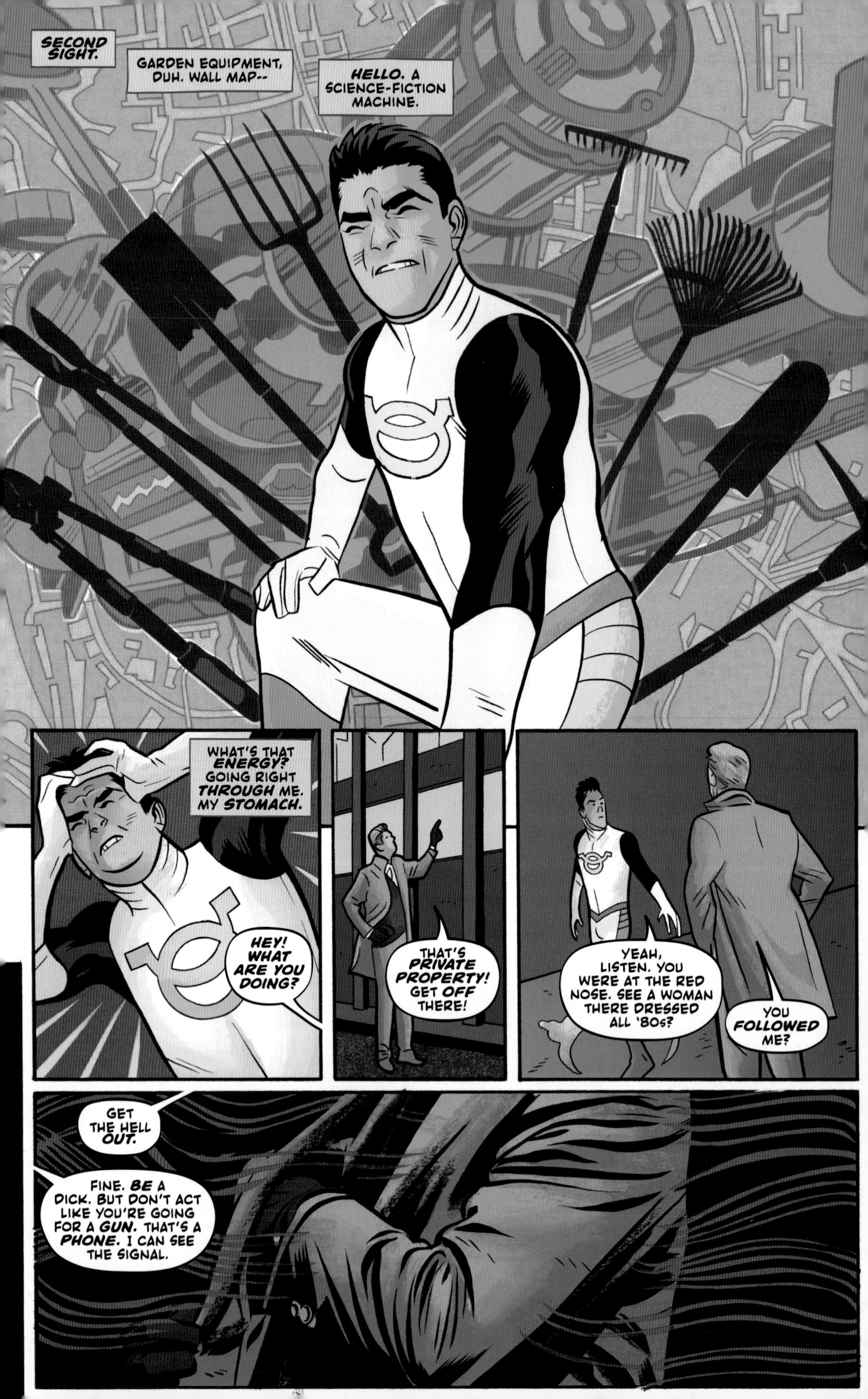
SECOND SIGHT.
GARDEN EQUIPMENT, DUH. WALL MAP--
HELLO. A SCIENCE-FICTION MACHINE.
WHAT'S THAT ENERGY? GOING RIGHT THROUGH ME. MY STOMACH.
HEY! WHAT ARE YOU DOING?
THAT'S PRIVATE PROPERTY! GET OFF THERE!
YEAH, LISTEN. YOU WERE AT THE RED NOSE. SEE A WOMAN THERE DRESSED ALL '80s?
YOU FOLLOWED ME?
GET THE HELL OUT.
FINE. BE A DICK. BUT DON'T ACT LIKE YOU'RE GOING FOR A GUN. THAT'S A PHONE. I CAN SEE THE SIGNAL.

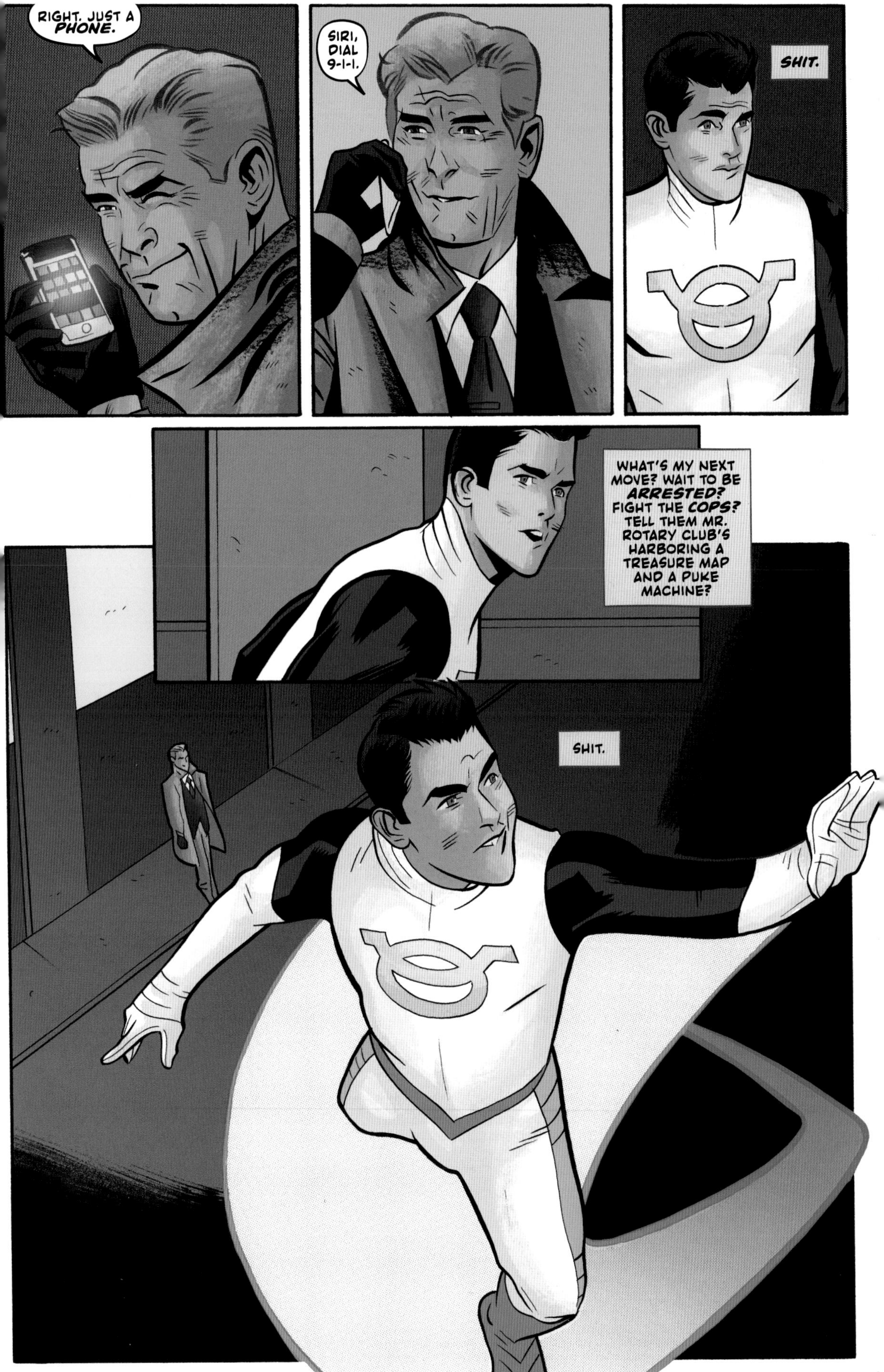
RIGHT. JUST A PHONE.
SIRI, DIAL 9-1-1.
SHIT.
WHAT'S MY NEXT MOVE? WAIT TO BE ARRESTED? FIGHT THE COPS? TELL THEM MR. ROTARY CLUB'S HARBORING A TREASURE MAP AND A PUKE MACHINE?
SHIT.

HEAVY CHEST? CHECK.

STIFF LEFT KNEE? CHECK.

SORE GUMS? CHECK.

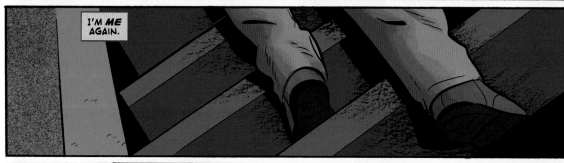

I'M *ME* AGAIN.

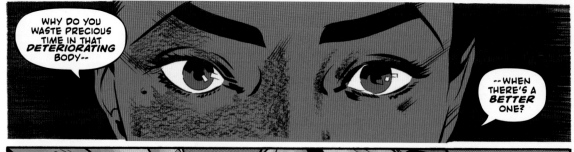

WHY DO YOU WASTE PRECIOUS TIME IN THAT *DETERIORATING* BODY--

--WHEN THERE'S A *BETTER* ONE?

AT LEAST I GOT A BIT OF THAT *BEER BUZZ* BACK.

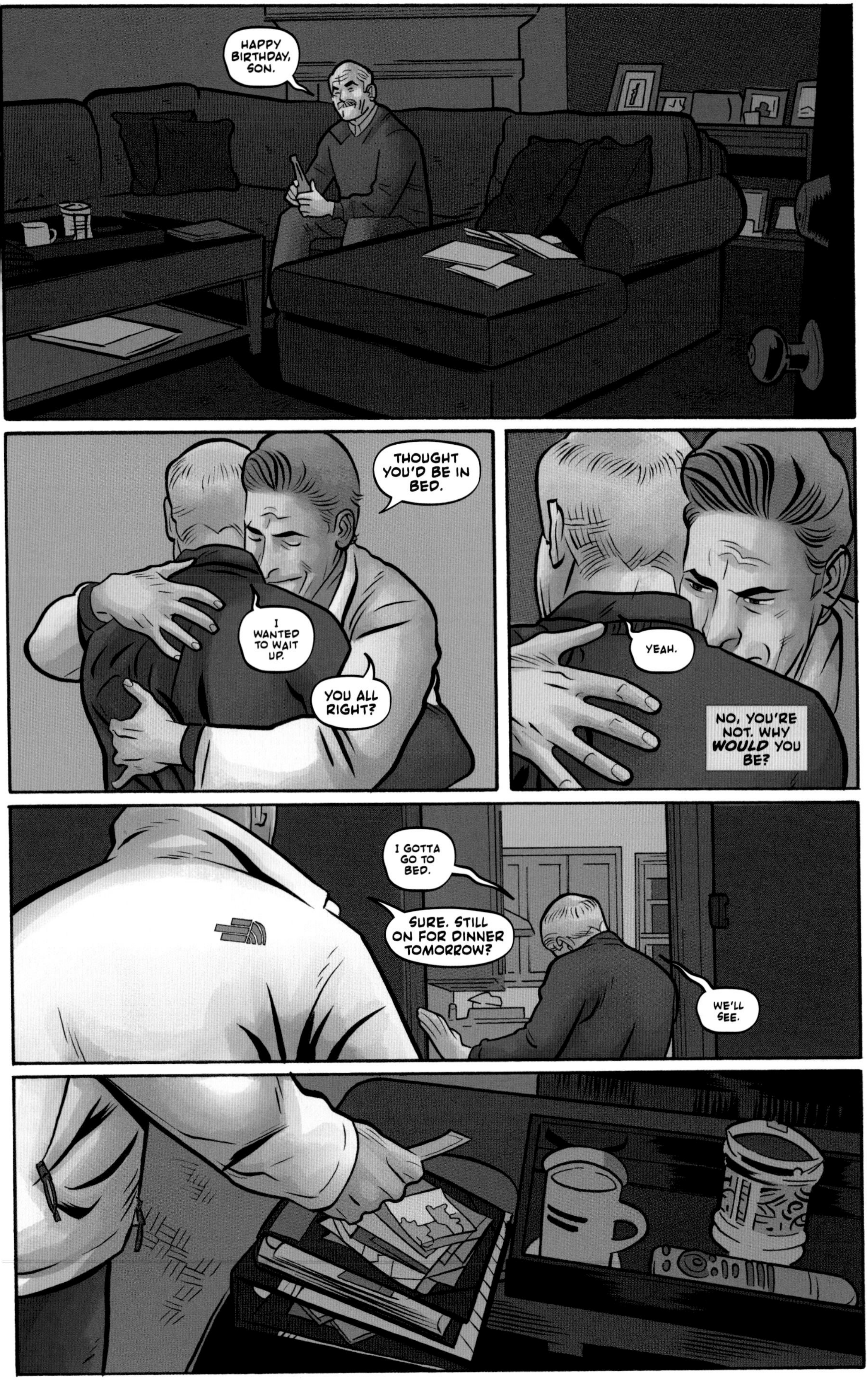
HAPPY BIRTHDAY, SON.
THOUGHT YOU'D BE IN BED.
I WANTED TO WAIT UP.
YOU ALL RIGHT?
YEAH.
NO, YOU'RE NOT. WHY *WOULD* YOU BE?
I GOTTA GO TO BED.
SURE. STILL ON FOR DINNER TOMORROW?
WE'LL SEE.

Chris, Rita & Perry
Chris' 15th Birthday
6/7/86

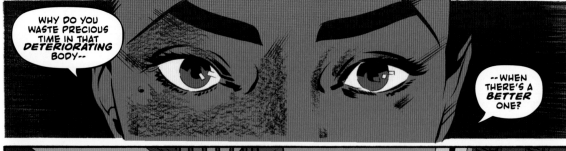

WHY DO YOU WASTE PRECIOUS TIME IN THAT *DETERIORATING* BODY--

--WHEN THERE'S A *BETTER* ONE?

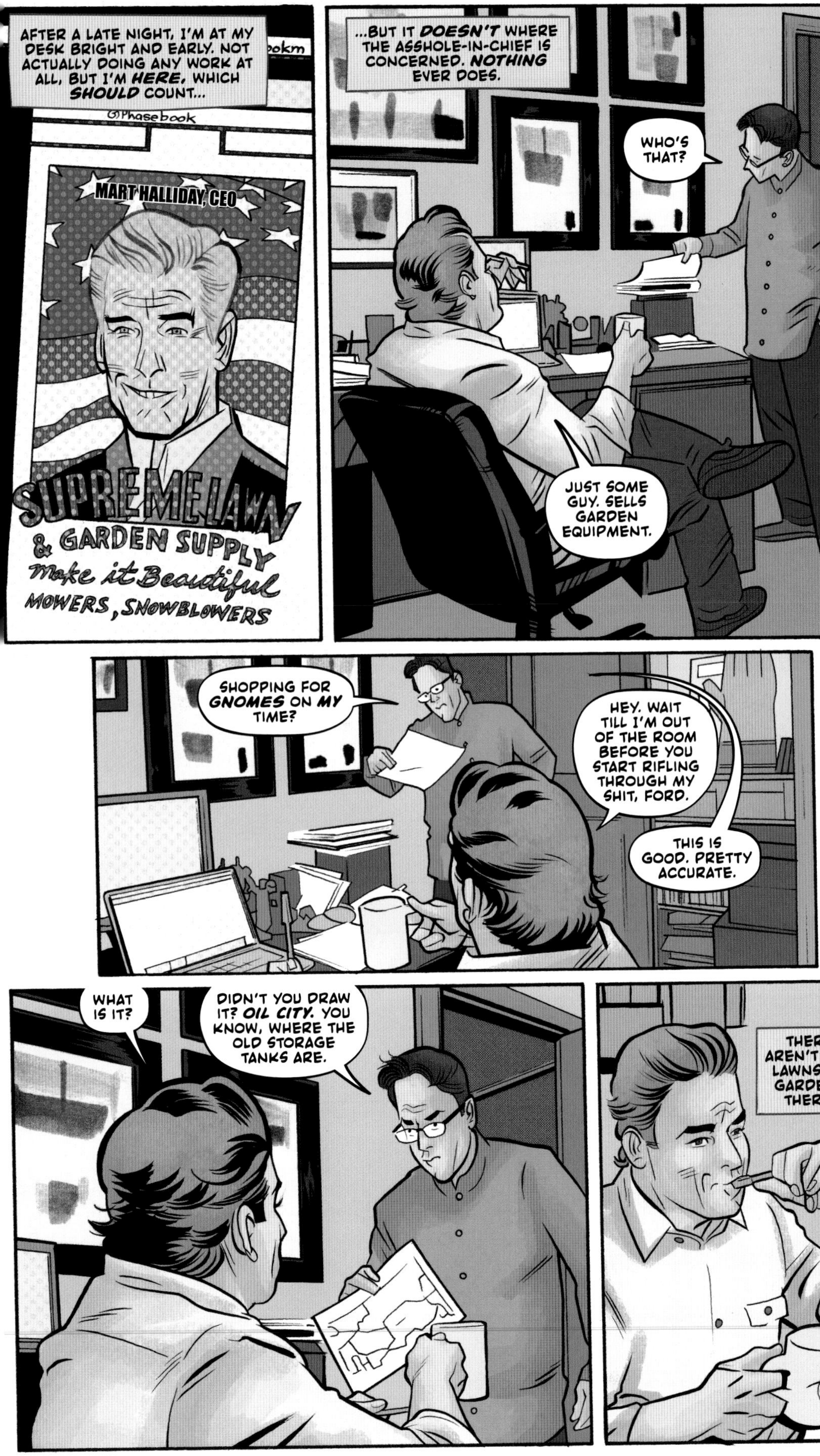
AFTER A LATE NIGHT, I'M AT MY DESK BRIGHT AND EARLY. NOT ACTUALLY DOING ANY WORK AT ALL, BUT I'M HERE, WHICH SHOULD COUNT...
Phasebook
MART HALLIDAY, CEO
SUPREME LAWN & GARDEN SUPPLY
Make it Beautiful
MOWERS, SNOWBLOWERS
...BUT IT DOESN'T WHERE THE ASSHOLE-IN-CHIEF IS CONCERNED. NOTHING EVER DOES.
WHO'S THAT?
JUST SOME GUY. SELLS GARDEN EQUIPMENT.
SHOPPING FOR GNOMES ON MY TIME?
HEY. WAIT TILL I'M OUT OF THE ROOM BEFORE YOU START RIFLING THROUGH MY SHIT, FORD.
THIS IS GOOD. PRETTY ACCURATE.
WHAT IS IT?
DIDN'T YOU DRAW IT? OIL CITY. YOU KNOW, WHERE THE OLD STORAGE TANKS ARE.
THERE AREN'T ANY LAWNS OR GARDENS THERE.

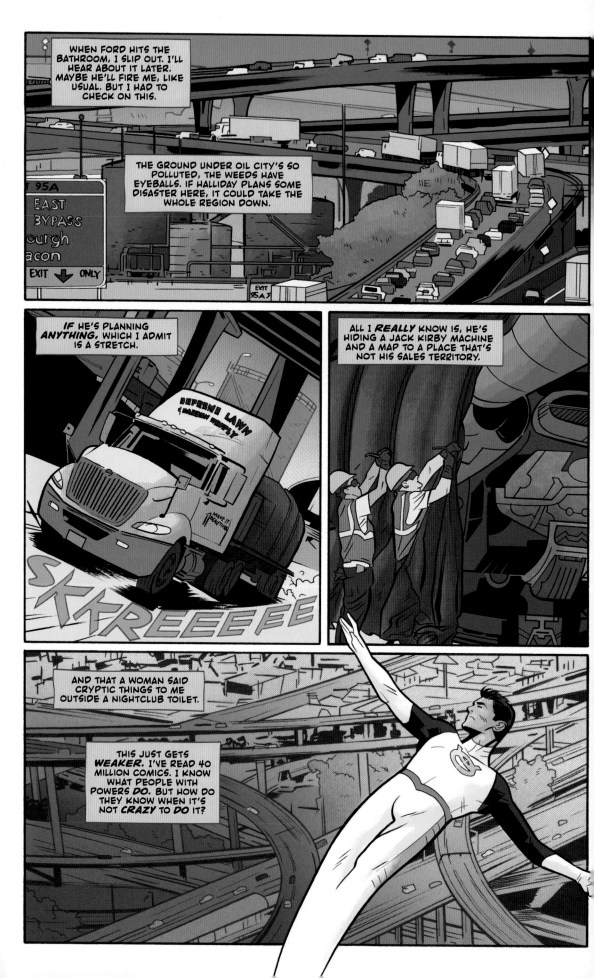

WHEN FORD HITS THE BATHROOM, I SLIP OUT. I'LL HEAR ABOUT IT LATER. MAYBE HE'LL FIRE ME, LIKE USUAL. BUT I HAD TO CHECK ON THIS.

THE GROUND UNDER OIL CITY'S SO POLLUTED, THE WEEDS HAVE EYEBALLS. IF HALLIDAY PLANS SOME DISASTER HERE, IT COULD TAKE THE WHOLE REGION DOWN.

95A
EAST
BYPASS
ourgh
acon
EXIT ⬇ ONLY

IF HE'S PLANNING *ANYTHING*, WHICH I ADMIT IS A STRETCH.

ALL I *REALLY* KNOW IS, HE'S HIDING A JACK KIRBY MACHINE AND A MAP TO A PLACE THAT'S NOT HIS SALES TERRITORY.

SKKREEEEE

AND THAT A WOMAN SAID CRYPTIC THINGS TO ME OUTSIDE A NIGHTCLUB TOILET.

THIS JUST GETS *WEAKER*. I'VE READ 40 MILLION COMICS. I KNOW WHAT PEOPLE WITH POWERS *DO*. BUT HOW DO THEY KNOW WHEN IT'S NOT *CRAZY* TO *DO* IT?

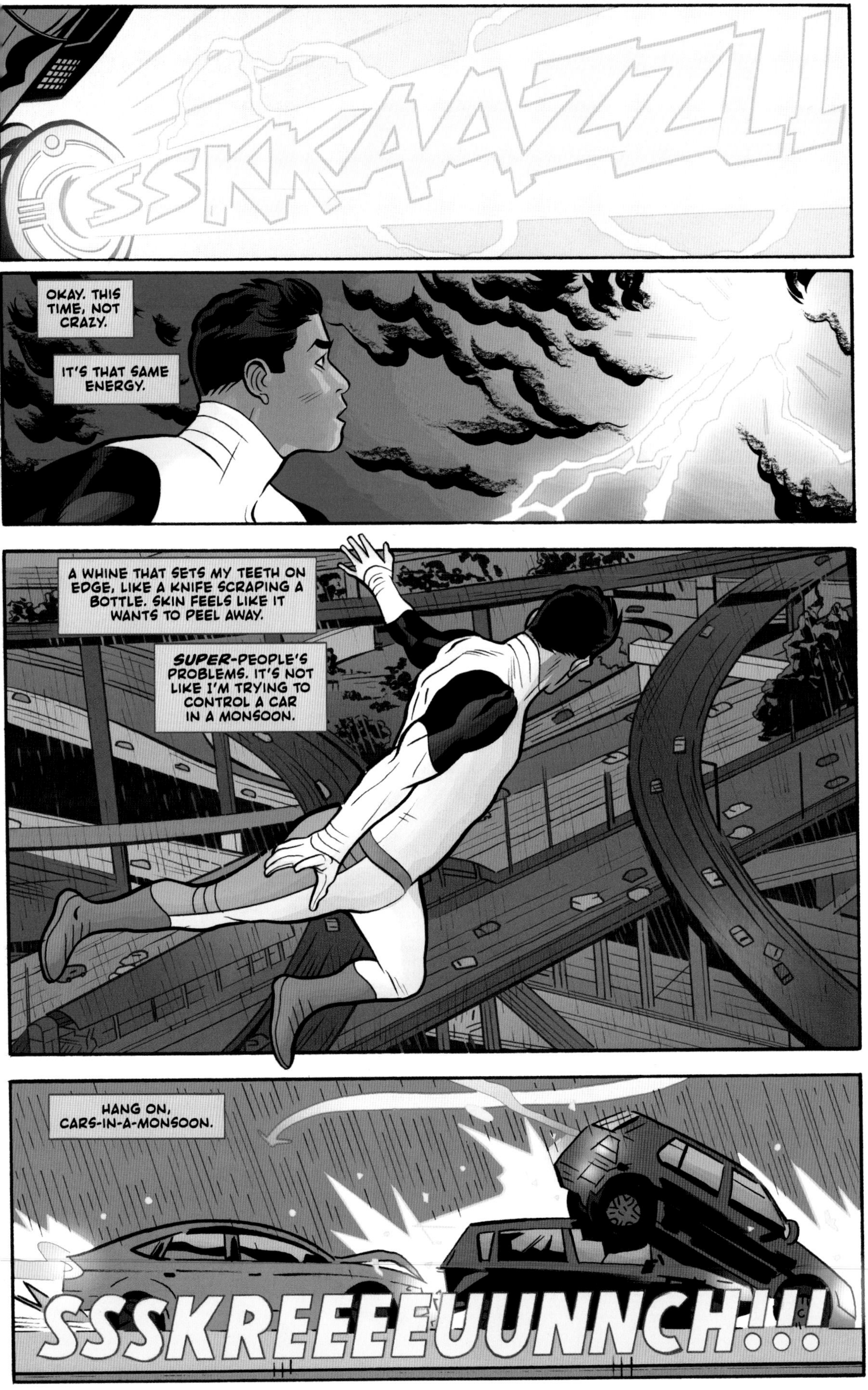
SSKAAZZL!
OKAY. THIS TIME, NOT CRAZY.
IT'S THAT SAME ENERGY.
A WHINE THAT SETS MY TEETH ON EDGE, LIKE A KNIFE SCRAPING A BOTTLE. SKIN FEELS LIKE IT WANTS TO PEEL AWAY.
SUPER-PEOPLE'S PROBLEMS. IT'S NOT LIKE I'M TRYING TO CONTROL A CAR IN A MONSOON.
HANG ON, CARS-IN-A-MONSOON.
SSSKREEEEEUUNNCH!!!

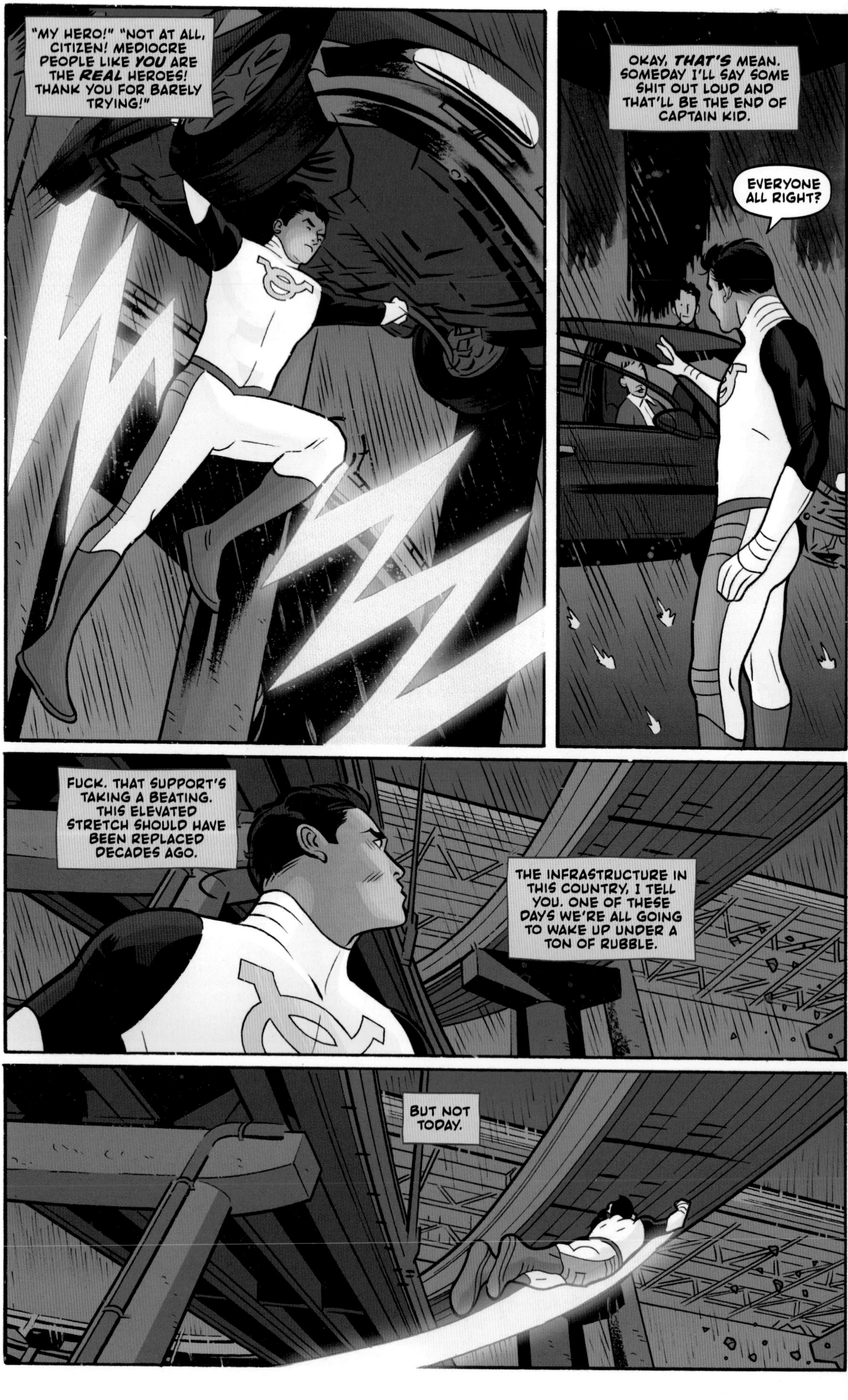
"MY HERO!" "NOT AT ALL, CITIZEN! MEDIOCRE PEOPLE LIKE YOU ARE THE REAL HEROES! THANK YOU FOR BARELY TRYING!"
OKAY, THAT'S MEAN. SOMEDAY I'LL SAY SOME SHIT OUT LOUD AND THAT'LL BE THE END OF CAPTAIN KID.
EVERYONE ALL RIGHT?
FUCK. THAT SUPPORT'S TAKING A BEATING. THIS ELEVATED STRETCH SHOULD HAVE BEEN REPLACED DECADES AGO.
THE INFRASTRUCTURE IN THIS COUNTRY, I TELL YOU. ONE OF THESE DAYS WE'RE ALL GOING TO WAKE UP UNDER A TON OF RUBBLE.
BUT NOT TODAY.

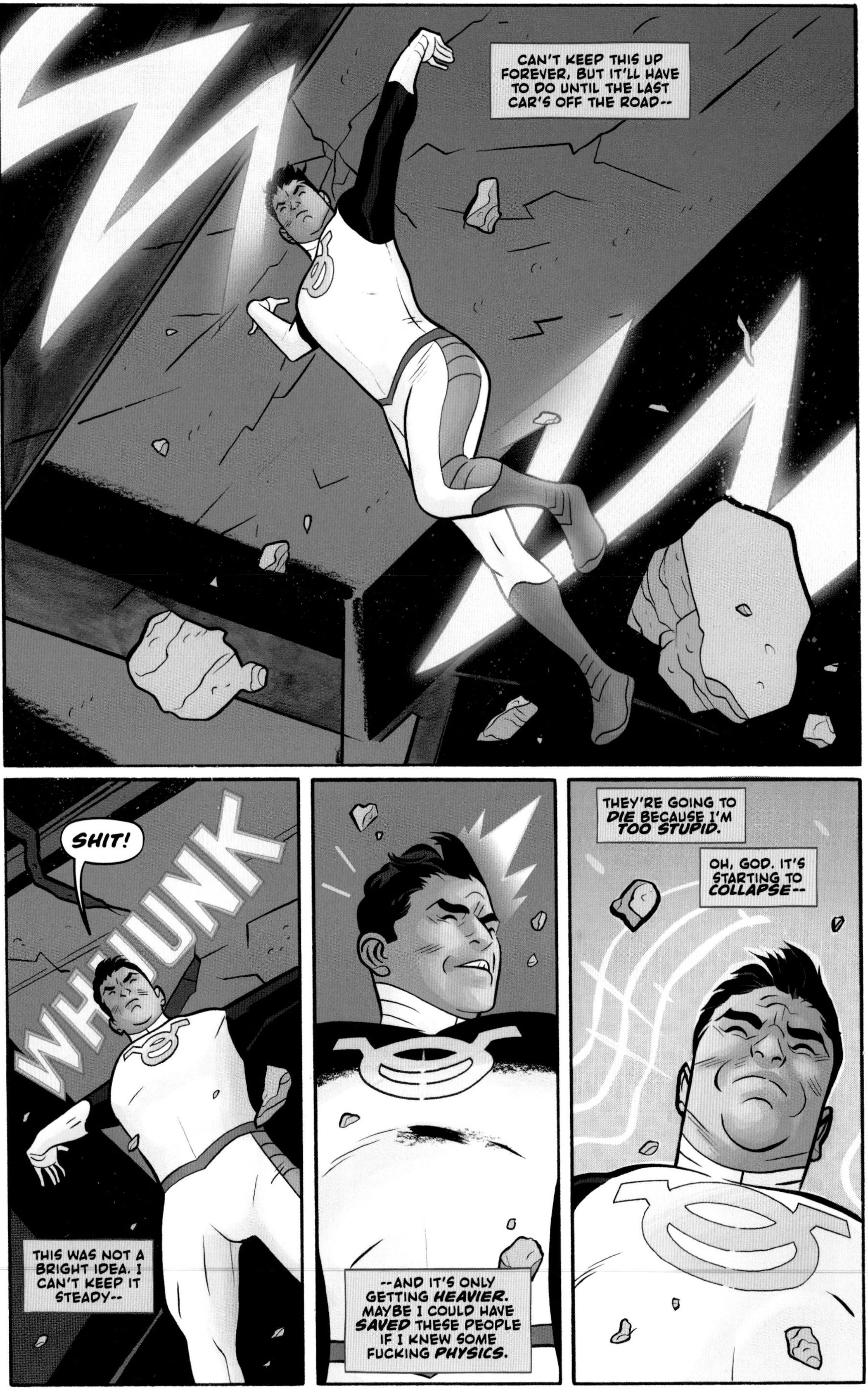

CAN'T KEEP THIS UP FOREVER, BUT IT'LL HAVE TO DO UNTIL THE LAST CAR'S OFF THE ROAD--
SHIT!
WHUNK
THIS WAS NOT A BRIGHT IDEA. I CAN'T KEEP IT STEADY--
--AND IT'S ONLY GETTING HEAVIER. MAYBE I COULD HAVE SAVED THESE PEOPLE IF I KNEW SOME FUCKING PHYSICS.
THEY'RE GOING TO DIE BECAUSE I'M TOO STUPID.
OH, GOD. IT'S STARTING TO COLLAPSE--

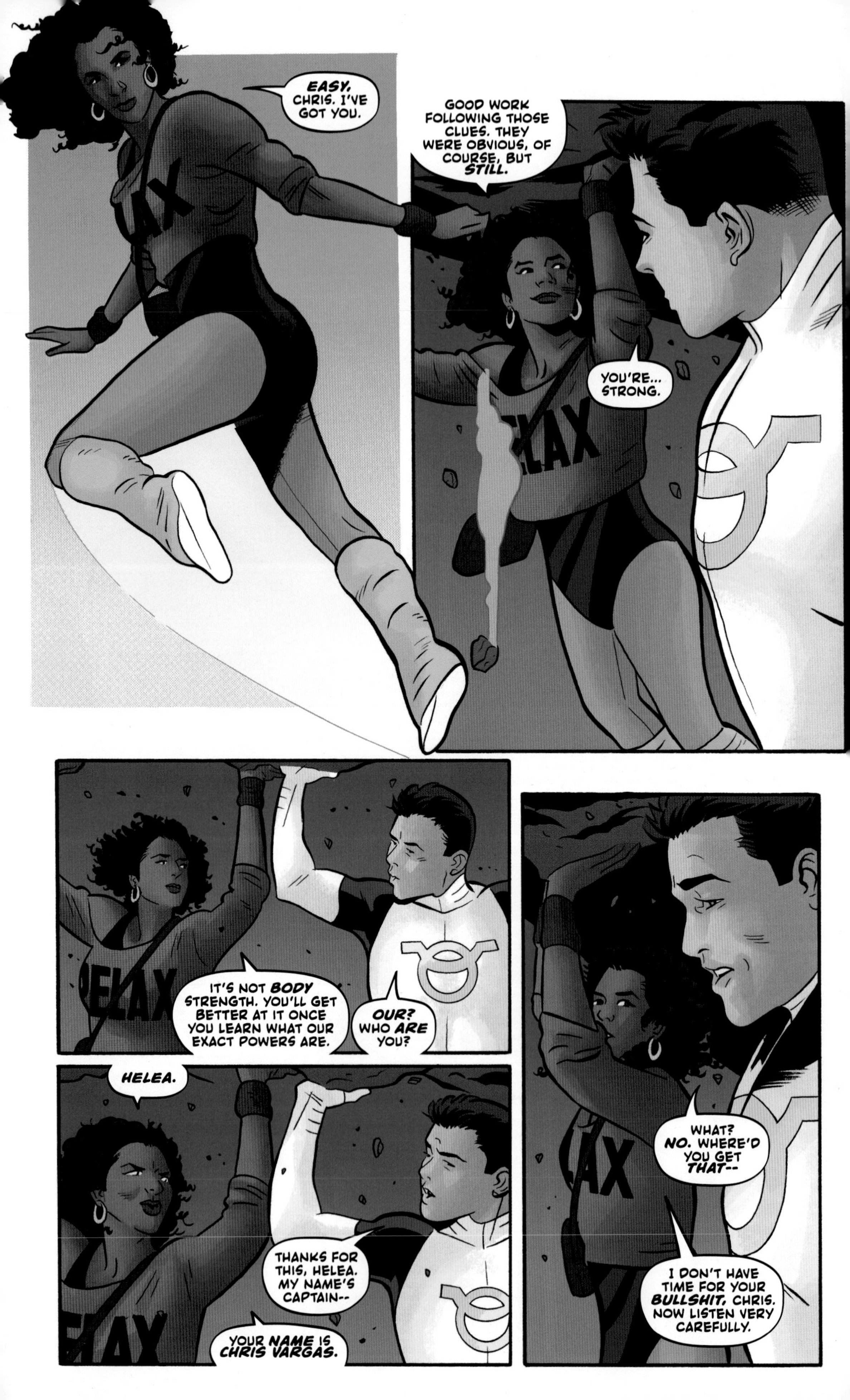
EASY, CHRIS. I'VE GOT YOU.
GOOD WORK FOLLOWING THOSE CLUES. THEY WERE OBVIOUS, OF COURSE, BUT STILL.
YOU'RE... STRONG.
IT'S NOT BODY STRENGTH. YOU'LL GET BETTER AT IT ONCE YOU LEARN WHAT OUR EXACT POWERS ARE.
OUR? WHO ARE YOU?
HELEA.
THANKS FOR THIS, HELEA. MY NAME'S CAPTAIN--
YOUR NAME IS CHRIS VARGAS.
WHAT? NO. WHERE'D YOU GET THAT--
I DON'T HAVE TIME FOR YOUR BULLSHIT, CHRIS. NOW LISTEN VERY CAREFULLY.

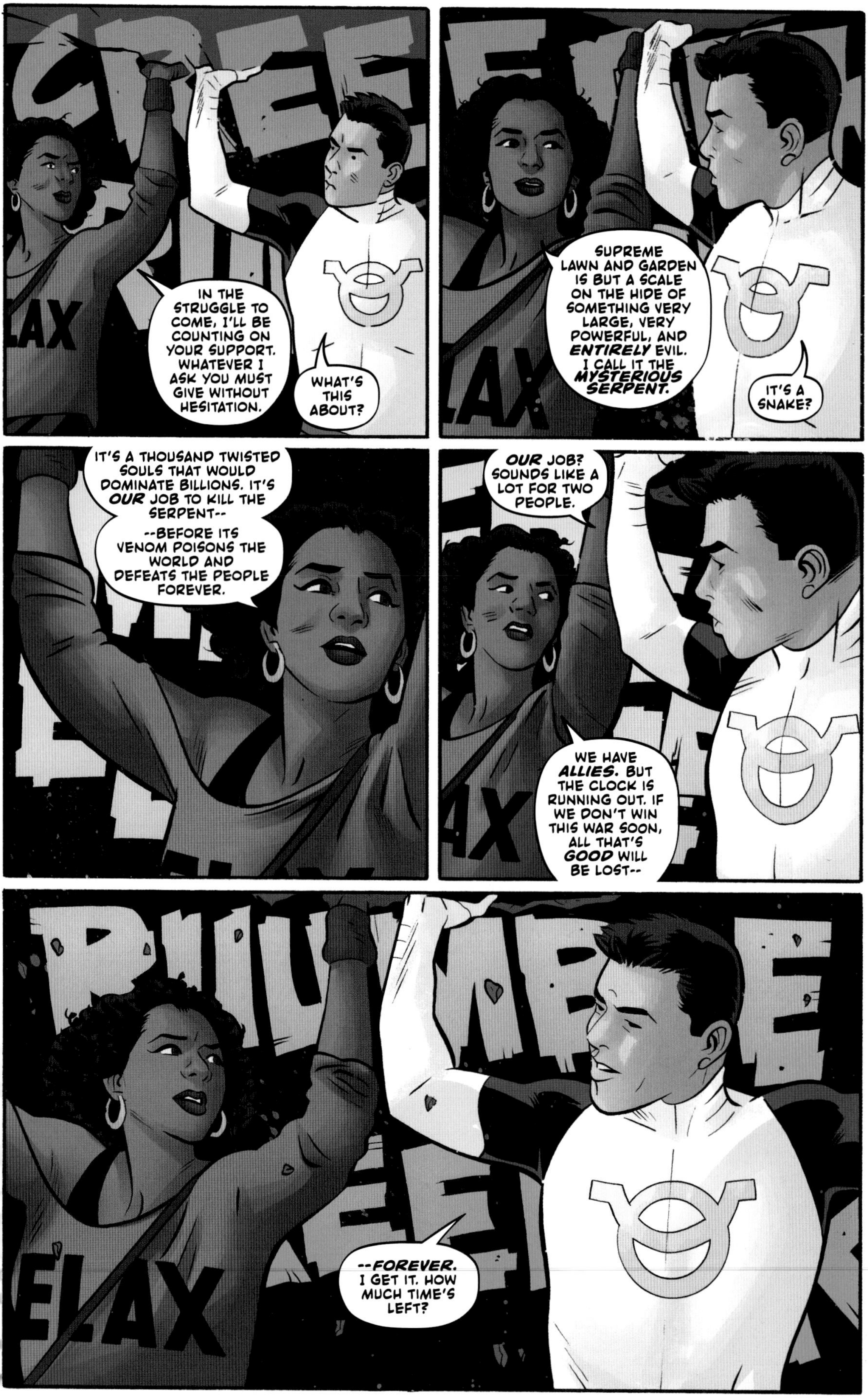
IN THE STRUGGLE TO COME, I'LL BE COUNTING ON YOUR SUPPORT. WHATEVER I ASK YOU MUST GIVE WITHOUT HESITATION.
WHAT'S THIS ABOUT?
SUPREME LAWN AND GARDEN IS BUT A SCALE ON THE HIDE OF SOMETHING VERY LARGE, VERY POWERFUL, AND ENTIRELY EVIL. I CALL IT THE MYSTERIOUS SERPENT.
IT'S A SNAKE?
IT'S A THOUSAND TWISTED SOULS THAT WOULD DOMINATE BILLIONS. IT'S OUR JOB TO KILL THE SERPENT--
--BEFORE ITS VENOM POISONS THE WORLD AND DEFEATS THE PEOPLE FOREVER.
OUR JOB? SOUNDS LIKE A LOT FOR TWO PEOPLE.
WE HAVE ALLIES. BUT THE CLOCK IS RUNNING OUT. IF WE DON'T WIN THIS WAR SOON, ALL THAT'S GOOD WILL BE LOST--
--FOREVER. I GET IT. HOW MUCH TIME'S LEFT?

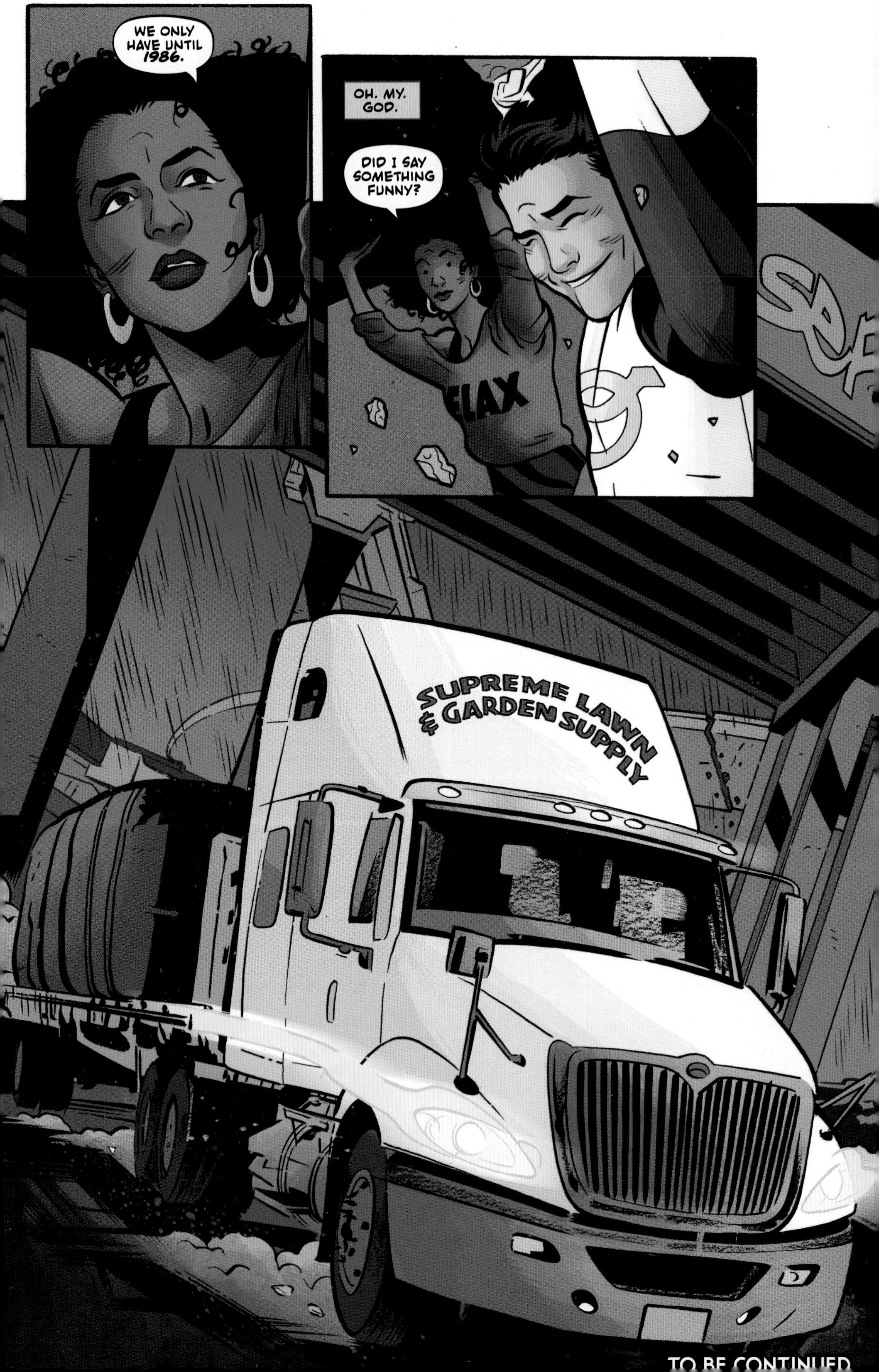
WE ONLY HAVE UNTIL 1986.
OH. MY. GOD.
DID I SAY SOMETHING FUNNY?
SUPREME LAWN & GARDEN SUPPLY
TO BE CONTINUED

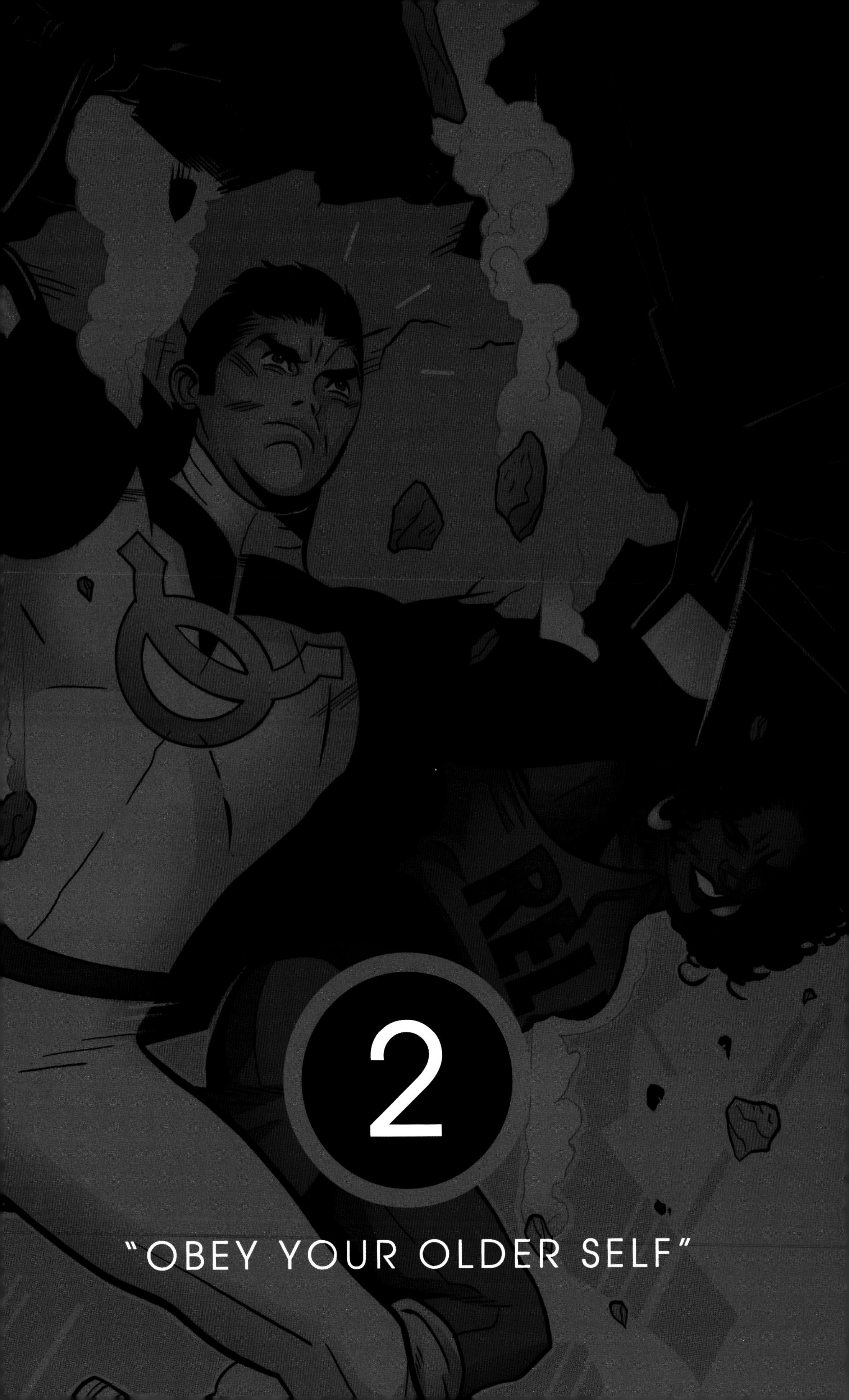

2

“OBEY YOUR OLDER SELF”

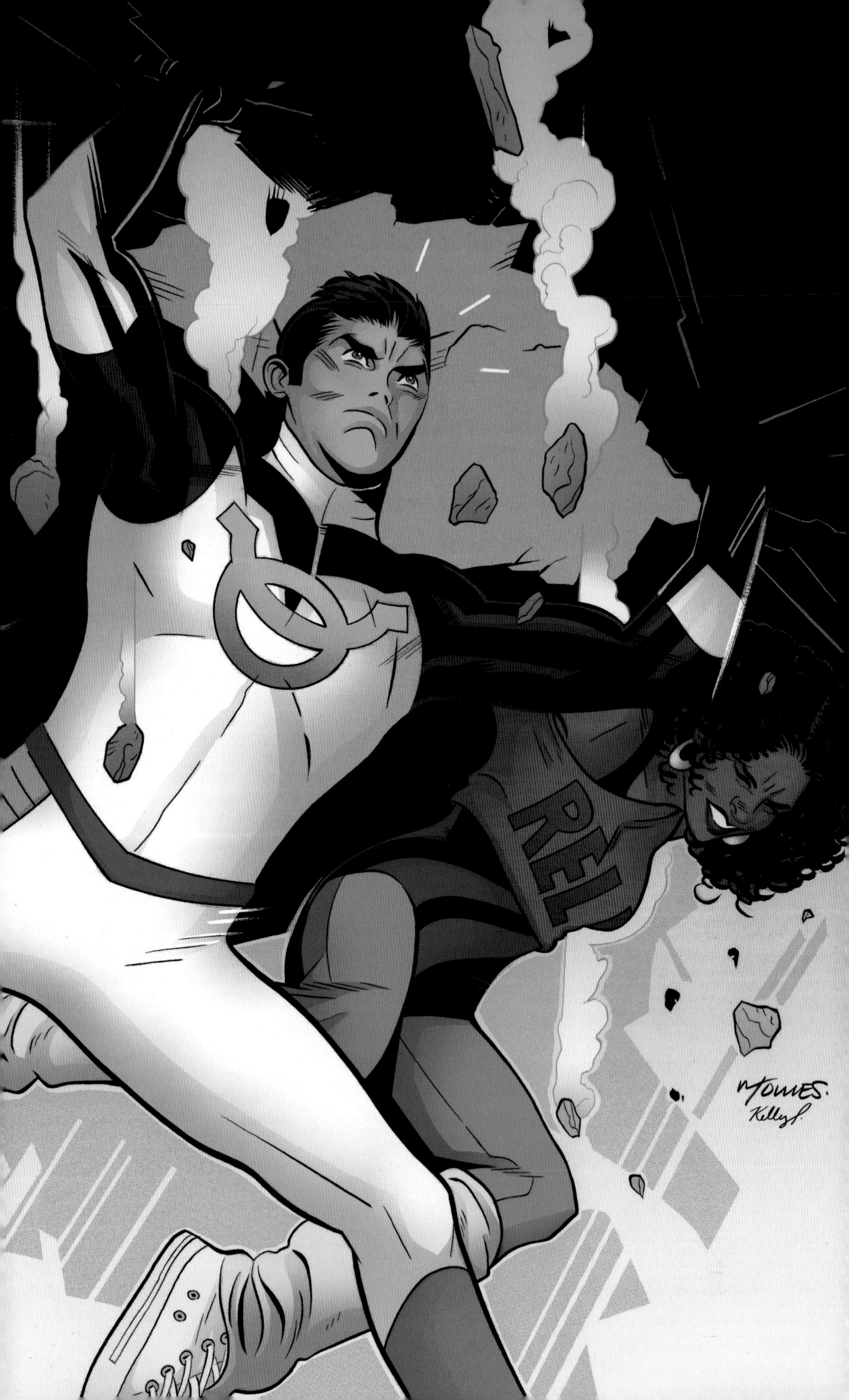
REL

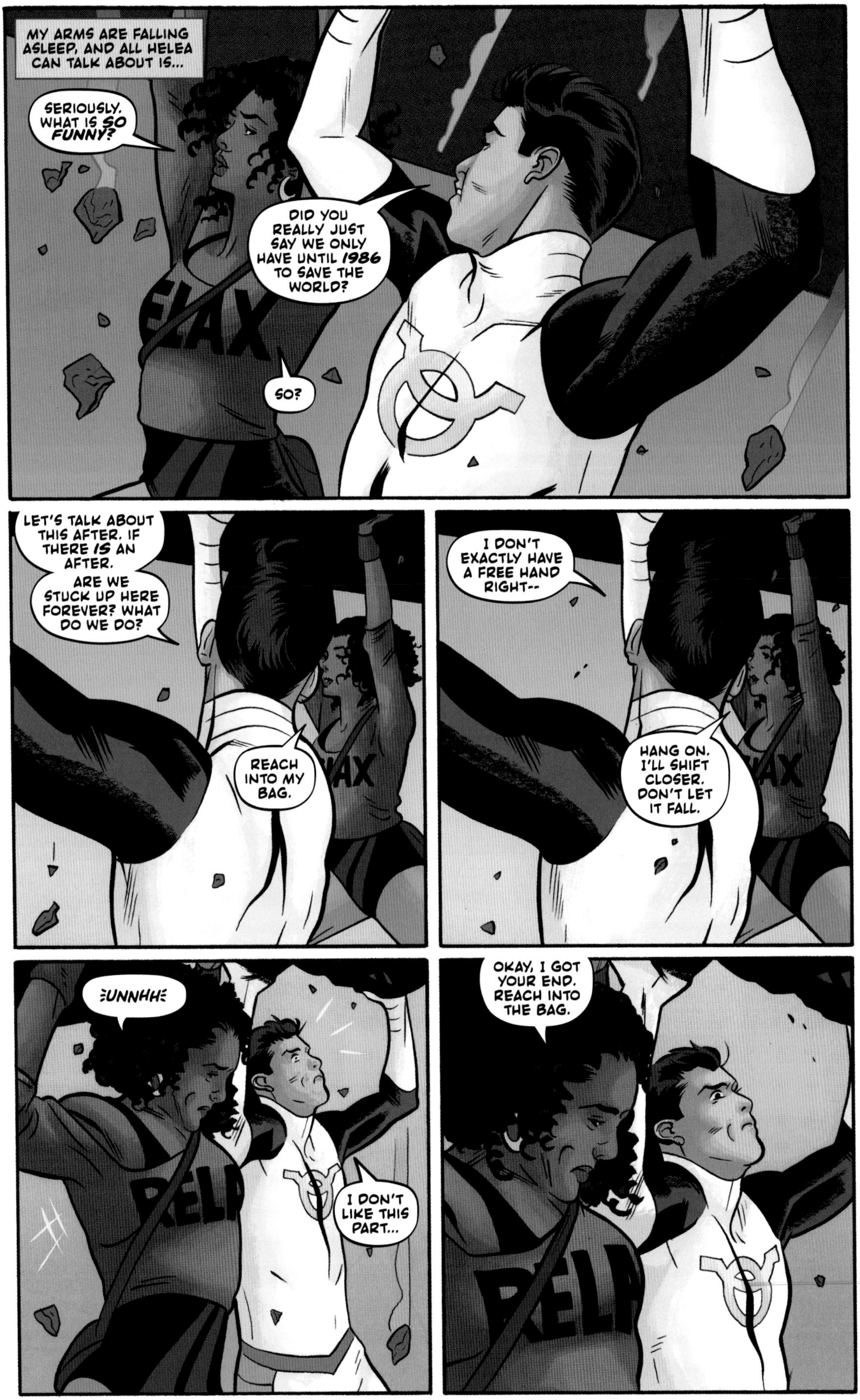
MY ARMS ARE FALLING ASLEEP, AND ALL HELEA CAN TALK ABOUT IS...
SERIOUSLY. WHAT IS *SO FUNNY?*
DID YOU REALLY JUST SAY WE ONLY HAVE UNTIL *1986* TO SAVE THE WORLD?
SO?
LET'S TALK ABOUT THIS AFTER. IF THERE *IS* AN AFTER.
ARE WE STUCK UP HERE FOREVER? WHAT DO WE DO?
REACH INTO MY BAG.
I DON'T EXACTLY HAVE A FREE HAND RIGHT--
HANG ON. I'LL SHIFT CLOSER. DON'T LET IT FALL.
UNNHH
I DON'T LIKE THIS PART...
OKAY, I GOT YOUR END. REACH INTO THE BAG.

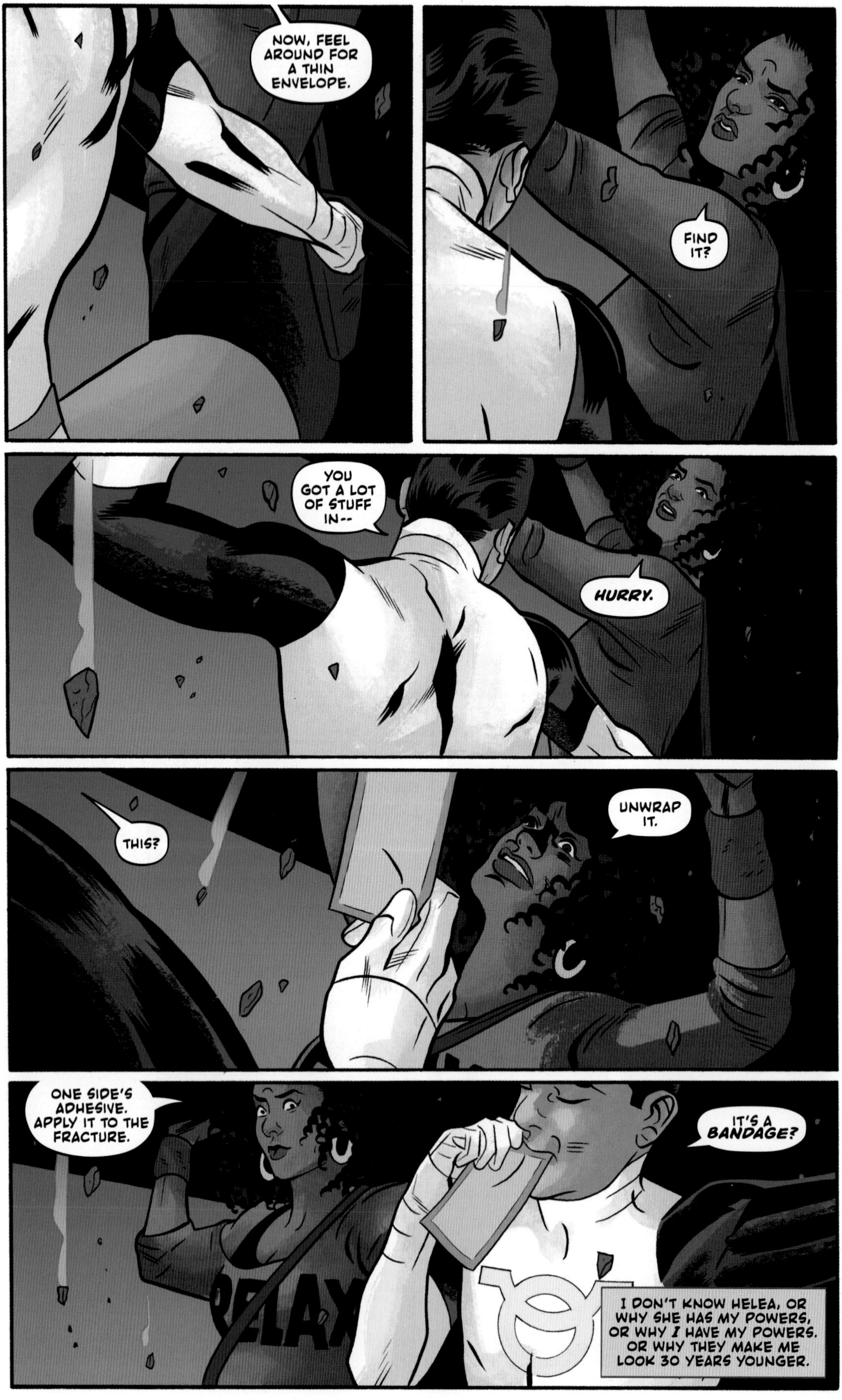
NOW, FEEL AROUND FOR A THIN ENVELOPE.
FIND IT?
YOU GOT A LOT OF STUFF IN--
HURRY.
THIS?
UNWRAP IT.
ONE SIDE'S ADHESIVE. APPLY IT TO THE FRACTURE.
IT'S A BANDAGE?
RELAX
I DON'T KNOW HELEA, OR WHY SHE HAS MY POWERS, OR WHY I HAVE MY POWERS. OR WHY THEY MAKE ME LOOK 30 YEARS YOUNGER.

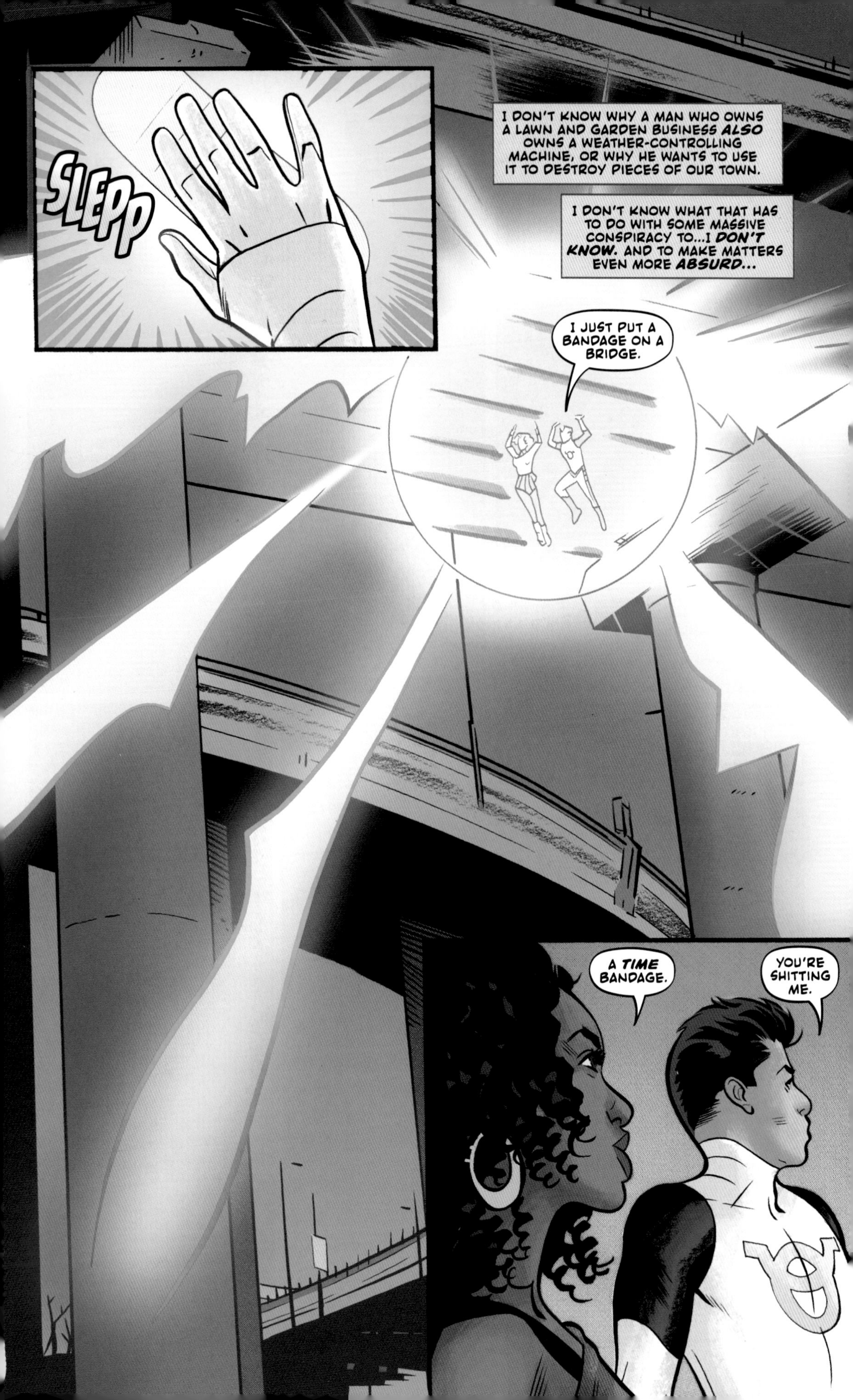
SLEPP
I DON'T KNOW WHY A MAN WHO OWNS A LAWN AND GARDEN BUSINESS ALSO OWNS A WEATHER-CONTROLLING MACHINE, OR WHY HE WANTS TO USE IT TO DESTROY PIECES OF OUR TOWN.
I DON'T KNOW WHAT THAT HAS TO DO WITH SOME MASSIVE CONSPIRACY TO...I DON'T KNOW. AND TO MAKE MATTERS EVEN MORE ABSURD...
I JUST PUT A BANDAGE ON A BRIDGE.
A TIME BANDAGE.
YOU'RE SHITTING ME.

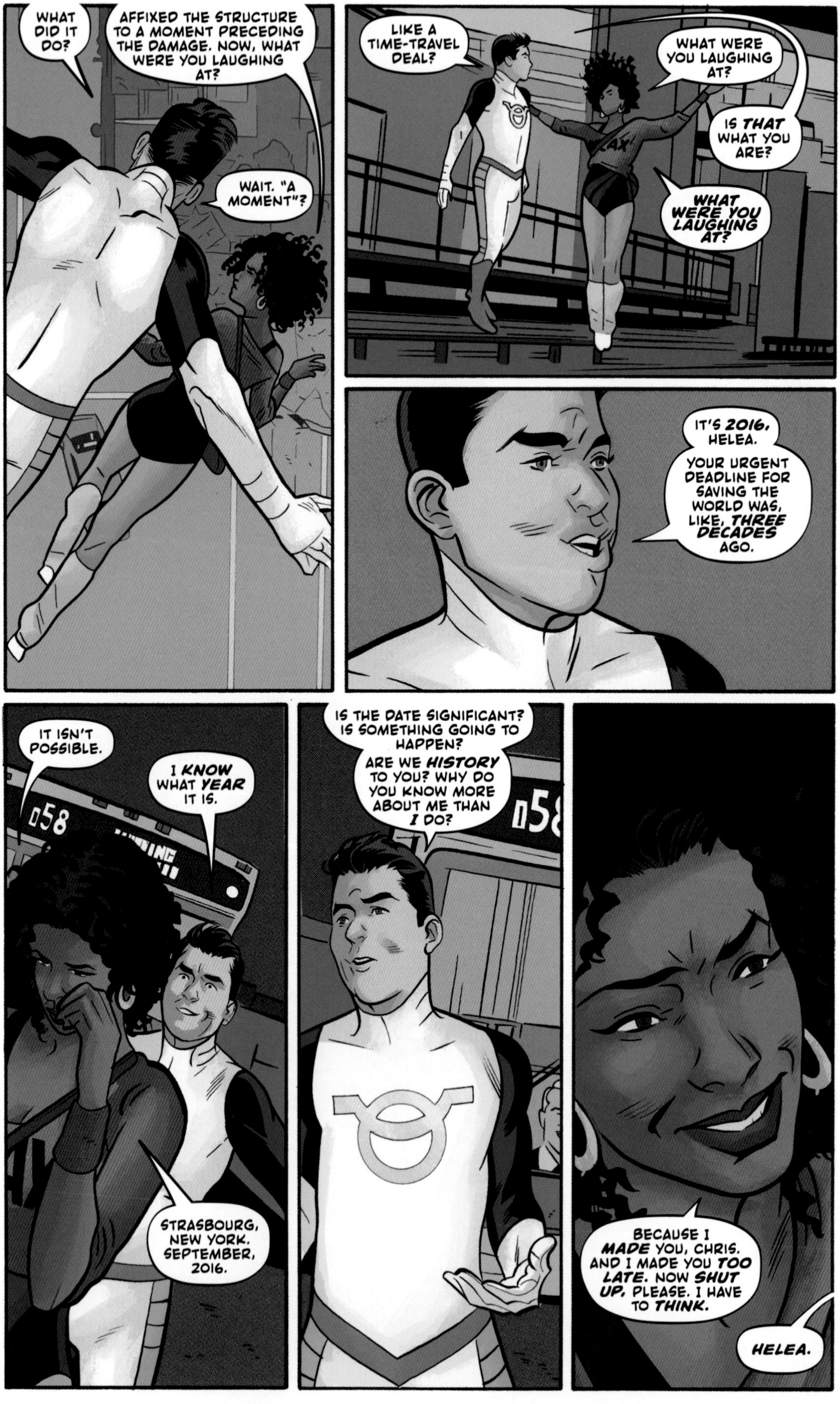
WHAT DID IT DO?
AFFIXED THE STRUCTURE TO A MOMENT PRECEDING THE DAMAGE. NOW, WHAT WERE YOU LAUGHING AT?
WAIT. "A MOMENT"?
LIKE A TIME-TRAVEL DEAL?
WHAT WERE YOU LAUGHING AT?
IS THAT WHAT YOU ARE?
WHAT WERE YOU LAUGHING AT?
IT'S 2016, HELEA.
YOUR URGENT DEADLINE FOR SAVING THE WORLD WAS, LIKE, THREE DECADES AGO.
IT ISN'T POSSIBLE.
I KNOW WHAT YEAR IT IS.
D58
STRASBOURG, NEW YORK. SEPTEMBER, 2016.
IS THE DATE SIGNIFICANT? IS SOMETHING GOING TO HAPPEN?
ARE WE HISTORY TO YOU? WHY DO YOU KNOW MORE ABOUT ME THAN I DO?
D58
BECAUSE I MADE YOU, CHRIS. AND I MADE YOU TOO LATE. NOW SHUT UP. PLEASE. I HAVE TO THINK.
HELEA.

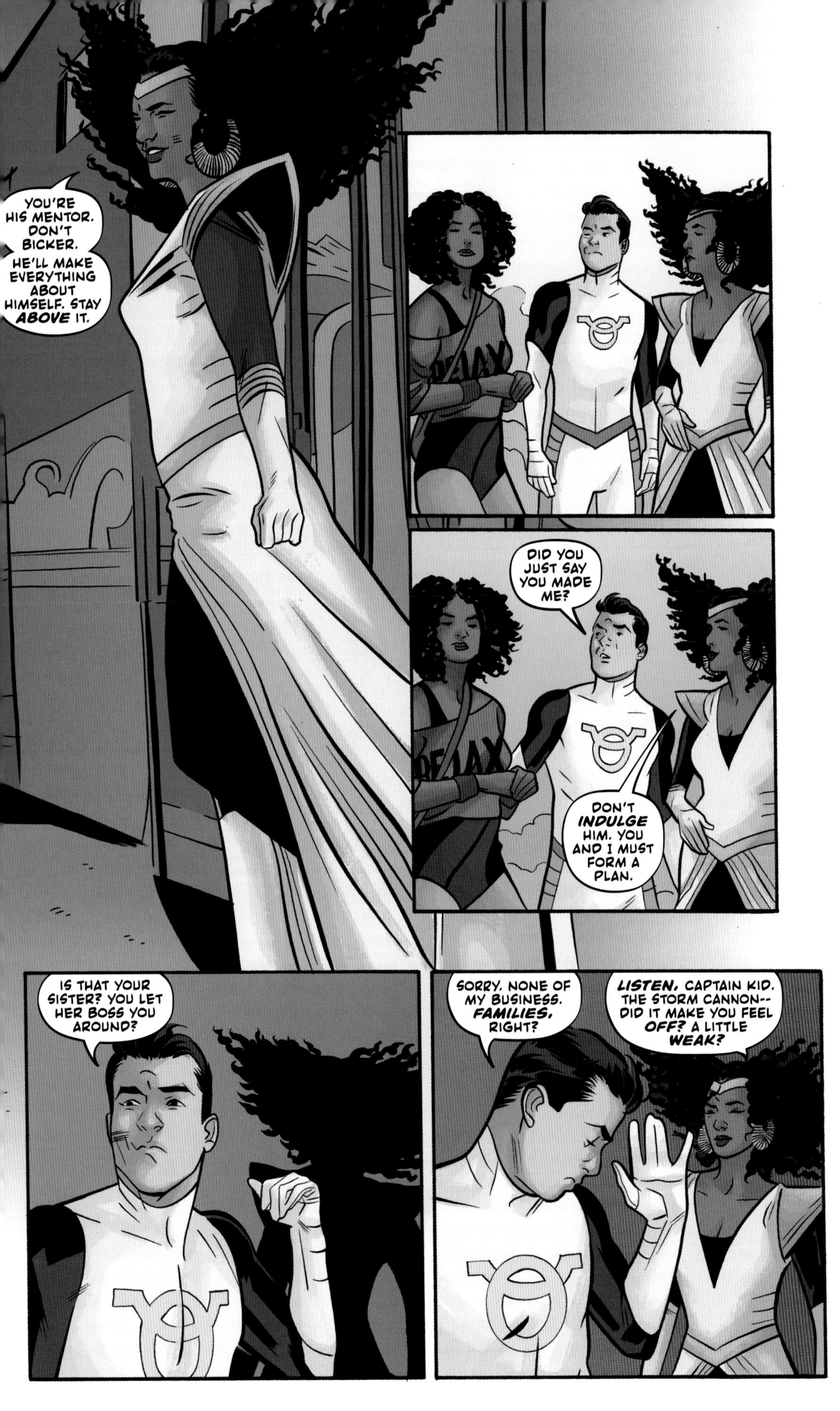
YOU'RE HIS MENTOR. DON'T BICKER.
HE'LL MAKE EVERYTHING ABOUT HIMSELF. STAY *ABOVE* IT.
DID YOU JUST SAY YOU MADE ME?
DON'T *INDULGE* HIM. YOU AND I MUST FORM A PLAN.
IS THAT YOUR SISTER? YOU LET HER BOSS YOU AROUND?
SORRY. NONE OF MY BUSINESS. *FAMILIES,* RIGHT?
LISTEN, CAPTAIN KID. THE STORM CANNON-- DID IT MAKE YOU FEEL *OFF?* A LITTLE *WEAK?*

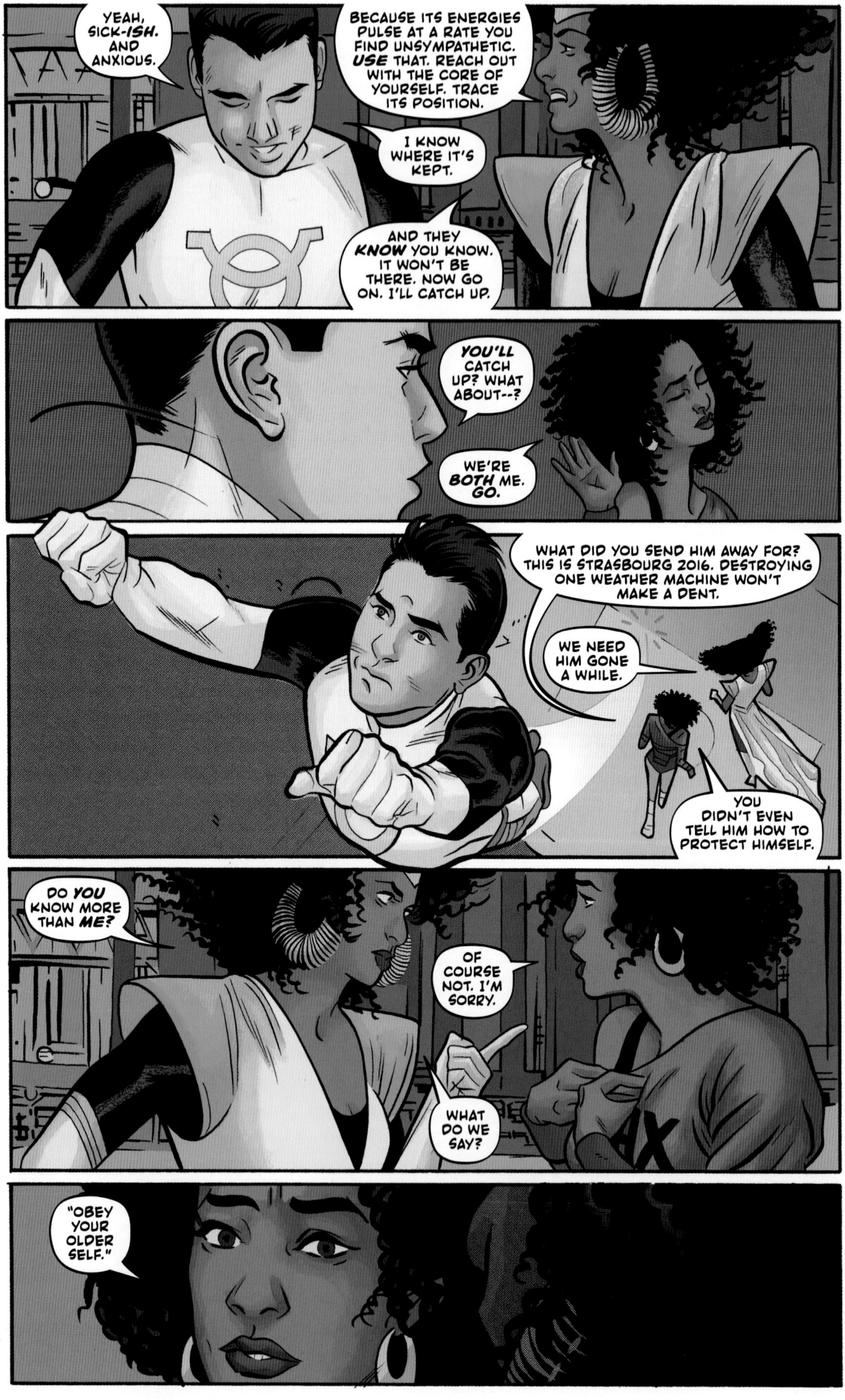
YEAH, SICK-*ISH.* AND ANXIOUS.
BECAUSE ITS ENERGIES PULSE AT A RATE YOU FIND UNSYMPATHETIC. *USE* THAT. REACH OUT WITH THE CORE OF YOURSELF. TRACE ITS POSITION.
I KNOW WHERE IT'S KEPT.
AND THEY *KNOW* YOU KNOW. IT WON'T BE THERE. NOW GO ON. I'LL CATCH UP.
YOU'LL CATCH UP? WHAT ABOUT--?
WE'RE *BOTH* ME. *GO.*
WHAT DID YOU SEND HIM AWAY FOR? THIS IS STRASBOURG 2016. DESTROYING ONE WEATHER MACHINE WON'T MAKE A DENT.
WE NEED HIM GONE A WHILE.
YOU DIDN'T EVEN TELL HIM HOW TO PROTECT HIMSELF.
DO *YOU* KNOW MORE THAN *ME?*
OF COURSE NOT. I'M SORRY.
WHAT DO WE SAY?
"OBEY YOUR OLDER SELF."

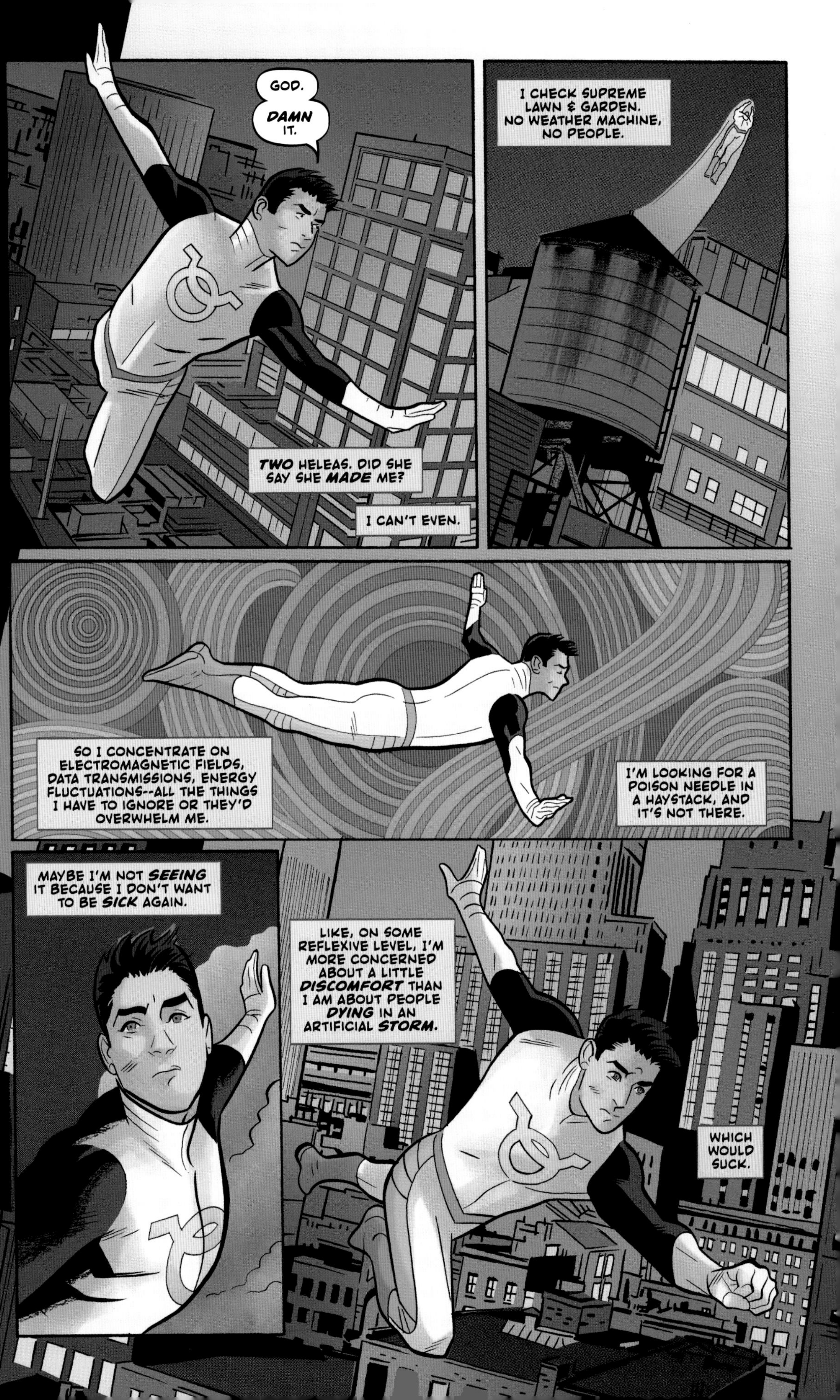
GOD.
DAMN IT.
TWO HELEAS. DID SHE SAY SHE MADE ME?
I CAN'T EVEN.
I CHECK SUPREME LAWN & GARDEN. NO WEATHER MACHINE, NO PEOPLE.
SO I CONCENTRATE ON ELECTROMAGNETIC FIELDS, DATA TRANSMISSIONS, ENERGY FLUCTUATIONS--ALL THE THINGS I HAVE TO IGNORE OR THEY'D OVERWHELM ME.
I'M LOOKING FOR A POISON NEEDLE IN A HAYSTACK, AND IT'S NOT THERE.
MAYBE I'M NOT SEEING IT BECAUSE I DON'T WANT TO BE SICK AGAIN.
LIKE, ON SOME REFLEXIVE LEVEL, I'M MORE CONCERNED ABOUT A LITTLE DISCOMFORT THAN I AM ABOUT PEOPLE DYING IN AN ARTIFICIAL STORM.
WHICH WOULD SUCK.

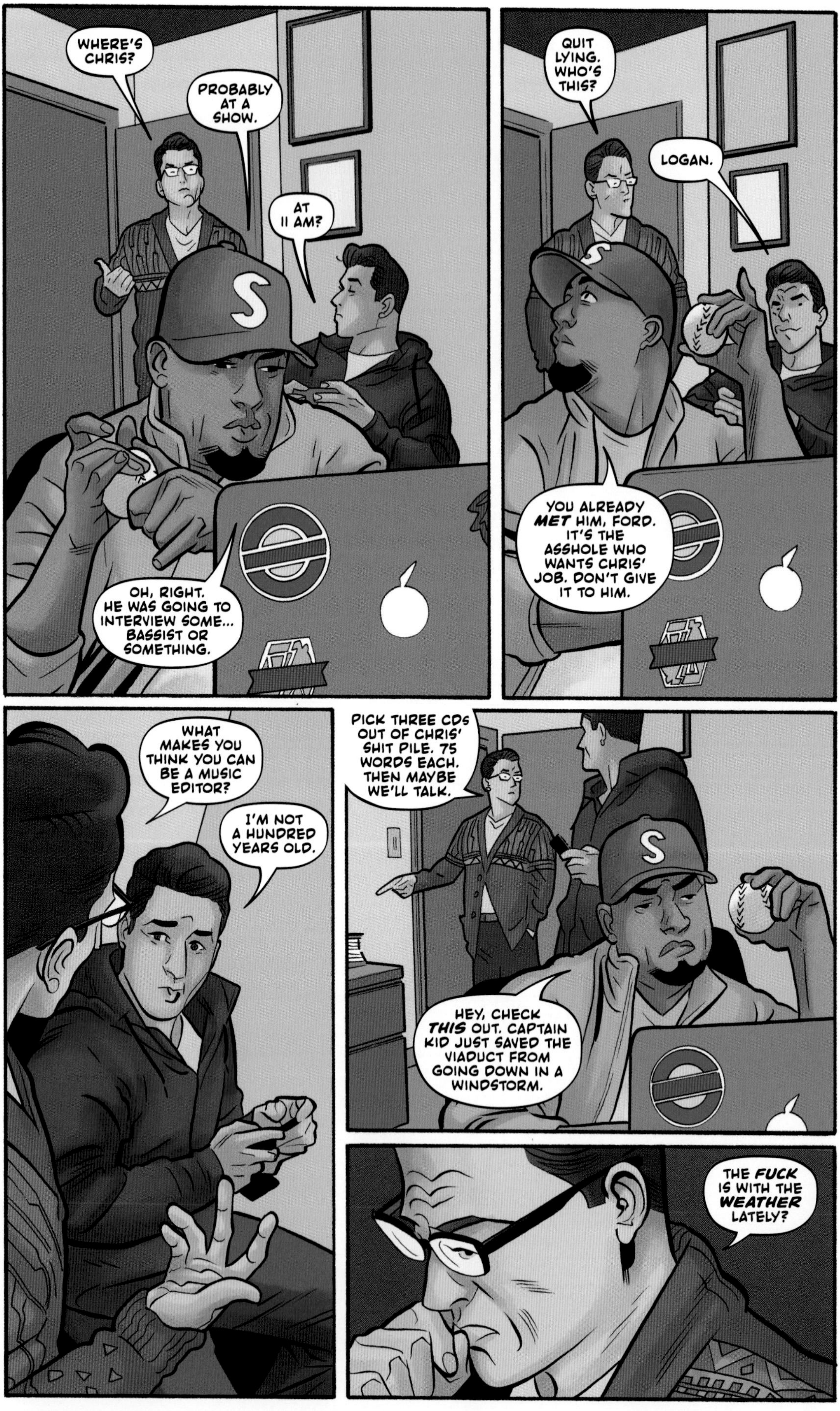
WHERE'S CHRIS?
PROBABLY AT A SHOW.
AT 11 AM?
OH, RIGHT. HE WAS GOING TO INTERVIEW SOME... BASSIST OR SOMETHING.
QUIT LYING. WHO'S THIS?
LOGAN.
YOU ALREADY MET HIM, FORD. IT'S THE ASSHOLE WHO WANTS CHRIS' JOB. DON'T GIVE IT TO HIM.
WHAT MAKES YOU THINK YOU CAN BE A MUSIC EDITOR?
I'M NOT A HUNDRED YEARS OLD.
PICK THREE CDs OUT OF CHRIS' SHIT PILE. 75 WORDS EACH. THEN MAYBE WE'LL TALK.
HEY, CHECK THIS OUT. CAPTAIN KID JUST SAVED THE VIADUCT FROM GOING DOWN IN A WINDSTORM.
THE FUCK IS WITH THE WEATHER LATELY?

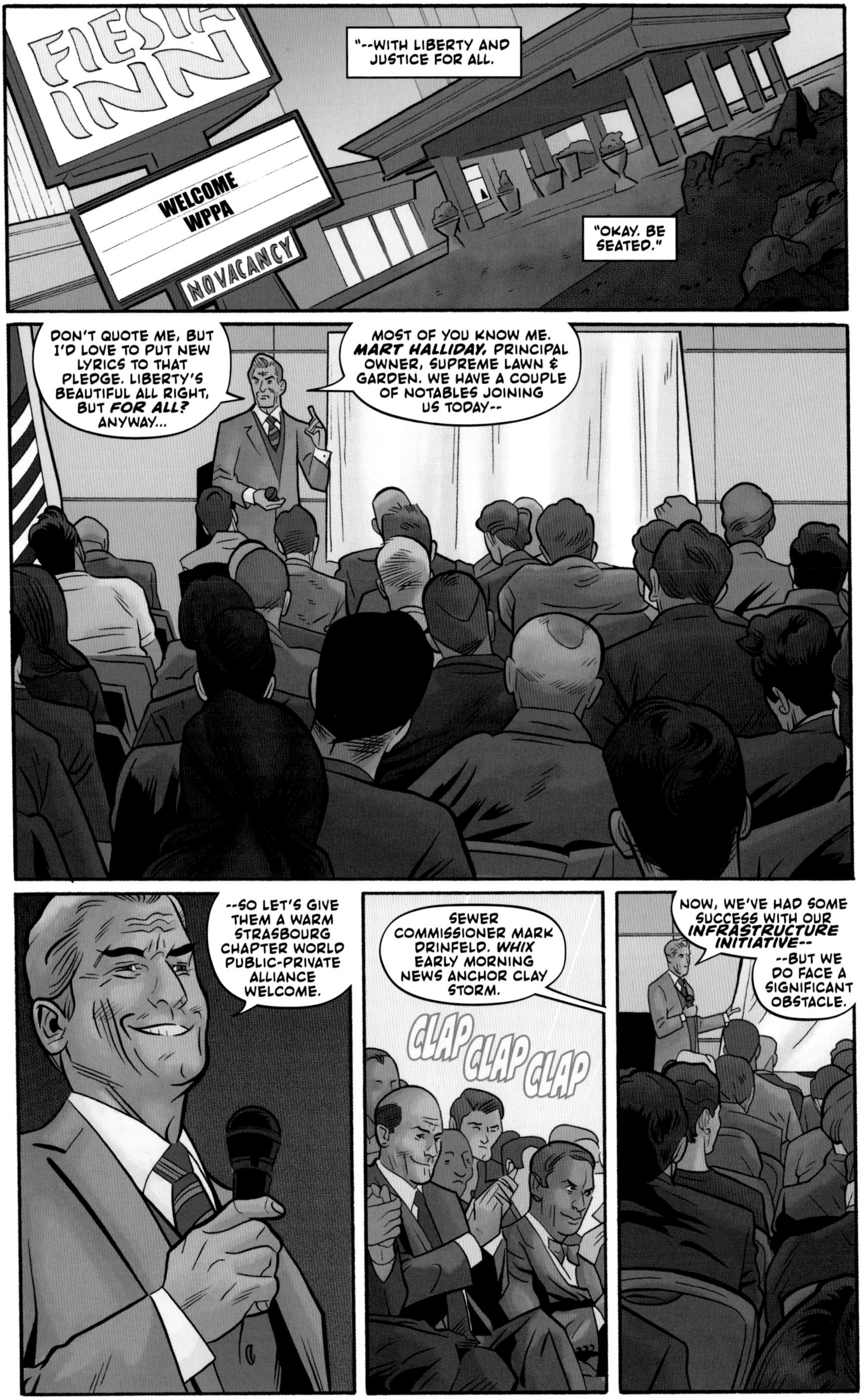
FIESTA INN
WELCOME WPPA
NO VACANCY
"--WITH LIBERTY AND JUSTICE FOR ALL.
"OKAY. BE SEATED."
DON'T QUOTE ME, BUT I'D LOVE TO PUT NEW LYRICS TO THAT PLEDGE. LIBERTY'S BEAUTIFUL ALL RIGHT, BUT FOR ALL? ANYWAY...
MOST OF YOU KNOW ME. MART HALLIDAY, PRINCIPAL OWNER, SUPREME LAWN & GARDEN. WE HAVE A COUPLE OF NOTABLES JOINING US TODAY--
--SO LET'S GIVE THEM A WARM STRASBOURG CHAPTER WORLD PUBLIC-PRIVATE ALLIANCE WELCOME.
SEWER COMMISSIONER MARK DRINFELD. WHIX EARLY MORNING NEWS ANCHOR CLAY STORM.
CLAP CLAP CLAP
NOW, WE'VE HAD SOME SUCCESS WITH OUR INFRASTRUCTURE INITIATIVE--
--BUT WE DO FACE A SIGNIFICANT OBSTACLE.

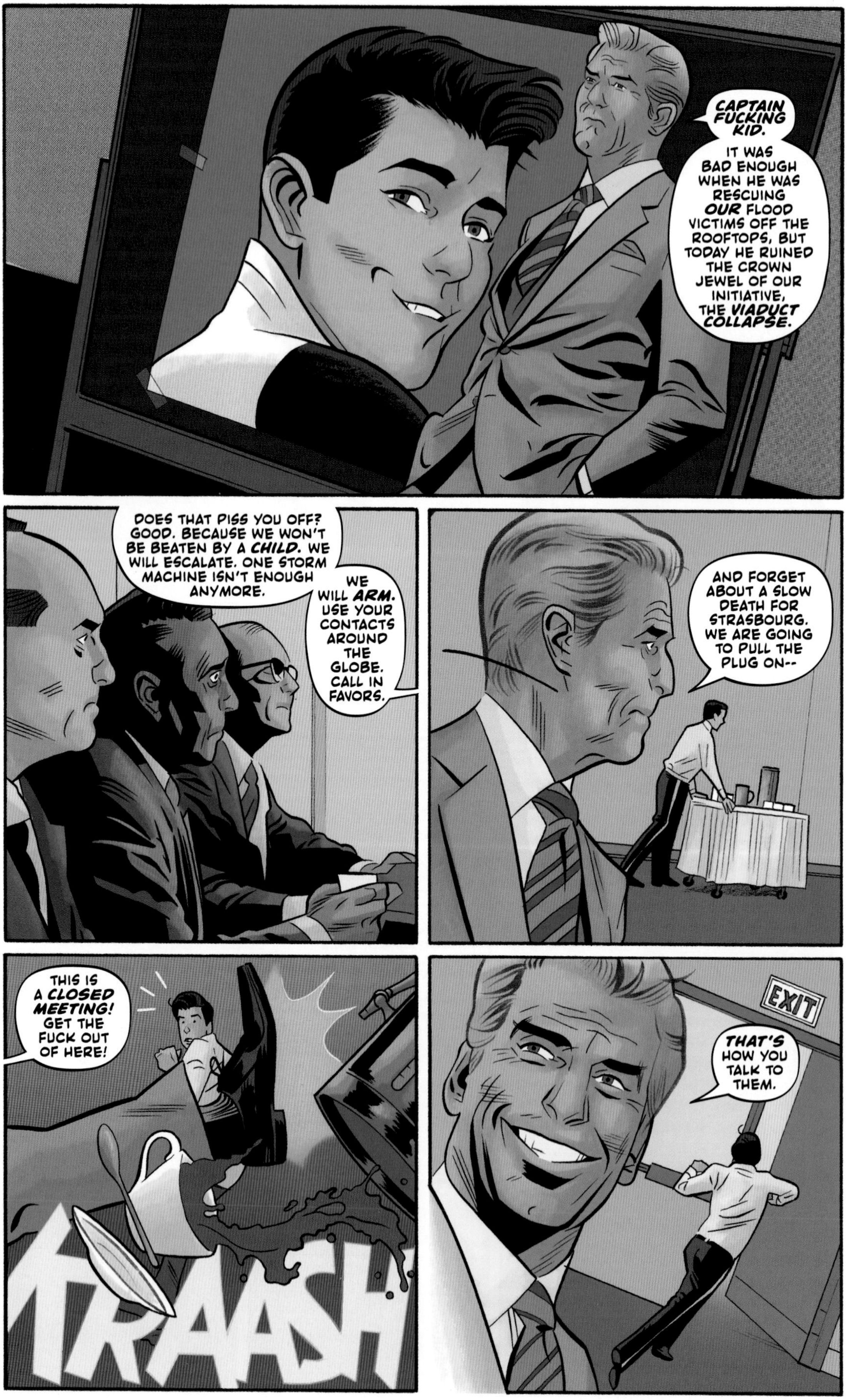

CAPTAIN FUCKING KID.
IT WAS BAD ENOUGH WHEN HE WAS RESCUING OUR FLOOD VICTIMS OFF THE ROOFTOPS, BUT TODAY HE RUINED THE CROWN JEWEL OF OUR INITIATIVE, THE VIADUCT COLLAPSE.
DOES THAT PISS YOU OFF? GOOD. BECAUSE WE WON'T BE BEATEN BY A CHILD. WE WILL ESCALATE. ONE STORM MACHINE ISN'T ENOUGH ANYMORE.
WE WILL ARM. USE YOUR CONTACTS AROUND THE GLOBE. CALL IN FAVORS.
AND FORGET ABOUT A SLOW DEATH FOR STRASBOURG. WE ARE GOING TO PULL THE PLUG ON--
THIS IS A CLOSED MEETING! GET THE FUCK OUT OF HERE!
TRAASH
EXIT
THAT'S HOW YOU TALK TO THEM.

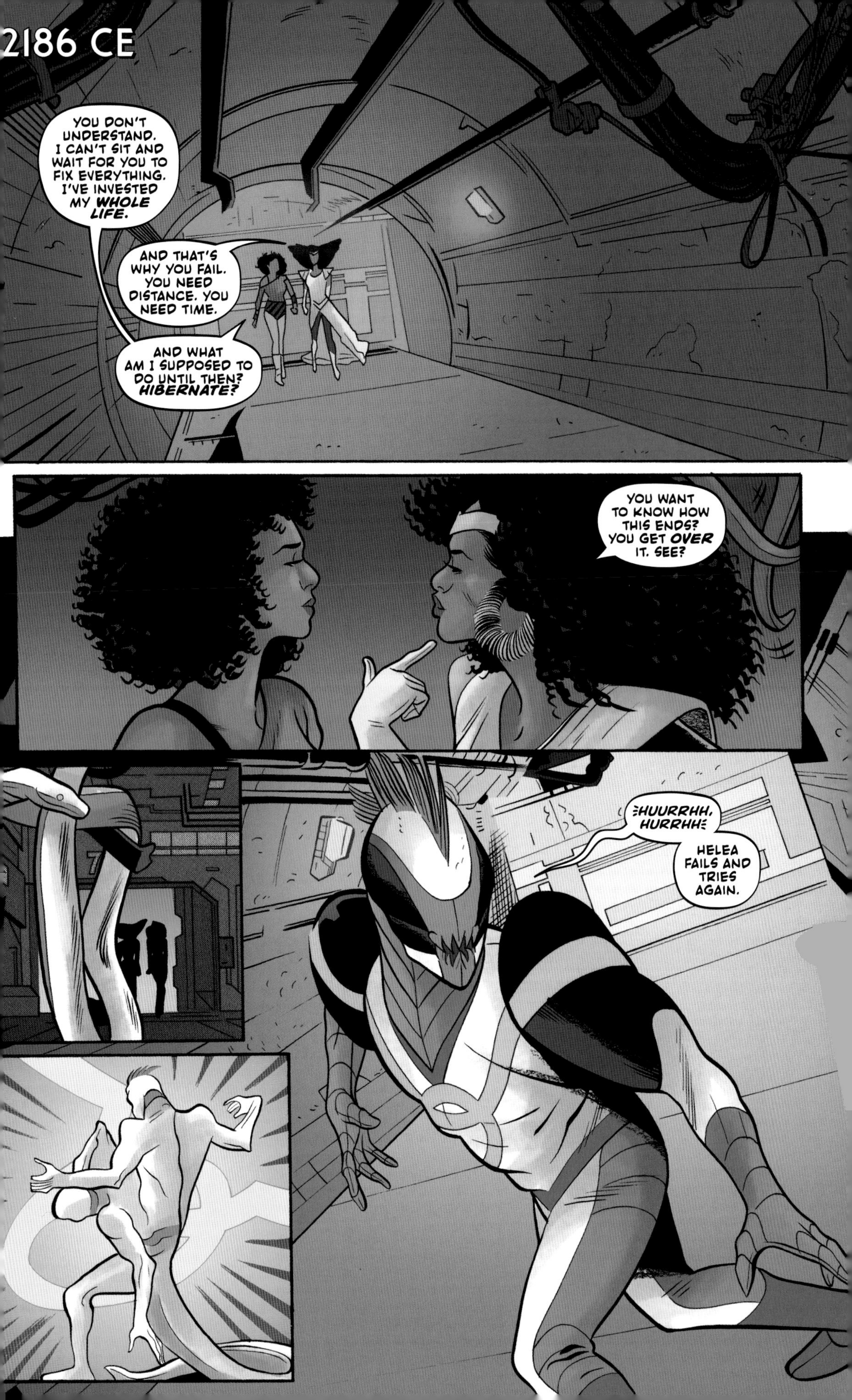
2186 CE
YOU DON'T UNDERSTAND. I CAN'T SIT AND WAIT FOR YOU TO FIX EVERYTHING. I'VE INVESTED MY WHOLE LIFE.
AND THAT'S WHY YOU FAIL. YOU NEED DISTANCE. YOU NEED TIME.
AND WHAT AM I SUPPOSED TO DO UNTIL THEN? HIBERNATE?
YOU WANT TO KNOW HOW THIS ENDS? YOU GET OVER IT. SEE?
HUURRHH, HURRHH
HELEA FAILS AND TRIES AGAIN.

SEARCHING FOR HOURS, ALL DEAD ENDS. I'D KEEP LOOKING, BUT I CAN'T MISS MY OWN *BIRTHDAY DINNER*.

VISUALIZE MY CHEST SYMBOL--

--AND I'M *ME* AGAIN.

EMOTIONALLY, A LITTLE CALMER. *PHYSICALLY*--

--NOT WHAT YOU'D CALL AN *UPGRADE*.

MAYA, YOU'RE HERE ALREADY. AM I LATE?

CHRIS, I CAN'T GO. I'M SORRY. I CAN'T.

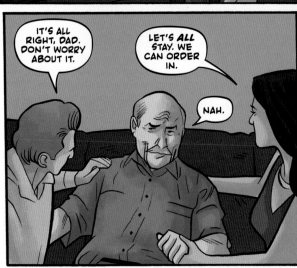

IT'S ALL RIGHT, DAD. DON'T WORRY ABOUT IT.

LET'S *ALL* STAY. WE CAN ORDER IN.

NAH.

I GOT MY BOOK. YOU GO OUT. IT'S CHRIS' BIRTHDAY. GO OUT.

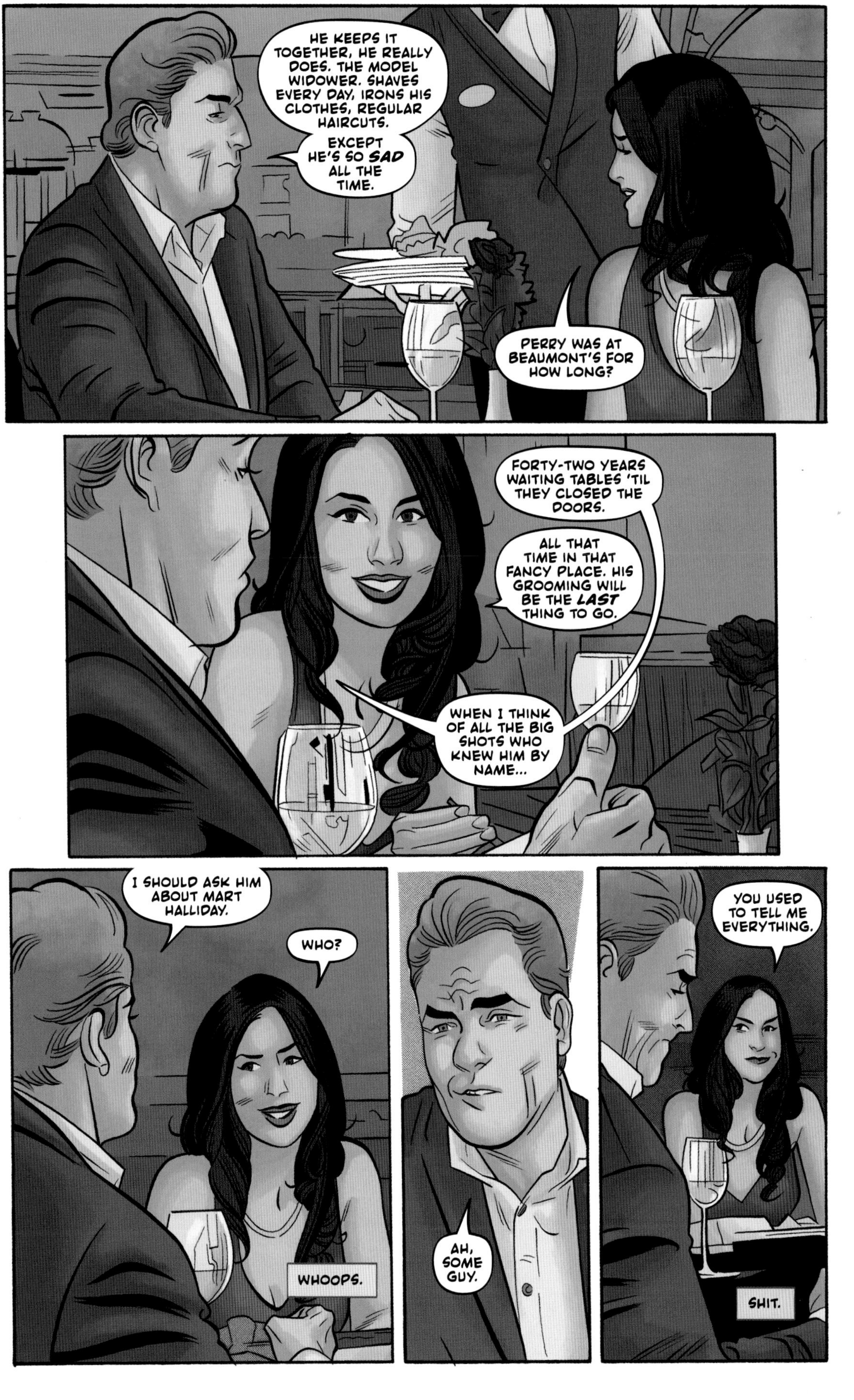
HE KEEPS IT TOGETHER, HE REALLY DOES. THE MODEL WIDOWER. SHAVES EVERY DAY, IRONS HIS CLOTHES, REGULAR HAIRCUTS.
EXCEPT HE'S SO SAD ALL THE TIME.
PERRY WAS AT BEAUMONT'S FOR HOW LONG?
FORTY-TWO YEARS WAITING TABLES 'TIL THEY CLOSED THE DOORS.
ALL THAT TIME IN THAT FANCY PLACE. HIS GROOMING WILL BE THE LAST THING TO GO.
WHEN I THINK OF ALL THE BIG SHOTS WHO KNEW HIM BY NAME...
I SHOULD ASK HIM ABOUT MART HALLIDAY.
WHO?
WHOOPS.
AH, SOME GUY.
YOU USED TO TELL ME EVERYTHING.
SHIT.

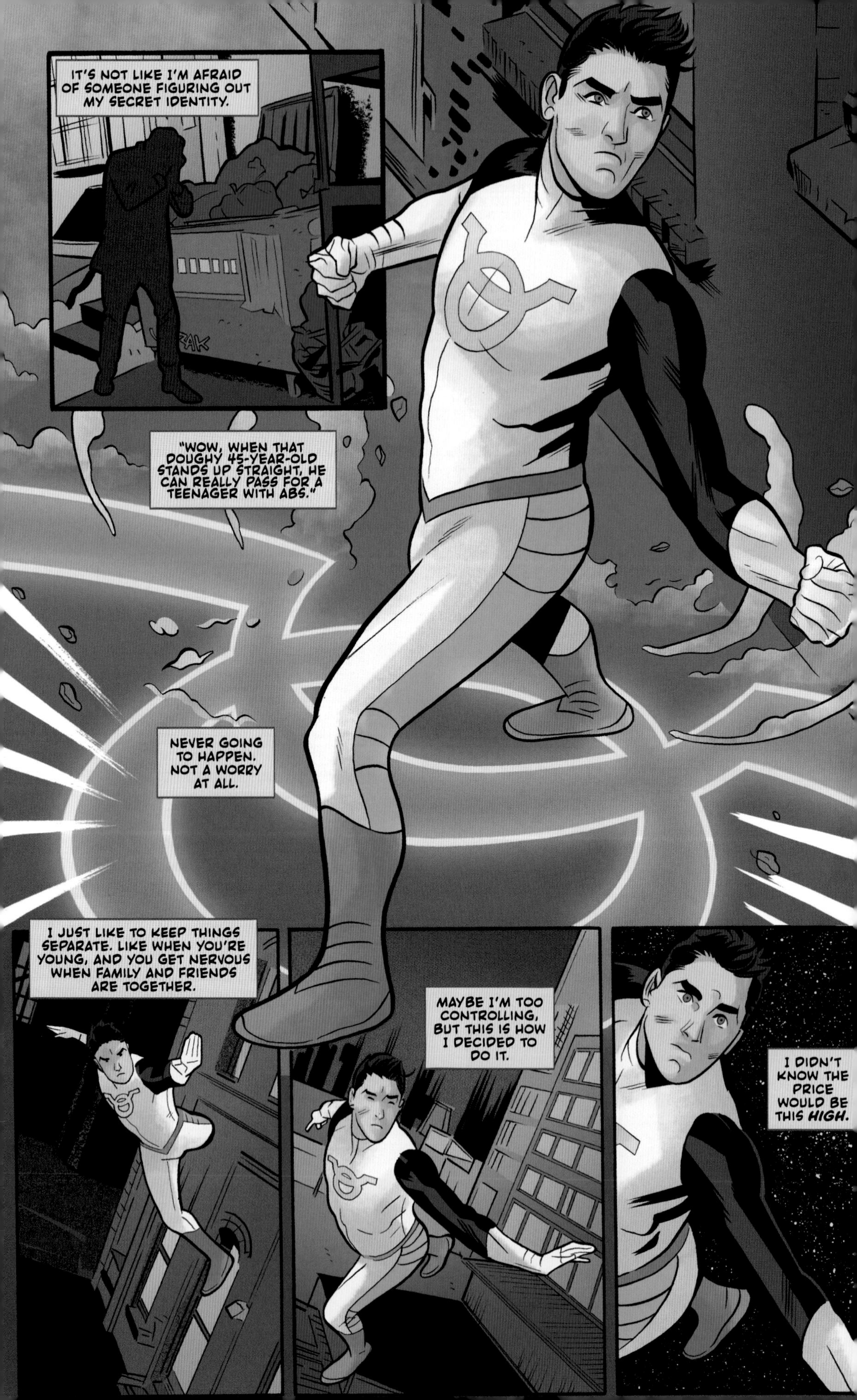
IT'S NOT LIKE I'M AFRAID OF SOMEONE FIGURING OUT MY SECRET IDENTITY.
"WOW, WHEN THAT DOUGHY 45-YEAR-OLD STANDS UP STRAIGHT, HE CAN REALLY PASS FOR A TEENAGER WITH ABS."
NEVER GOING TO HAPPEN. NOT A WORRY AT ALL.
I JUST LIKE TO KEEP THINGS SEPARATE. LIKE WHEN YOU'RE YOUNG, AND YOU GET NERVOUS WHEN FAMILY AND FRIENDS ARE TOGETHER.
MAYBE I'M TOO CONTROLLING, BUT THIS IS HOW I DECIDED TO DO IT.
I DIDN'T KNOW THE PRICE WOULD BE THIS *HIGH*.

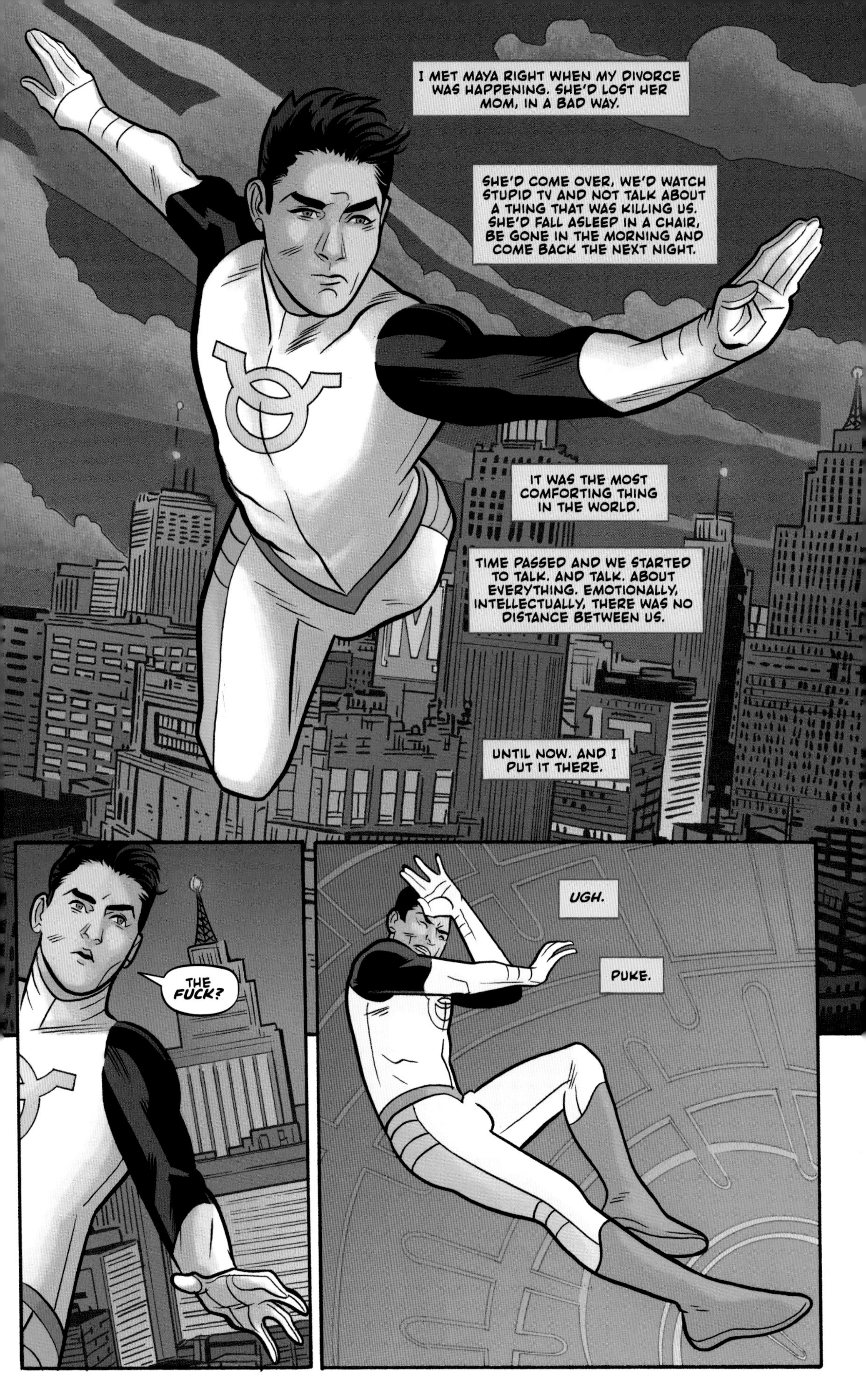

I MET MAYA RIGHT WHEN MY DIVORCE WAS HAPPENING. SHE'D LOST HER MOM, IN A BAD WAY.
SHE'D COME OVER, WE'D WATCH STUPID TV AND NOT TALK ABOUT A THING THAT WAS KILLING US. SHE'D FALL ASLEEP IN A CHAIR, BE GONE IN THE MORNING AND COME BACK THE NEXT NIGHT.
IT WAS THE MOST COMFORTING THING IN THE WORLD.
TIME PASSED AND WE STARTED TO TALK. AND TALK. ABOUT EVERYTHING. EMOTIONALLY, INTELLECTUALLY, THERE WAS NO DISTANCE BETWEEN US.
UNTIL NOW. AND I PUT IT THERE.
THE *FUCK?*
UGH.
PUKE.

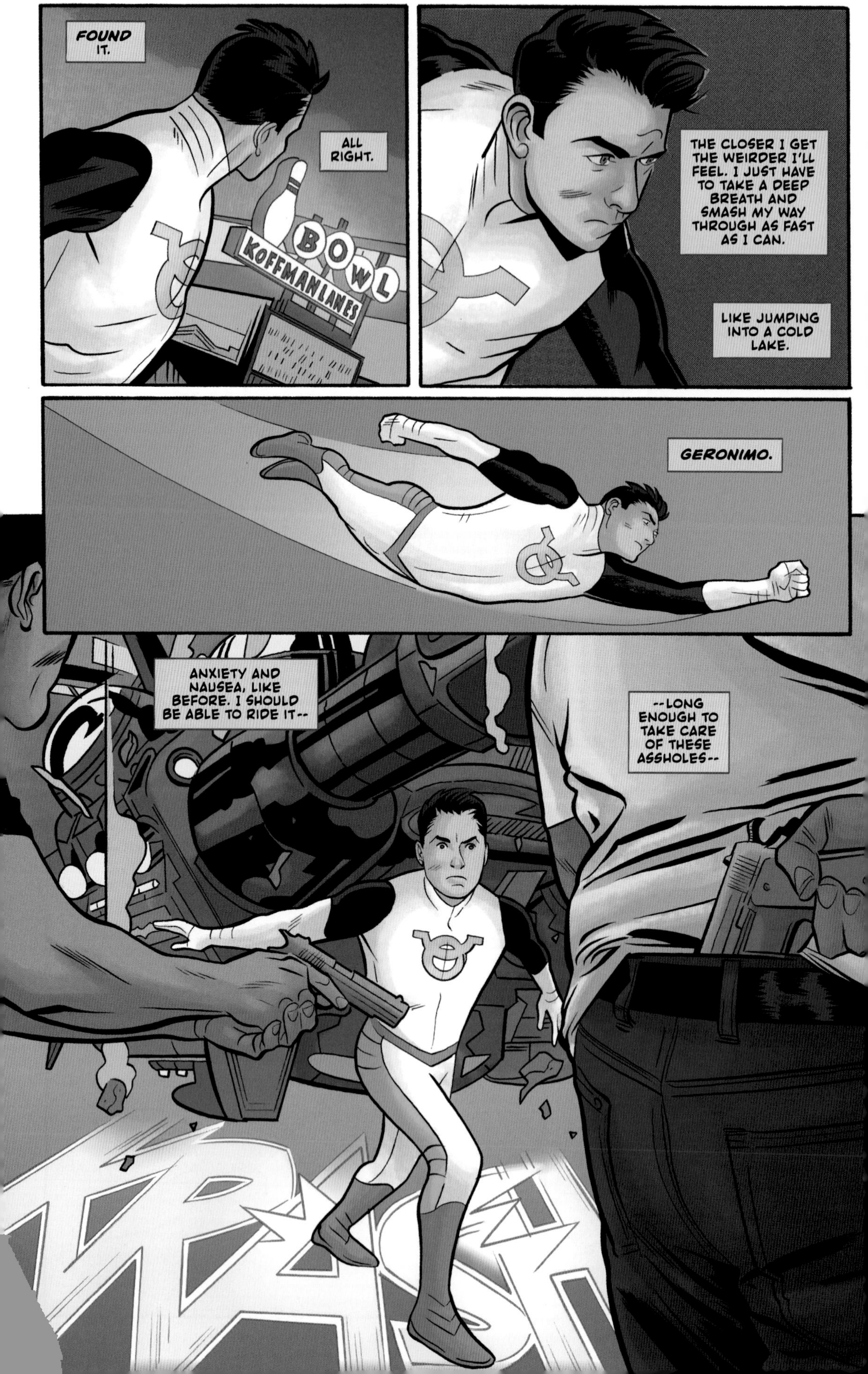
FOUND IT.
ALL RIGHT.
BOWL
KOFFMAN LANES
THE CLOSER I GET THE WEIRDER I'LL FEEL. I JUST HAVE TO TAKE A DEEP BREATH AND SMASH MY WAY THROUGH AS FAST AS I CAN.
LIKE JUMPING INTO A COLD LAKE.
GERONIMO.
ANXIETY AND NAUSEA, LIKE BEFORE. I SHOULD BE ABLE TO RIDE IT--
--LONG ENOUGH TO TAKE CARE OF THESE ASSHOLES--

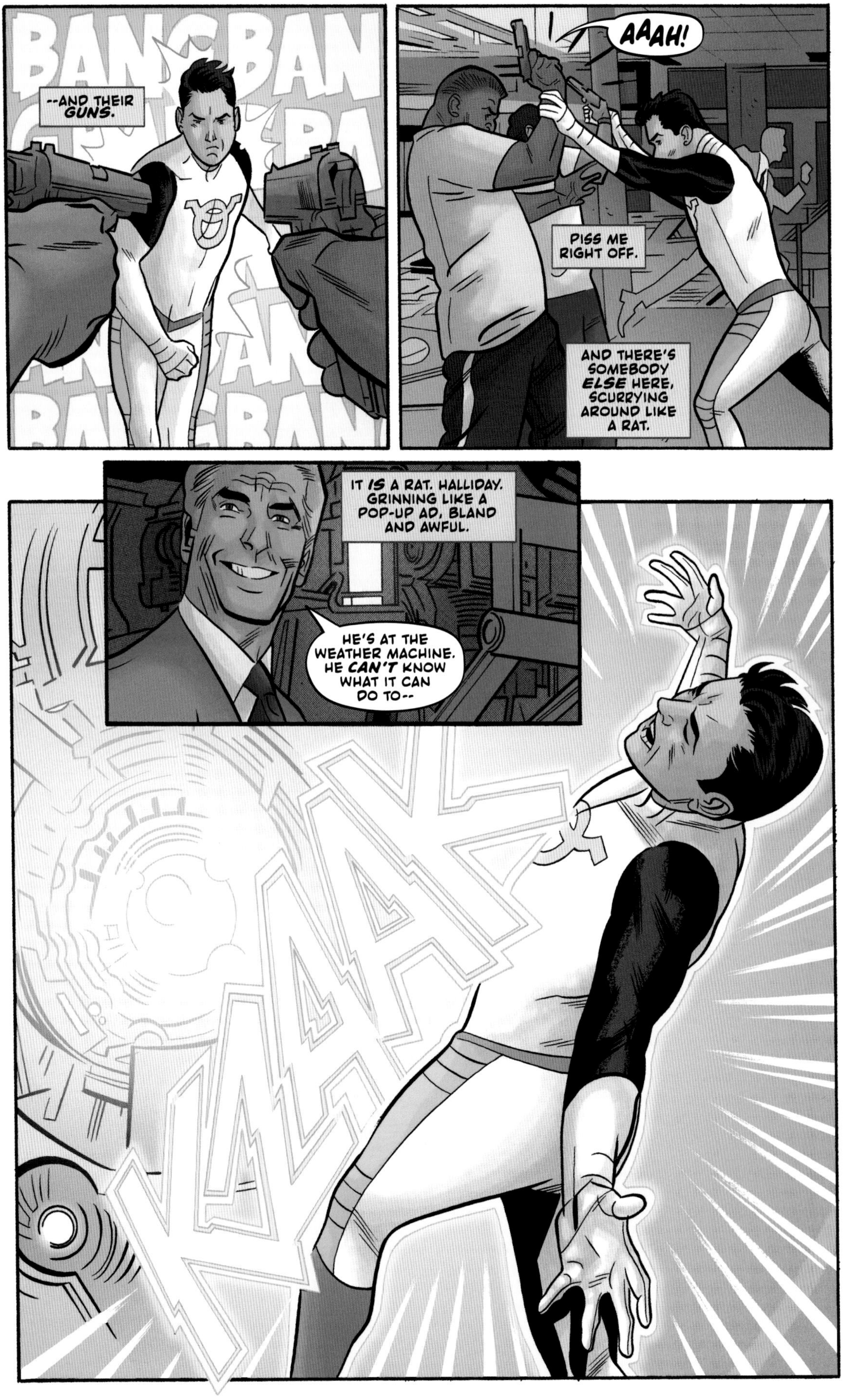
--AND THEIR GUNS.
AAAH!
PISS ME RIGHT OFF.
AND THERE'S SOMEBODY ELSE HERE, SCURRYING AROUND LIKE A RAT.
IT IS A RAT. HALLIDAY. GRINNING LIKE A POP-UP AD, BLAND AND AWFUL.
HE'S AT THE WEATHER MACHINE. HE CAN'T KNOW WHAT IT CAN DO TO--

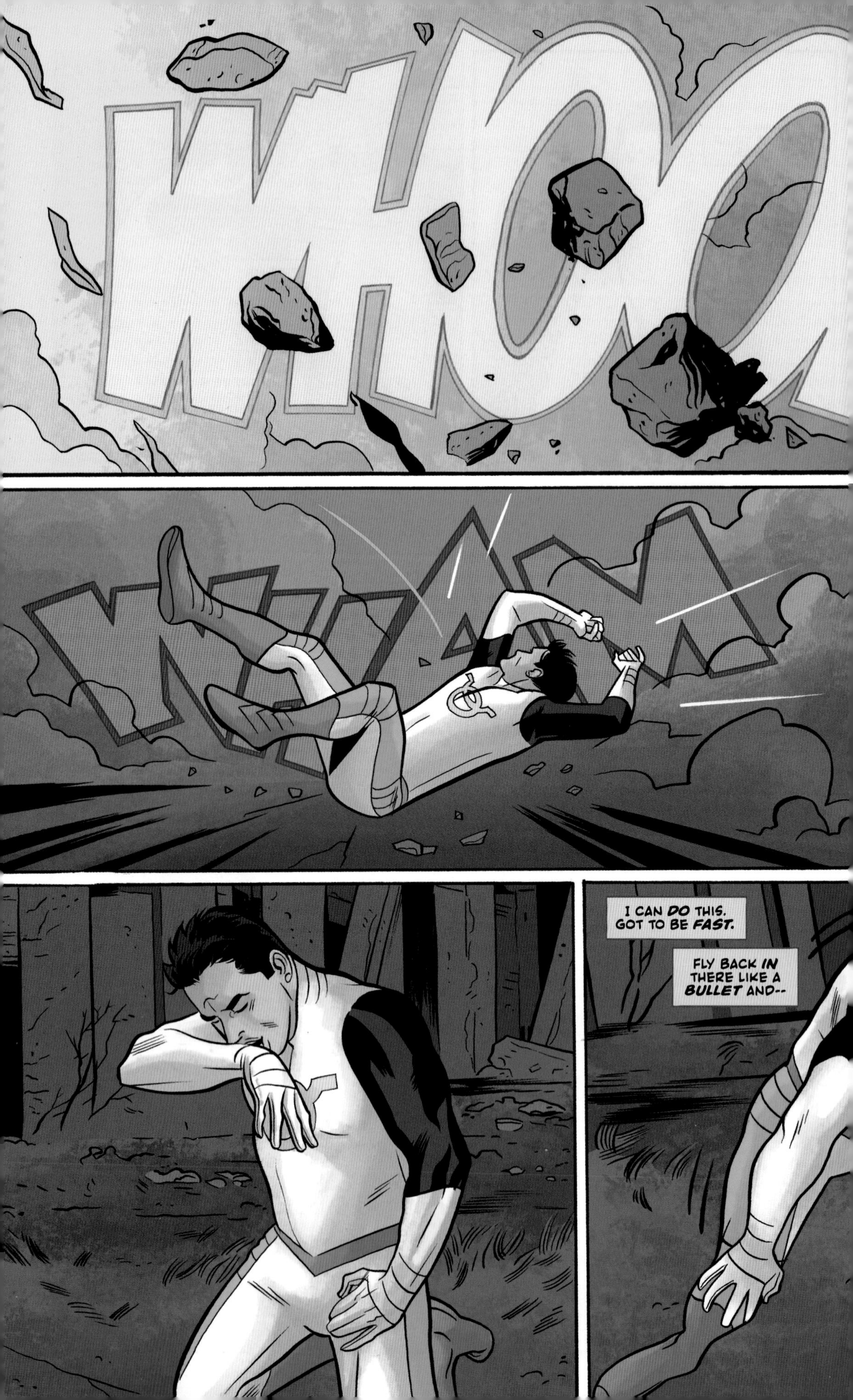
WHOO
I CAN *DO* THIS. GOT TO BE *FAST.*
FLY BACK *IN* THERE LIKE A *BULLET* AND--

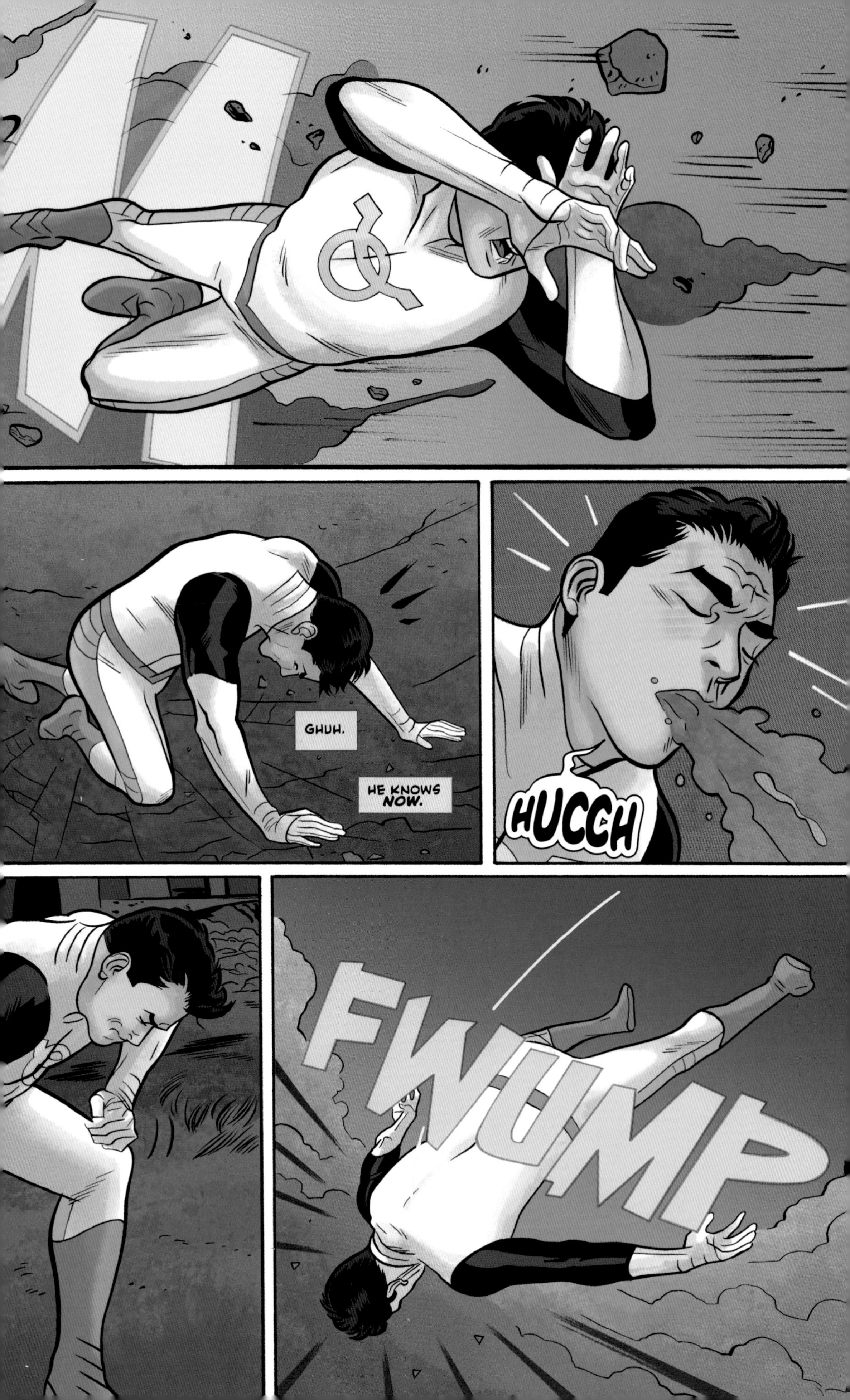
GHUH.
HE KNOWS NOW.
HUCCGH
FWUMP

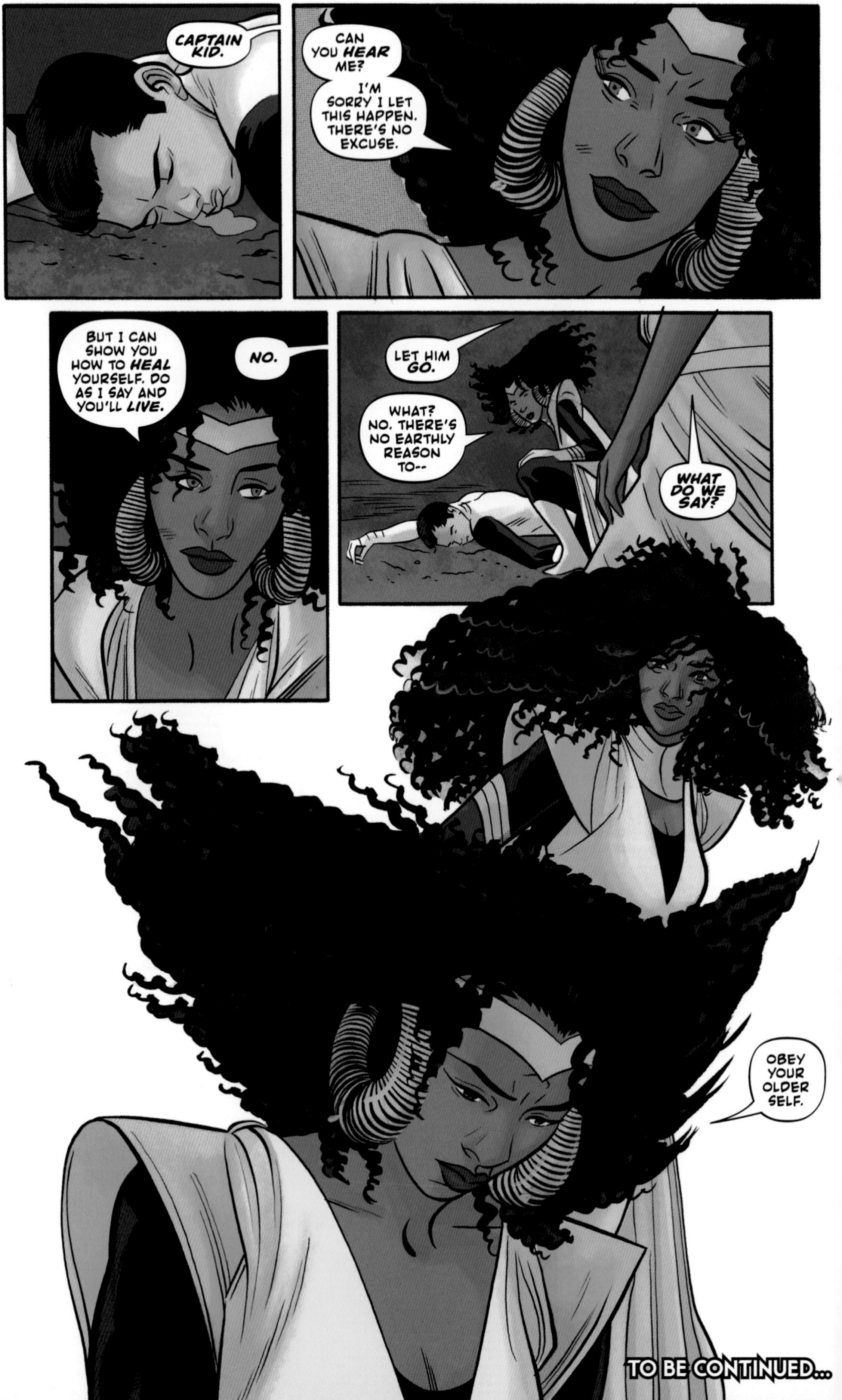
CAPTAIN KID.
CAN YOU HEAR ME?
I'M SORRY I LET THIS HAPPEN. THERE'S NO EXCUSE.
BUT I CAN SHOW YOU HOW TO HEAL YOURSELF. DO AS I SAY AND YOU'LL LIVE.
NO.
LET HIM GO.
WHAT? NO. THERE'S NO EARTHLY REASON TO--
WHAT DO WE SAY?
OBEY YOUR OLDER SELF.
TO BE CONTINUED...

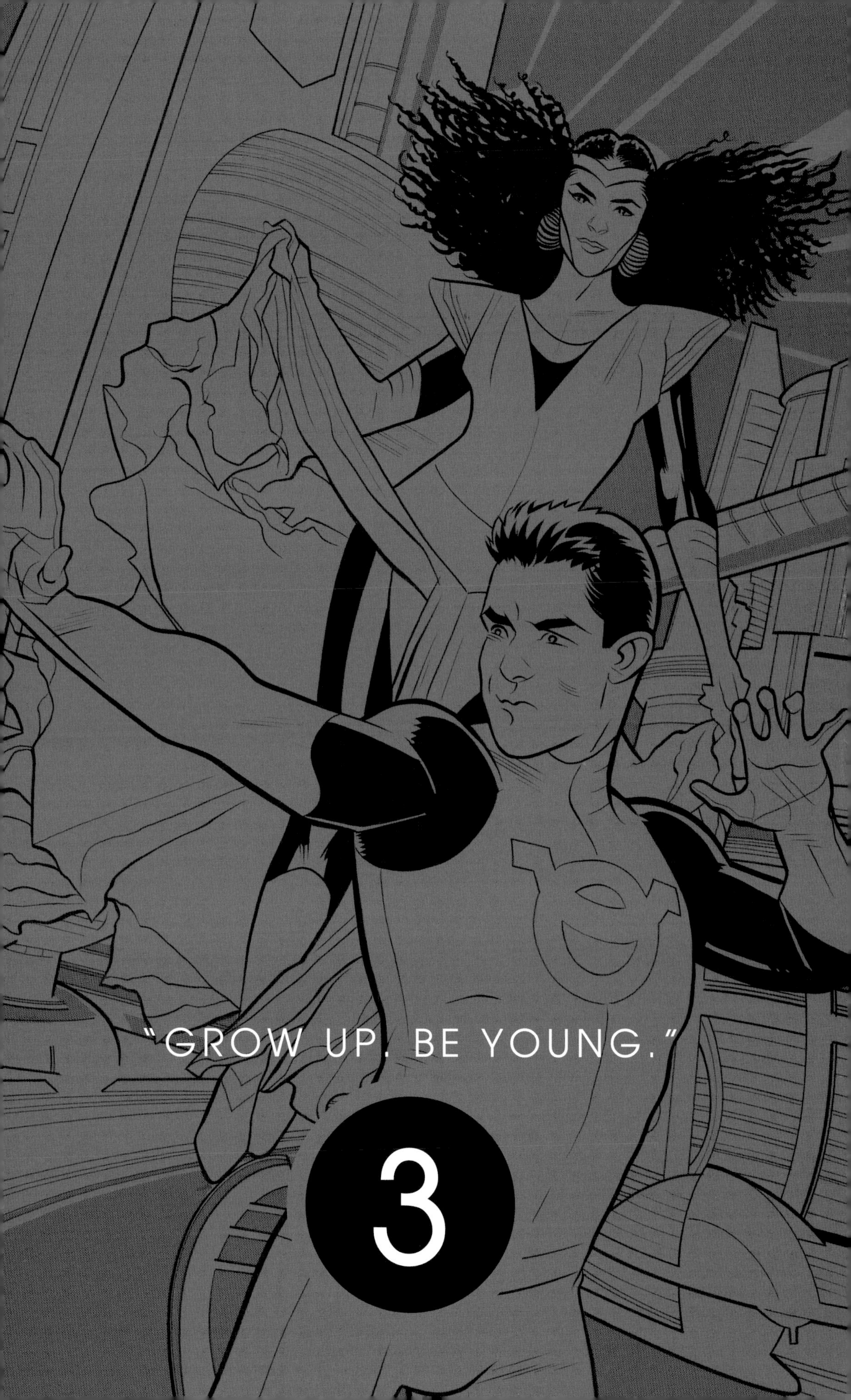
"GROW UP. BE YOUNG."
3

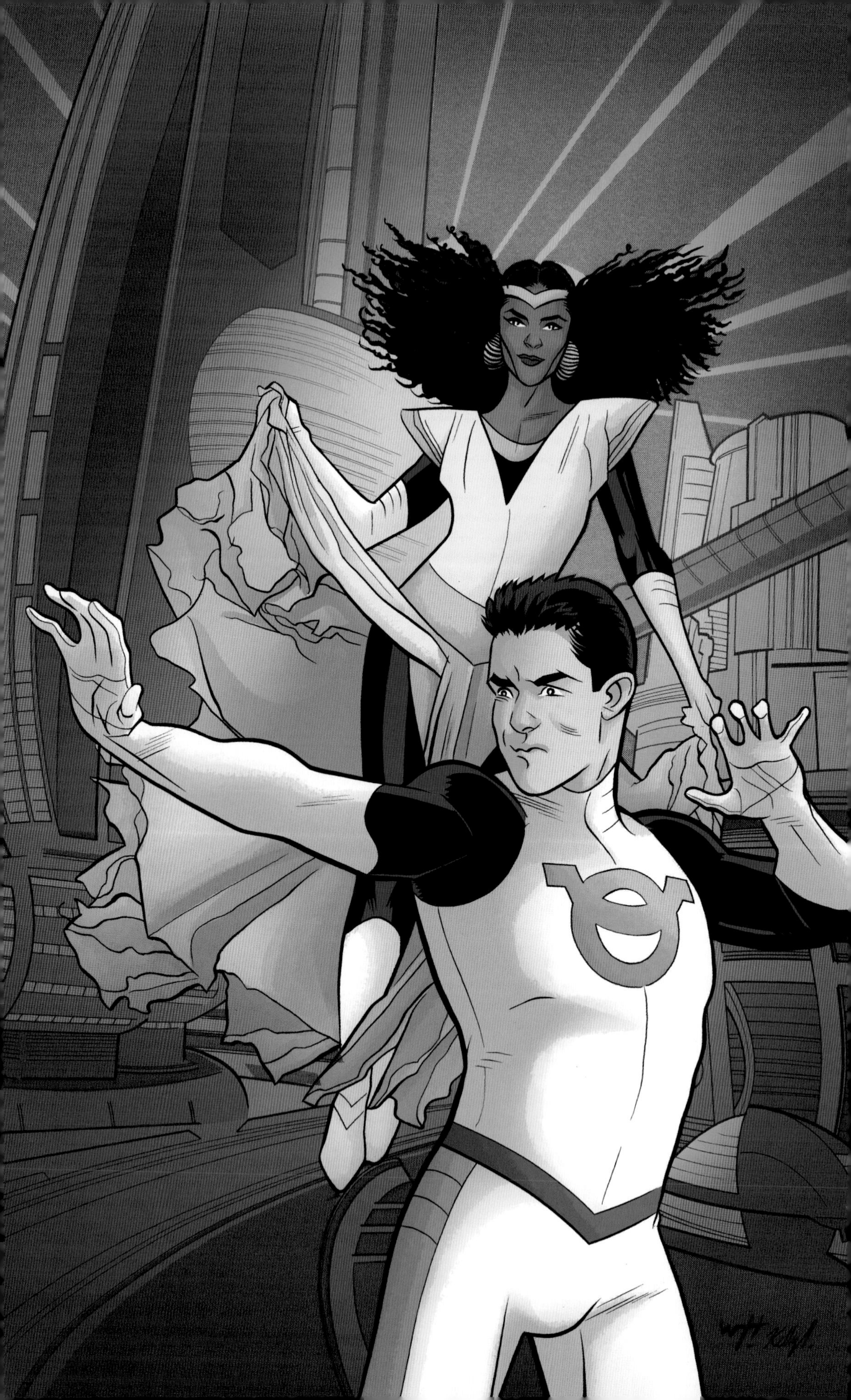

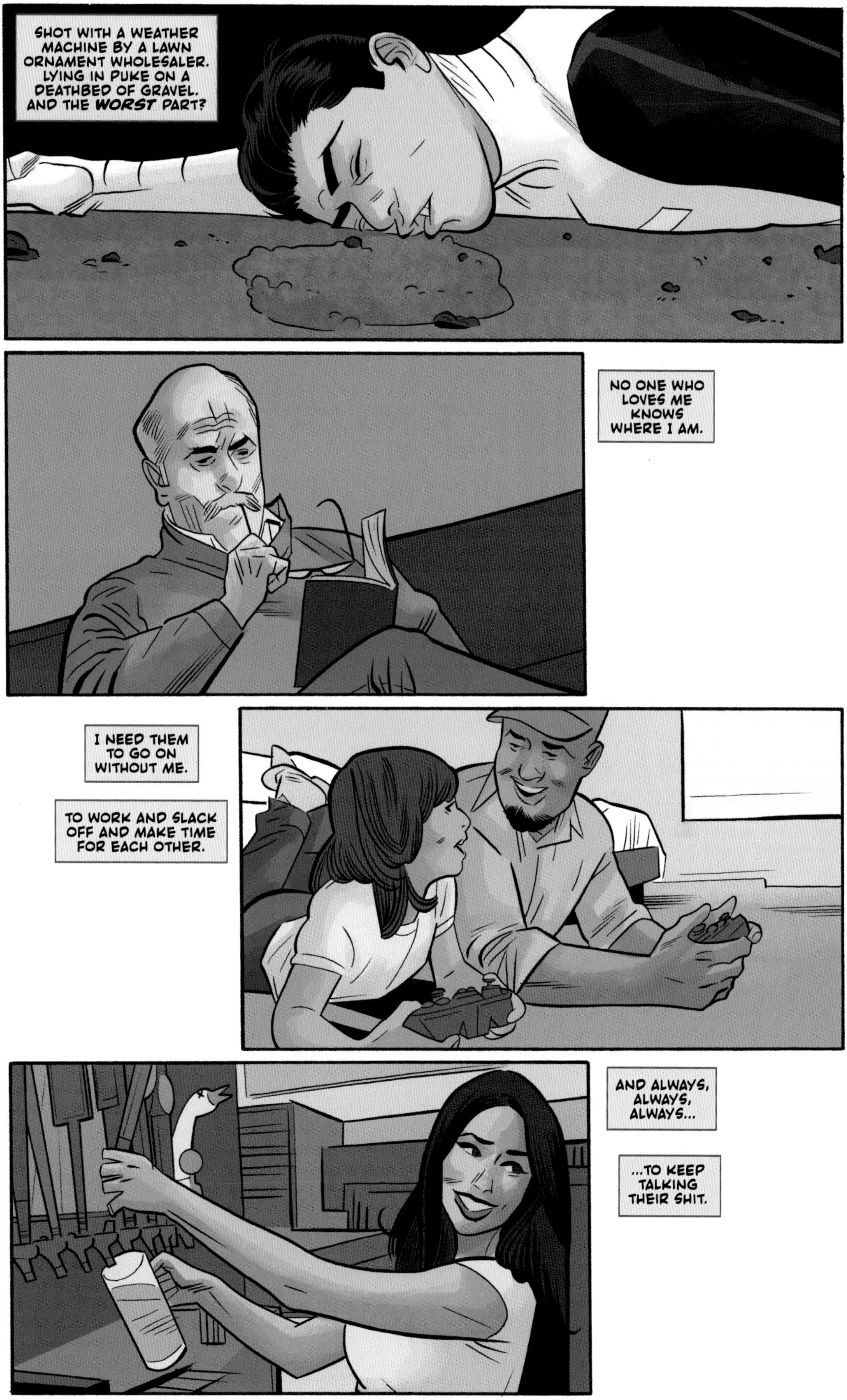

SHOT WITH A WEATHER MACHINE BY A LAWN ORNAMENT WHOLESALER. LYING IN PUKE ON A DEATHBED OF GRAVEL. AND THE *WORST* PART?
NO ONE WHO LOVES ME KNOWS WHERE I AM.
I NEED THEM TO GO ON WITHOUT ME.
TO WORK AND SLACK OFF AND MAKE TIME FOR EACH OTHER.
AND ALWAYS, ALWAYS, ALWAYS...
...TO KEEP TALKING THEIR SHIT.

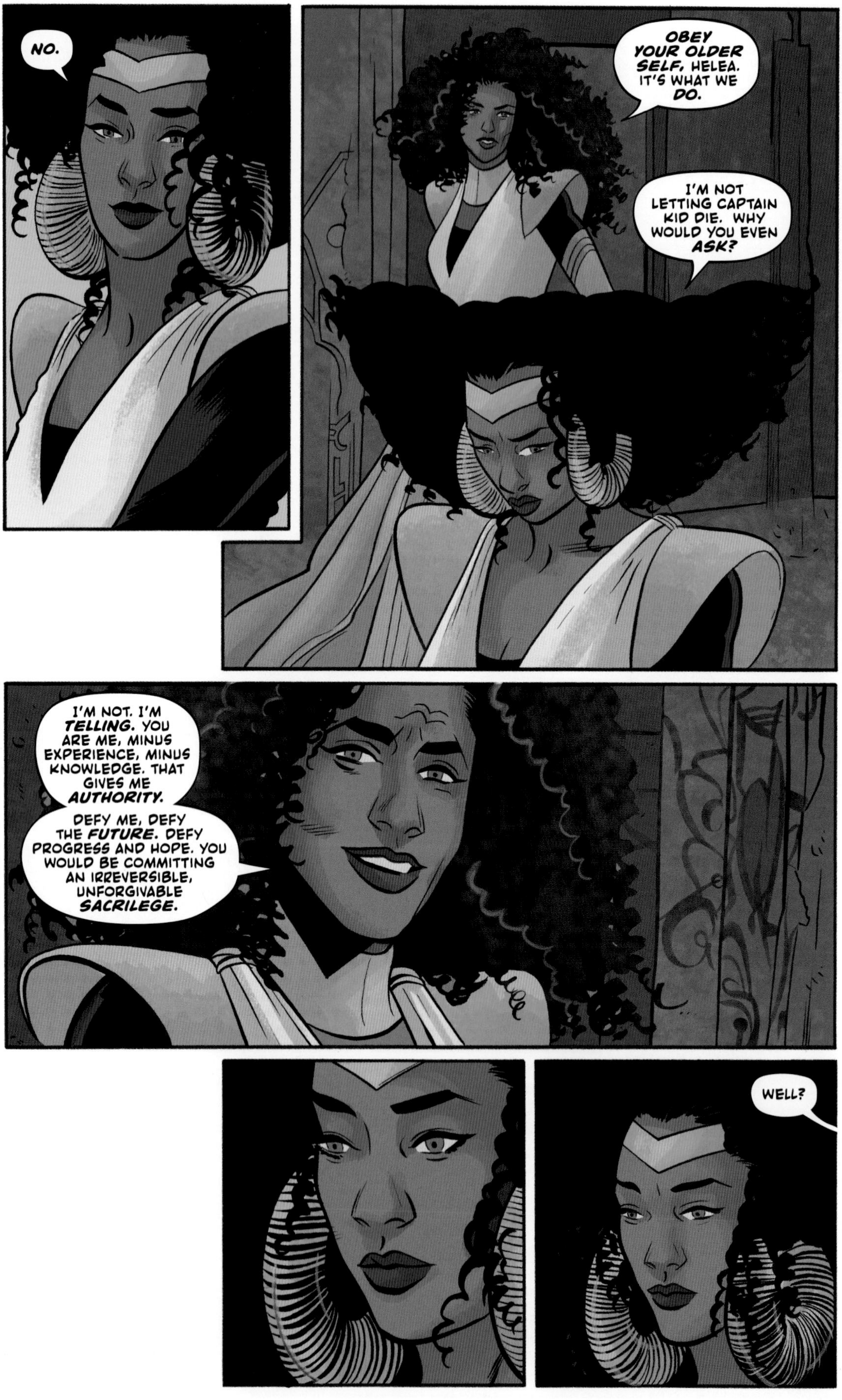
NO.
OBEY YOUR OLDER SELF, HELEA. IT'S WHAT WE DO.
I'M NOT LETTING CAPTAIN KID DIE. WHY WOULD YOU EVEN ASK?
I'M NOT. I'M TELLING. YOU ARE ME, MINUS EXPERIENCE, MINUS KNOWLEDGE. THAT GIVES ME AUTHORITY.
DEFY ME, DEFY THE FUTURE. DEFY PROGRESS AND HOPE. YOU WOULD BE COMMITTING AN IRREVERSIBLE, UNFORGIVABLE SACRILEGE.
WELL?

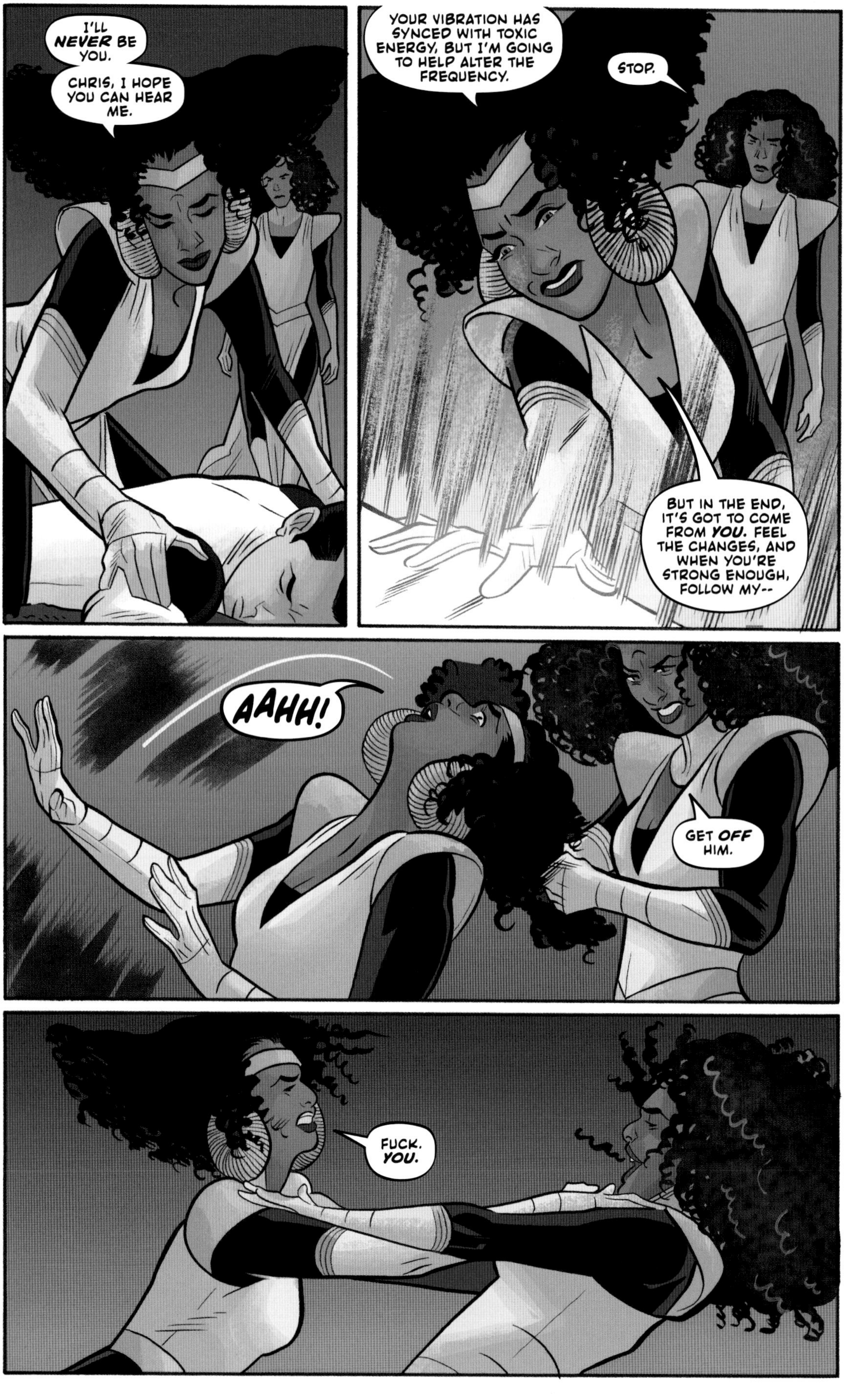
I'LL **NEVER** BE YOU.
CHRIS, I HOPE YOU CAN HEAR ME.
YOUR VIBRATION HAS SYNCED WITH TOXIC ENERGY, BUT I'M GOING TO HELP ALTER THE FREQUENCY.
STOP.
BUT IN THE END, IT'S GOT TO COME FROM **YOU.** FEEL THE CHANGES, AND WHEN YOU'RE STRONG ENOUGH, FOLLOW MY--
AAHH!
GET **OFF** HIM.
FUCK. **YOU.**

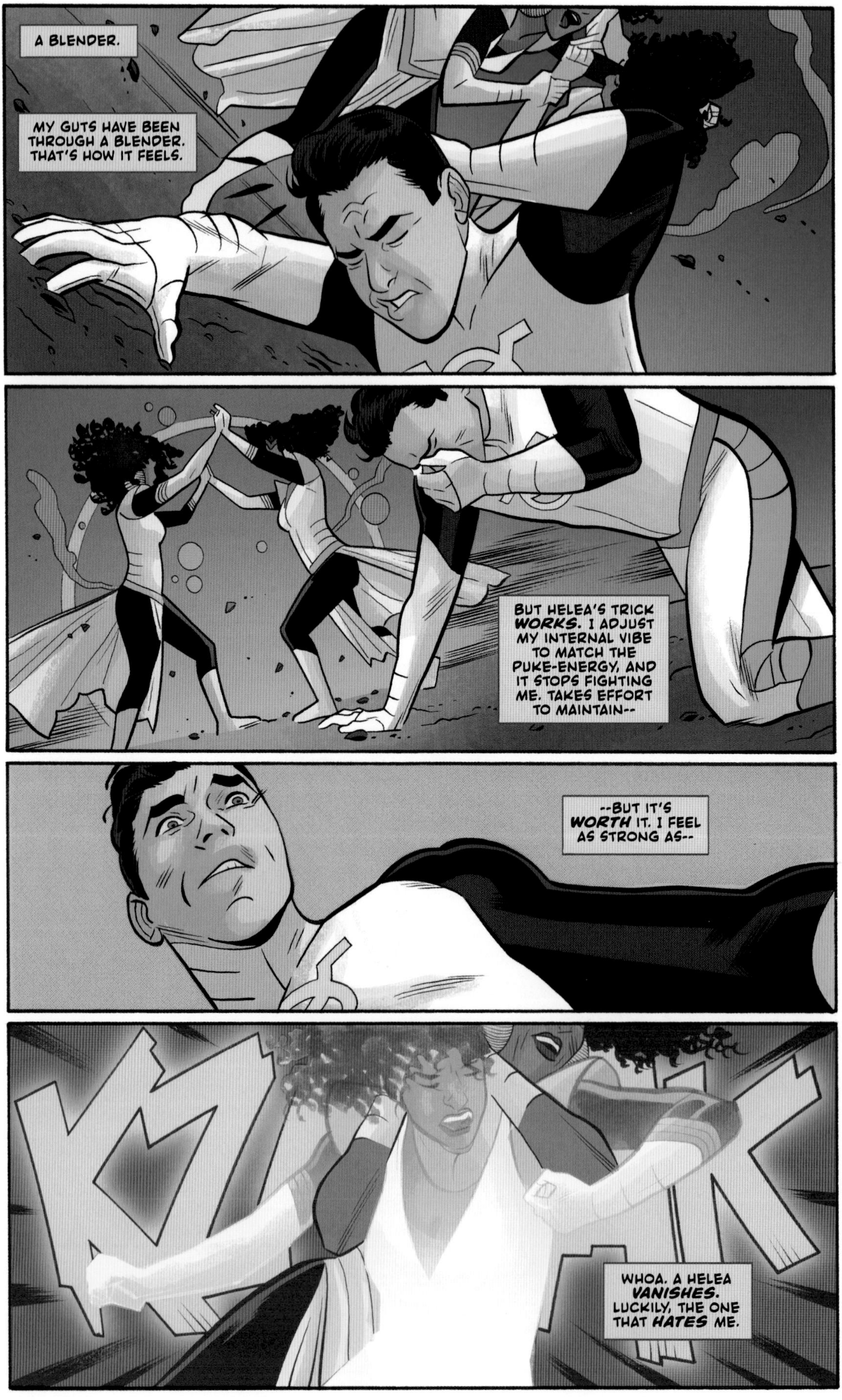
A BLENDER.
MY GUTS HAVE BEEN THROUGH A BLENDER. THAT'S HOW IT FEELS.
BUT HELEA'S TRICK **WORKS.** I ADJUST MY INTERNAL VIBE TO MATCH THE PUKE-ENERGY, AND IT STOPS FIGHTING ME. TAKES EFFORT TO MAINTAIN--
--BUT IT'S **WORTH** IT. I FEEL AS STRONG AS--
WHOA. A HELEA **VANISHES.** LUCKILY, THE ONE THAT **HATES** ME.

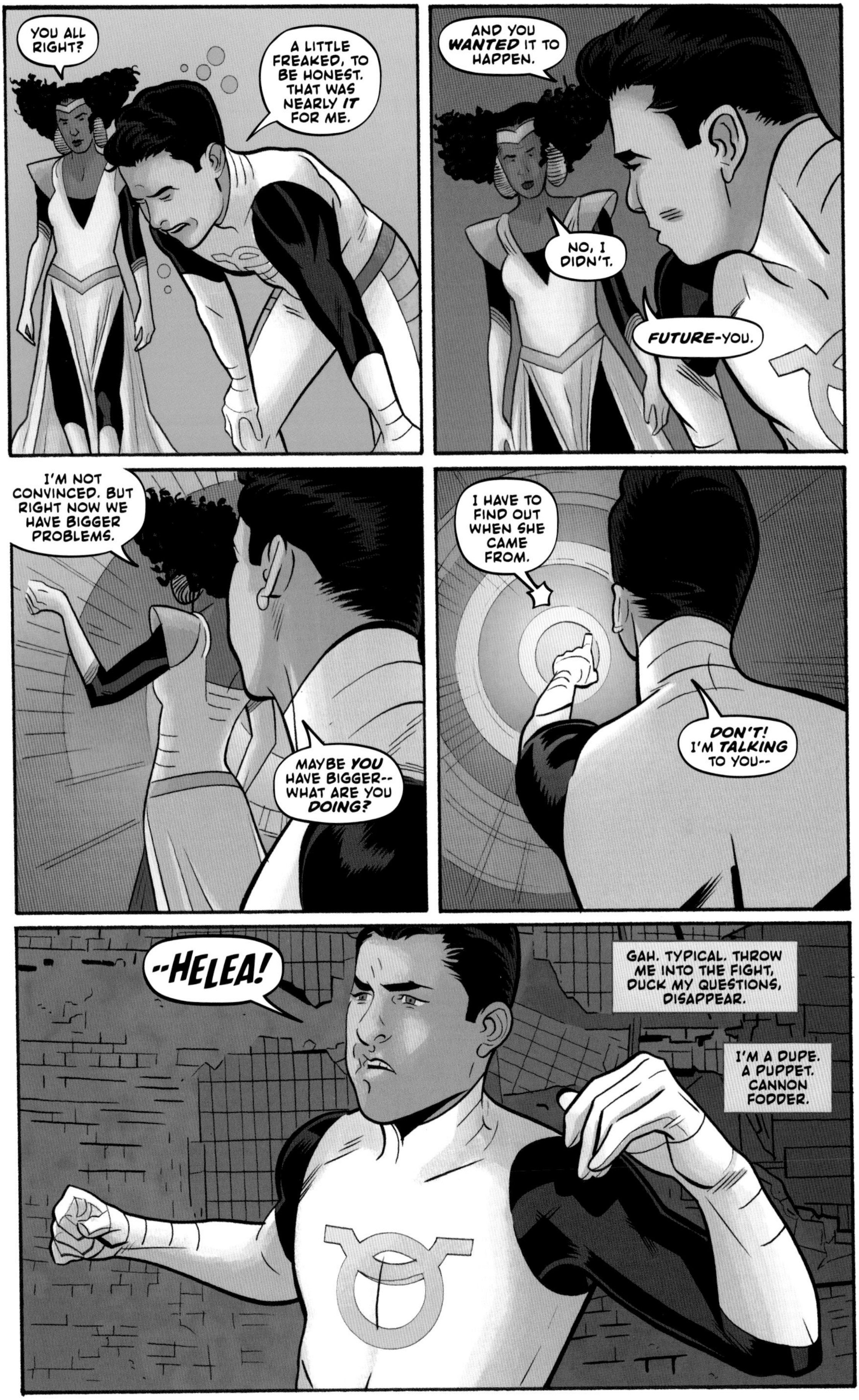
YOU ALL RIGHT?
A LITTLE FREAKED, TO BE HONEST. THAT WAS NEARLY *IT* FOR ME.
AND YOU *WANTED* IT TO HAPPEN.
NO, I DIDN'T.
FUTURE-YOU.
I'M NOT CONVINCED. BUT RIGHT NOW WE HAVE BIGGER PROBLEMS.
MAYBE *YOU* HAVE BIGGER-- WHAT ARE YOU *DOING?*
I HAVE TO FIND OUT WHEN SHE CAME FROM.
DON'T! I'M *TALKING* TO YOU--
--HELEA!
GAH. TYPICAL. THROW ME INTO THE FIGHT, DUCK MY QUESTIONS, DISAPPEAR.
I'M A DUPE. A PUPPET. CANNON FODDER.

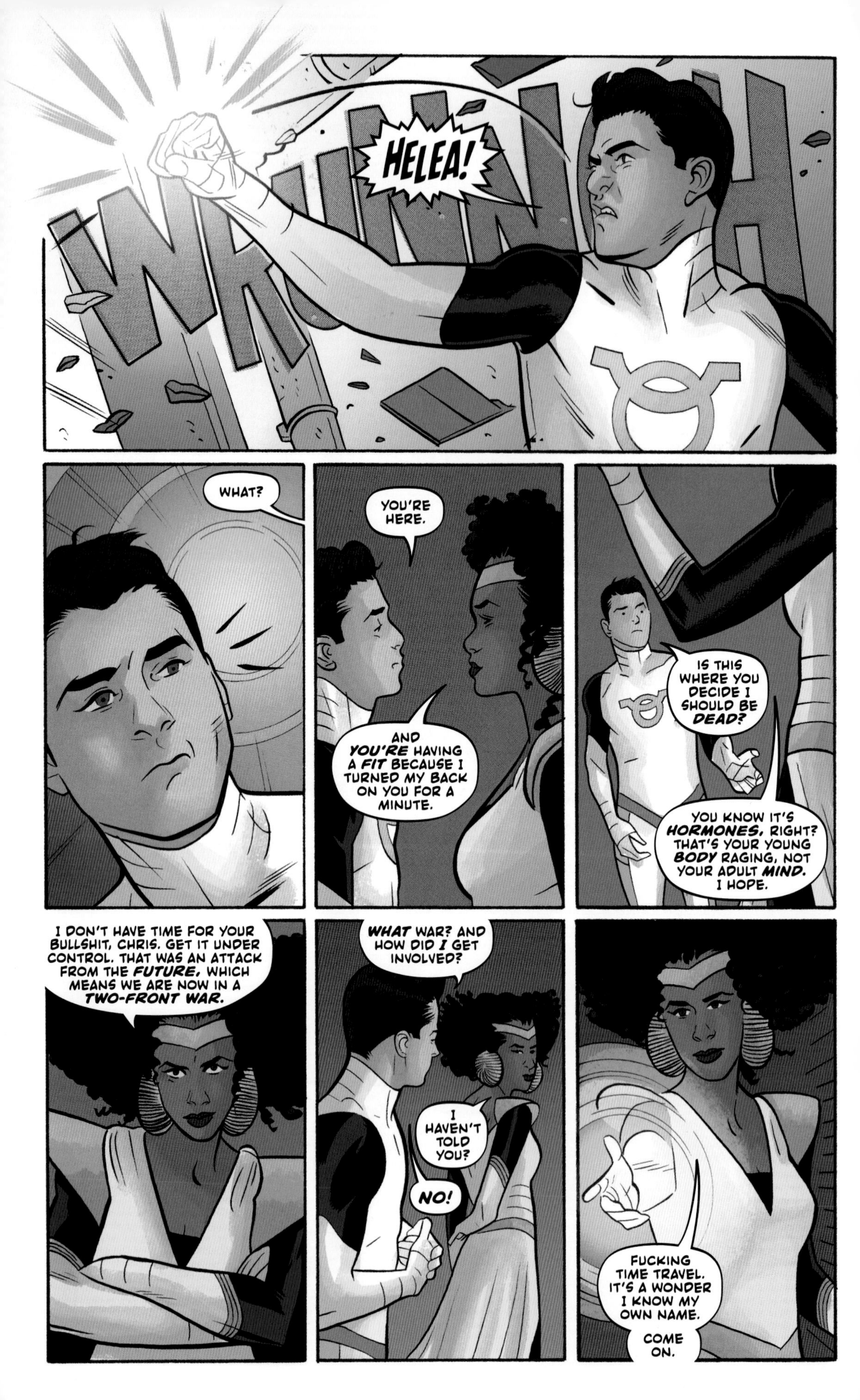
WHUMMM
HELEA!
WHAT?
YOU'RE HERE.
AND YOU'RE HAVING A FIT BECAUSE I TURNED MY BACK ON YOU FOR A MINUTE.
IS THIS WHERE YOU DECIDE I SHOULD BE DEAD?
YOU KNOW IT'S HORMONES, RIGHT? THAT'S YOUR YOUNG BODY RAGING, NOT YOUR ADULT MIND. I HOPE.
I DON'T HAVE TIME FOR YOUR BULLSHIT, CHRIS. GET IT UNDER CONTROL. THAT WAS AN ATTACK FROM THE FUTURE, WHICH MEANS WE ARE NOW IN A TWO-FRONT WAR.
WHAT WAR? AND HOW DID I GET INVOLVED?
I HAVEN'T TOLD YOU?
NO!
FUCKING TIME TRAVEL. IT'S A WONDER I KNOW MY OWN NAME.
COME ON.

WHY *SHOULD* I?

LISTEN-- WHEN I WAS YOUNGER, I LIKED KEEPING PEOPLE IN THE DARK. I *THOUGHT* IT MADE THE PROBLEMS I HAD TO MANAGE *SIMPLER*...

...BUT, IF I'M BEING HONEST, I REALLY GOT OFF ON THE *CONTROL* IT GAVE ME. EVEN THOUGH THAT FEELING IS COMPLETELY AT ODDS WITH THE WORLD I FIGHT TO BUILD.

THAT WAS THE HELEA YOU MET *BEFORE*. I'VE GROWN SINCE.

LET ME SHOW YOU.

SHOW ME *WHAT?*

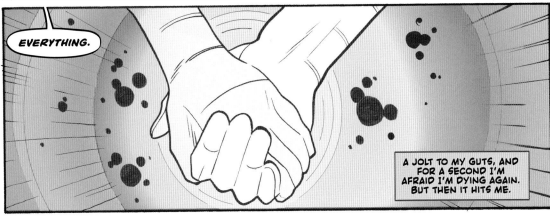

EVERYTHING.

A JOLT TO MY GUTS, AND FOR A SECOND I'M AFRAID I'M DYING AGAIN. BUT THEN IT HITS ME.

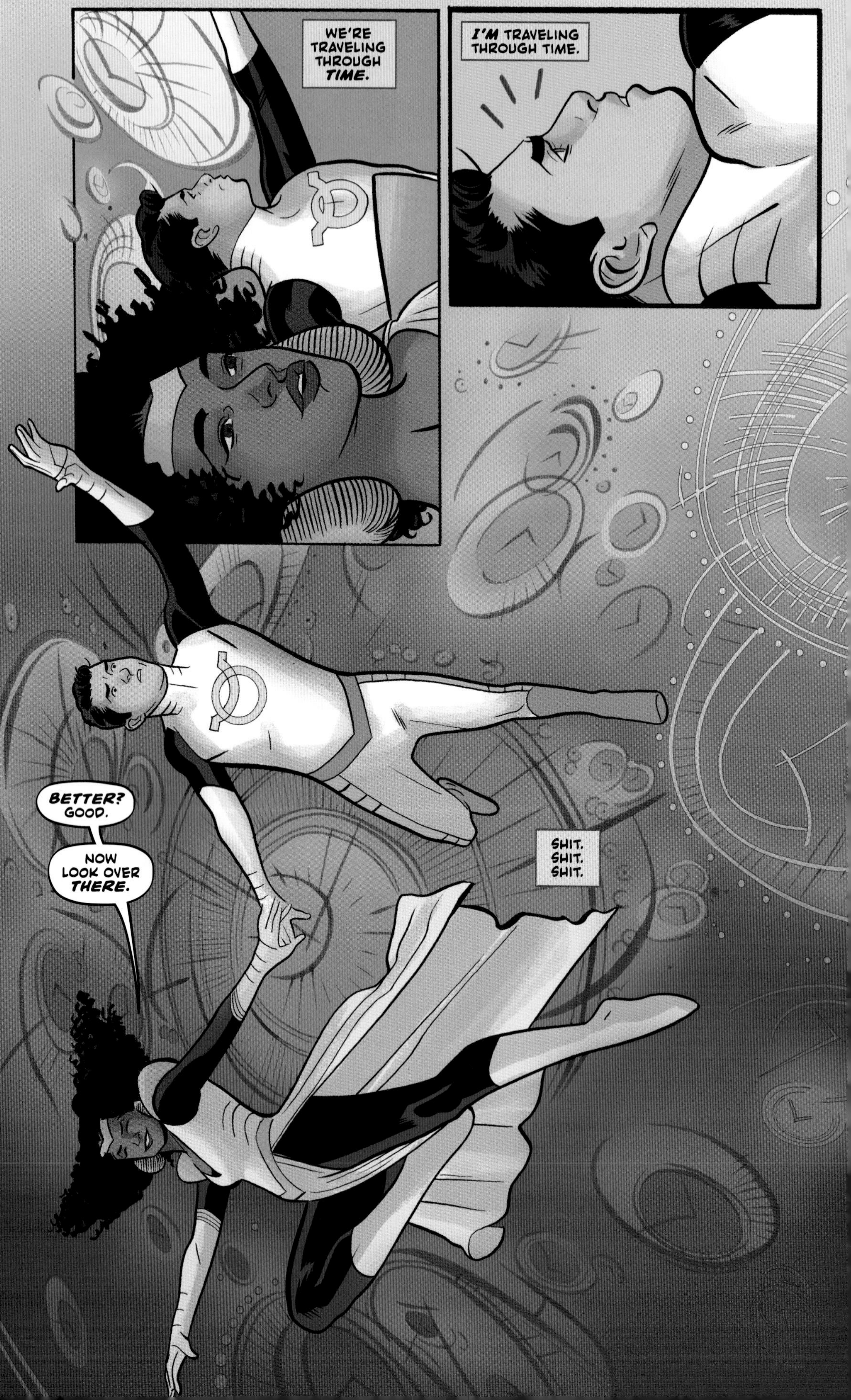
WE'RE TRAVELING THROUGH TIME.
I'M TRAVELING THROUGH TIME.
BETTER? GOOD.
NOW LOOK OVER THERE.
SHIT. SHIT. SHIT.

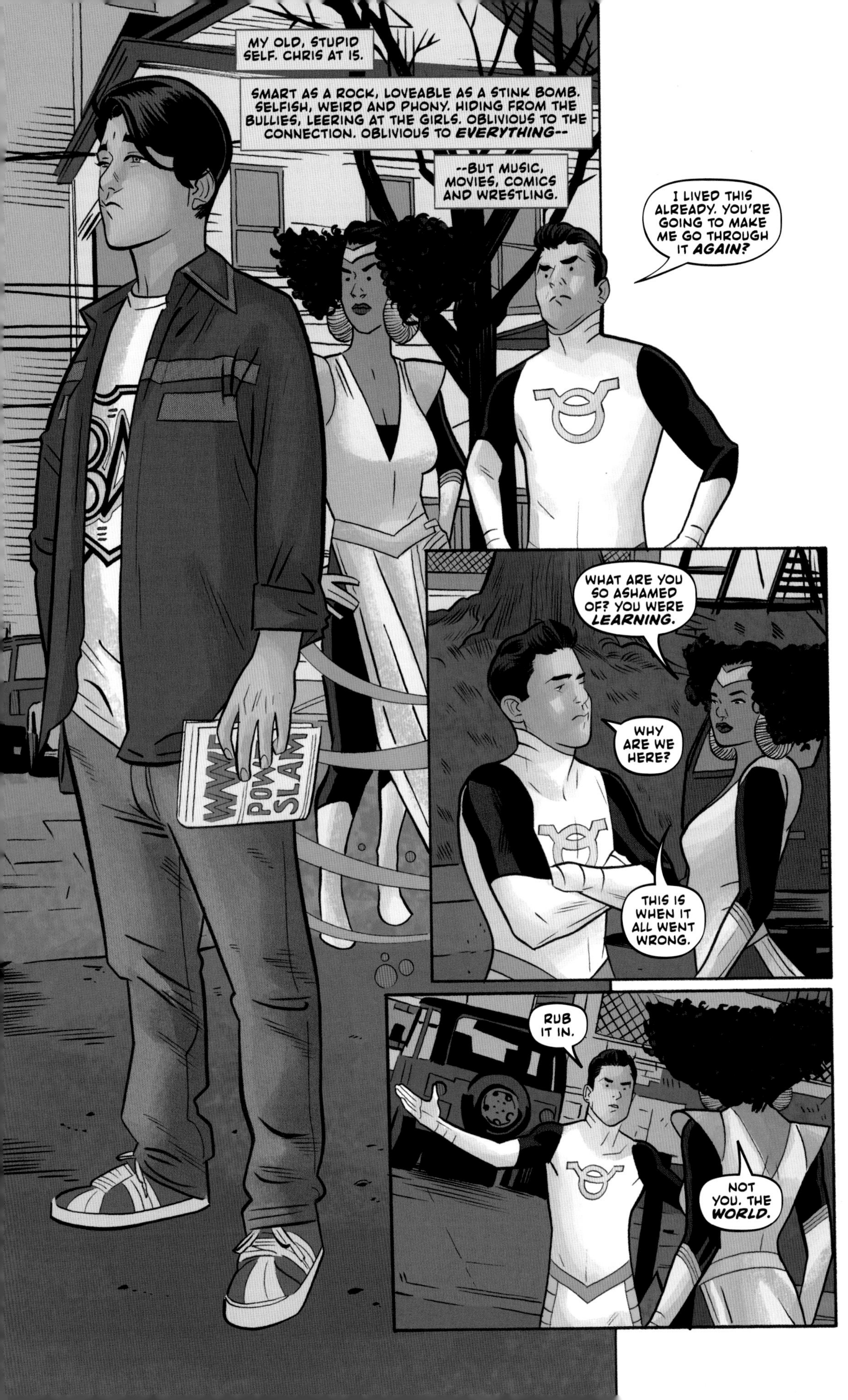
MY OLD, STUPID SELF. CHRIS AT 15.
SMART AS A ROCK, LOVEABLE AS A STINK BOMB. SELFISH, WEIRD AND PHONY. HIDING FROM THE BULLIES, LEERING AT THE GIRLS. OBLIVIOUS TO THE CONNECTION. OBLIVIOUS TO EVERYTHING--
--BUT MUSIC, MOVIES, COMICS AND WRESTLING.
I LIVED THIS ALREADY. YOU'RE GOING TO MAKE ME GO THROUGH IT AGAIN?
WWF POWER SLAM
WHAT ARE YOU SO ASHAMED OF? YOU WERE LEARNING.
WHY ARE WE HERE?
THIS IS WHEN IT ALL WENT WRONG.
RUB IT IN.
NOT YOU. THE WORLD.

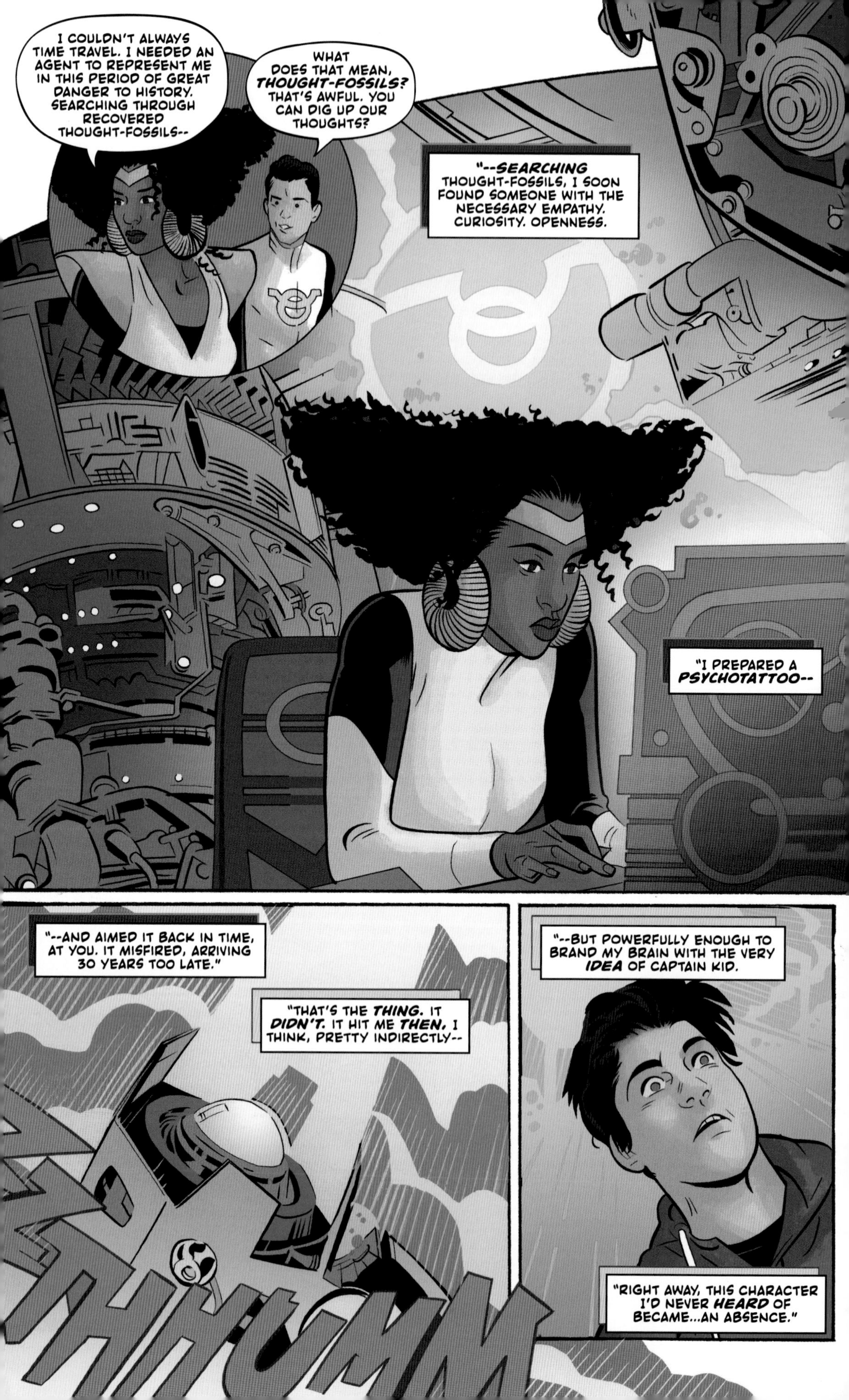

I COULDN'T ALWAYS TIME TRAVEL. I NEEDED AN AGENT TO REPRESENT ME IN THIS PERIOD OF GREAT DANGER TO HISTORY. SEARCHING THROUGH RECOVERED THOUGHT-FOSSILS--
WHAT DOES THAT MEAN, THOUGHT-FOSSILS? THAT'S AWFUL. YOU CAN DIG UP OUR THOUGHTS?
"--SEARCHING THOUGHT-FOSSILS, I SOON FOUND SOMEONE WITH THE NECESSARY EMPATHY. CURIOSITY. OPENNESS.
"I PREPARED A PSYCHOTATTOO--
"--AND AIMED IT BACK IN TIME, AT YOU. IT MISFIRED, ARRIVING 30 YEARS TOO LATE."
"THAT'S THE THING. IT DIDN'T. IT HIT ME THEN. I THINK, PRETTY INDIRECTLY--
THHUMM
"--BUT POWERFULLY ENOUGH TO BRAND MY BRAIN WITH THE VERY IDEA OF CAPTAIN KID.
"RIGHT AWAY, THIS CHARACTER I'D NEVER HEARD OF BECAME...AN ABSENCE."

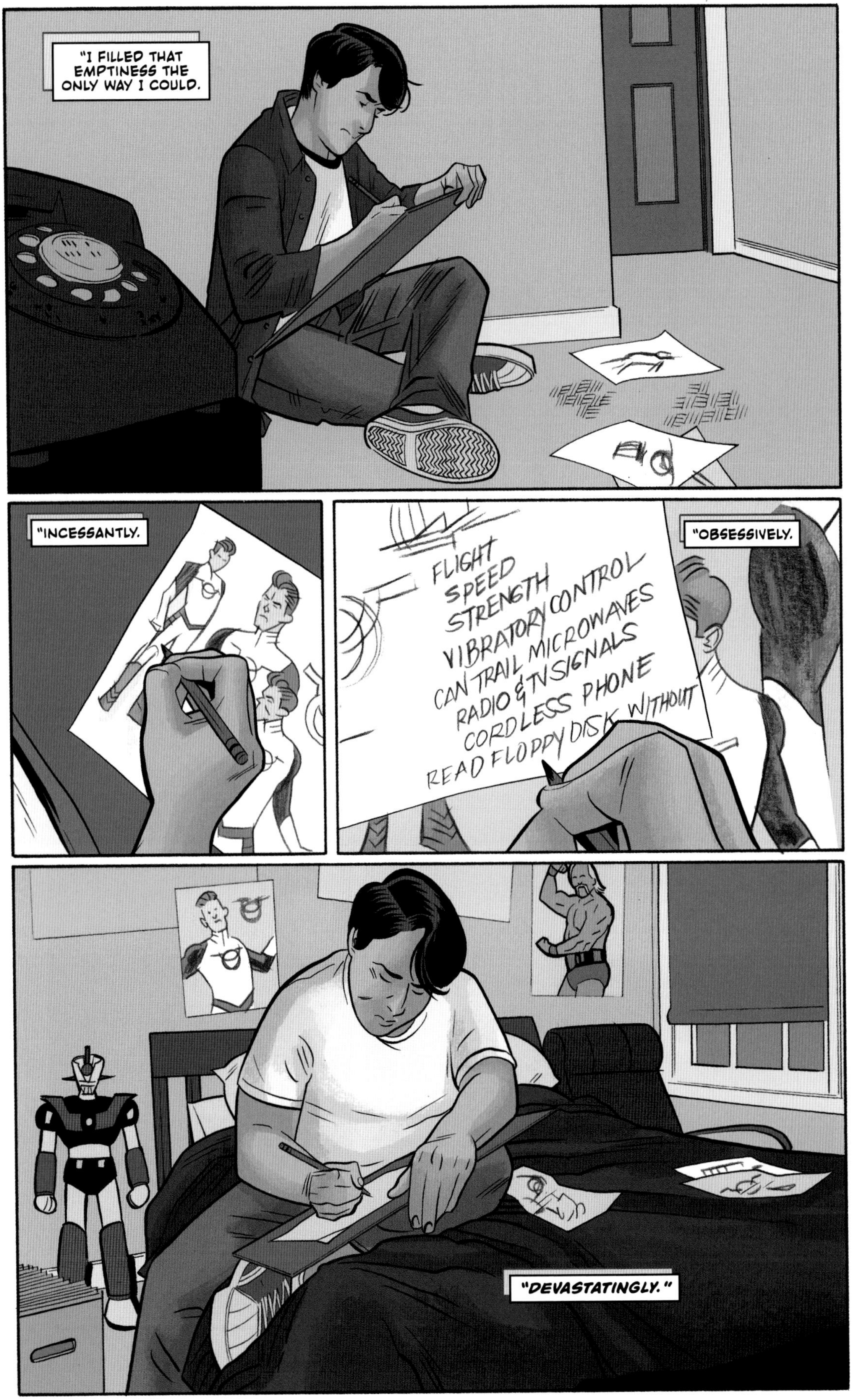
"I FILLED THAT EMPTINESS THE ONLY WAY I COULD.
"INCESSANTLY.
"OBSESSIVELY.
FLIGHT
SPEED
STRENGTH
VIBRATORY CONTROL
CAN TRAIL MICROWAVES
RADIO & TV SIGNALS
CORDLESS PHONE
READ FLOPPY DISK WITHOUT
"DEVASTATINGLY."

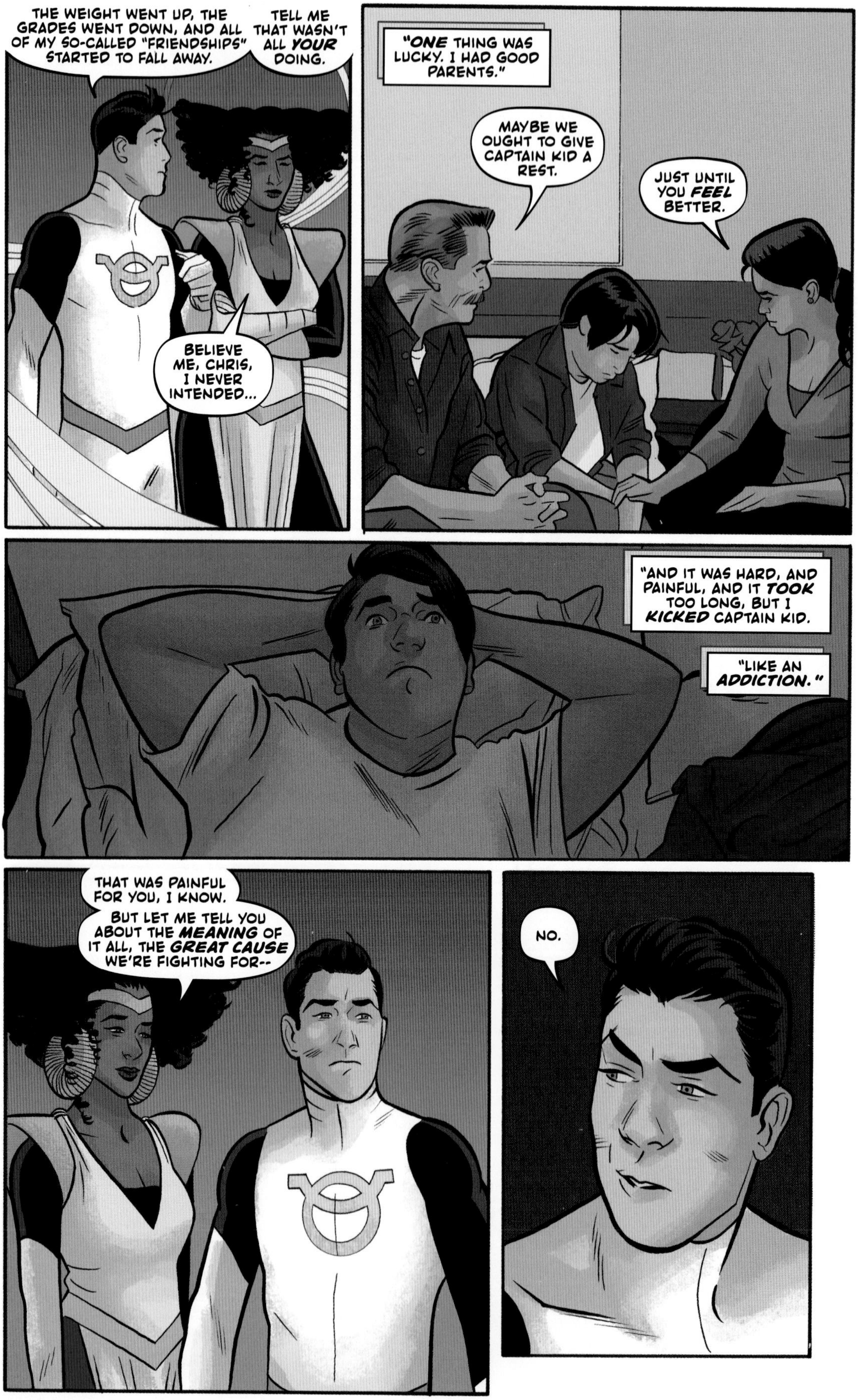
THE WEIGHT WENT UP, THE GRADES WENT DOWN, AND ALL OF MY SO-CALLED "FRIENDSHIPS" STARTED TO FALL AWAY.
TELL ME THAT WASN'T ALL *YOUR* DOING.
BELIEVE ME, CHRIS, I NEVER INTENDED...
"*ONE* THING WAS LUCKY. I HAD GOOD PARENTS."
MAYBE WE OUGHT TO GIVE CAPTAIN KID A REST.
JUST UNTIL YOU *FEEL* BETTER.
"AND IT WAS HARD, AND PAINFUL, AND IT *TOOK* TOO LONG, BUT I *KICKED* CAPTAIN KID.
"LIKE AN *ADDICTION.*"
THAT WAS PAINFUL FOR YOU, I KNOW.
BUT LET ME TELL YOU ABOUT THE *MEANING* OF IT ALL, THE *GREAT CAUSE* WE'RE FIGHTING FOR--
NO.

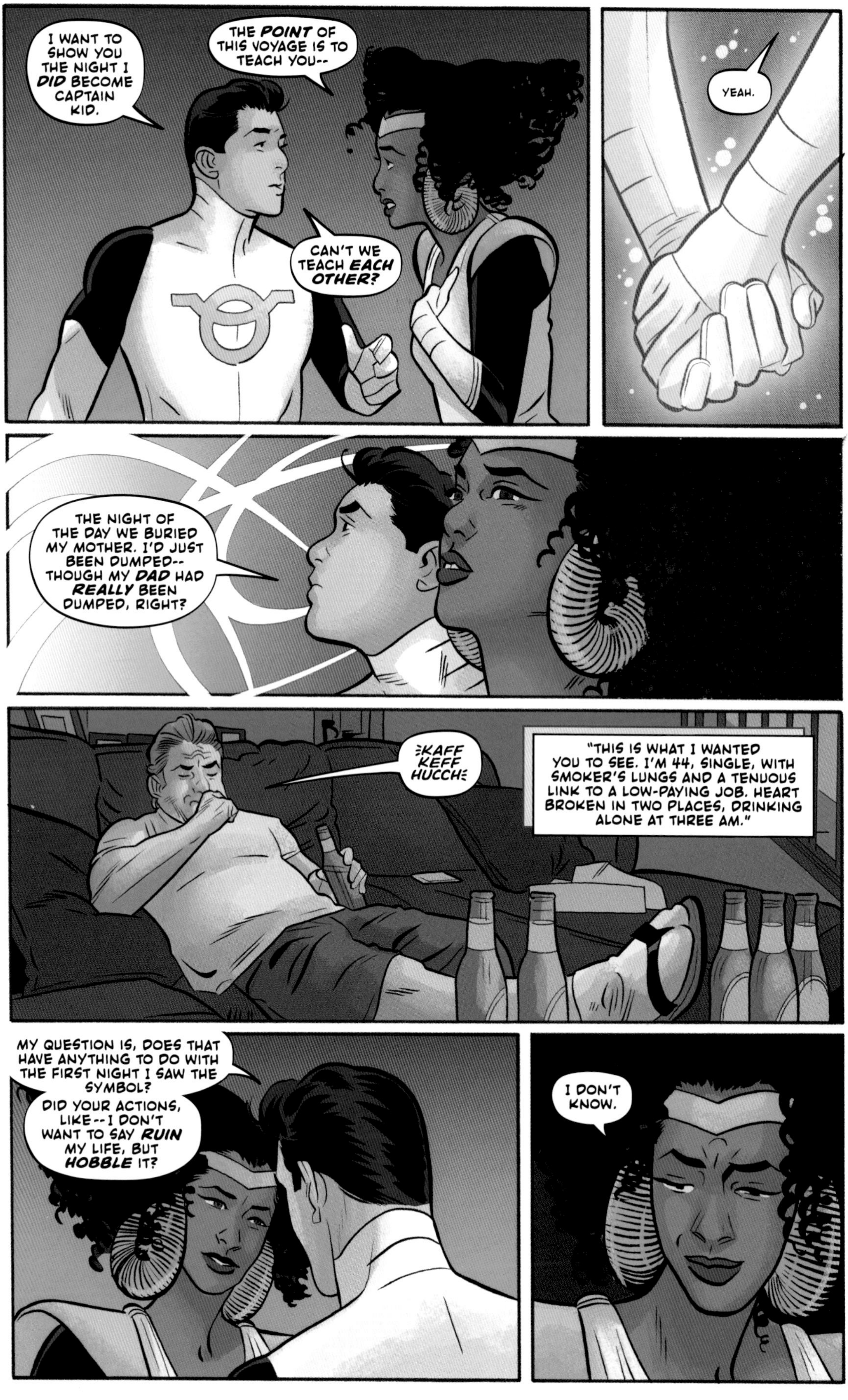
I WANT TO SHOW YOU THE NIGHT I *DID* BECOME CAPTAIN KID.
THE *POINT* OF THIS VOYAGE IS TO TEACH YOU--
CAN'T WE TEACH *EACH OTHER?*
YEAH.
THE NIGHT OF THE DAY WE BURIED MY MOTHER. I'D JUST BEEN DUMPED--THOUGH MY *DAD* HAD *REALLY* BEEN DUMPED, RIGHT?
KAFF KEFF HUCCH
"THIS IS WHAT I WANTED YOU TO SEE. I'M 44, SINGLE, WITH SMOKER'S LUNGS AND A TENUOUS LINK TO A LOW-PAYING JOB. HEART BROKEN IN TWO PLACES, DRINKING ALONE AT THREE AM."
MY QUESTION IS, DOES THAT HAVE ANYTHING TO DO WITH THE FIRST NIGHT I SAW THE SYMBOL?
DID YOUR ACTIONS, LIKE--I DON'T WANT TO SAY *RUIN* MY LIFE, BUT *HOBBLE* IT?
I DON'T KNOW.

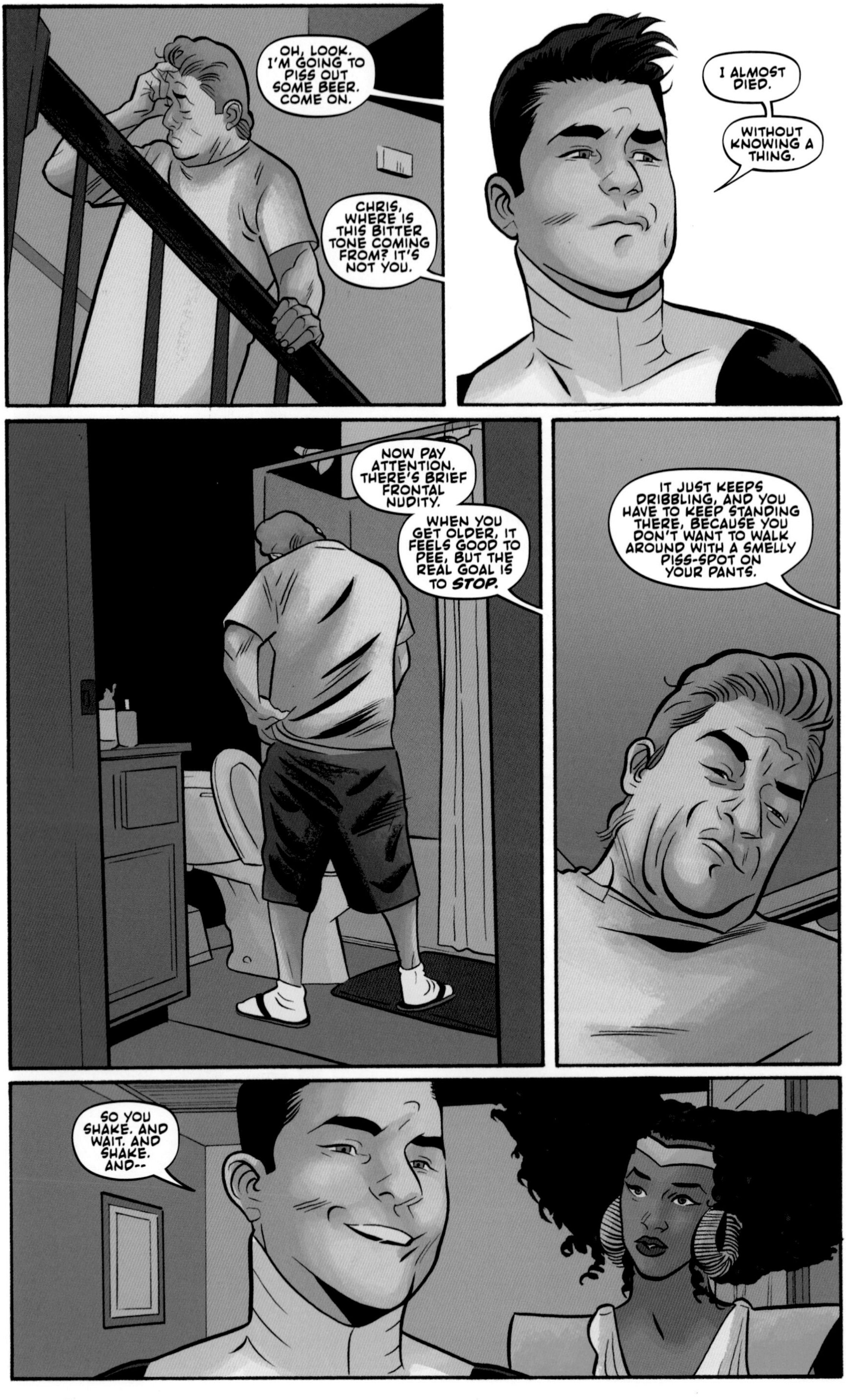
OH, LOOK. I'M GOING TO PISS OUT SOME BEER. COME ON.
CHRIS, WHERE IS THIS BITTER TONE COMING FROM? IT'S NOT YOU.
I ALMOST DIED.
WITHOUT KNOWING A THING.
NOW PAY ATTENTION. THERE'S BRIEF FRONTAL NUDITY.
WHEN YOU GET OLDER, IT FEELS GOOD TO PEE, BUT THE REAL GOAL IS TO *STOP.*
IT JUST KEEPS DRIBBLING, AND YOU HAVE TO KEEP STANDING THERE, BECAUSE YOU DON'T WANT TO WALK AROUND WITH A SMELLY PISS-SPOT ON YOUR PANTS.
SO YOU SHAKE. AND WAIT. AND SHAKE. AND--

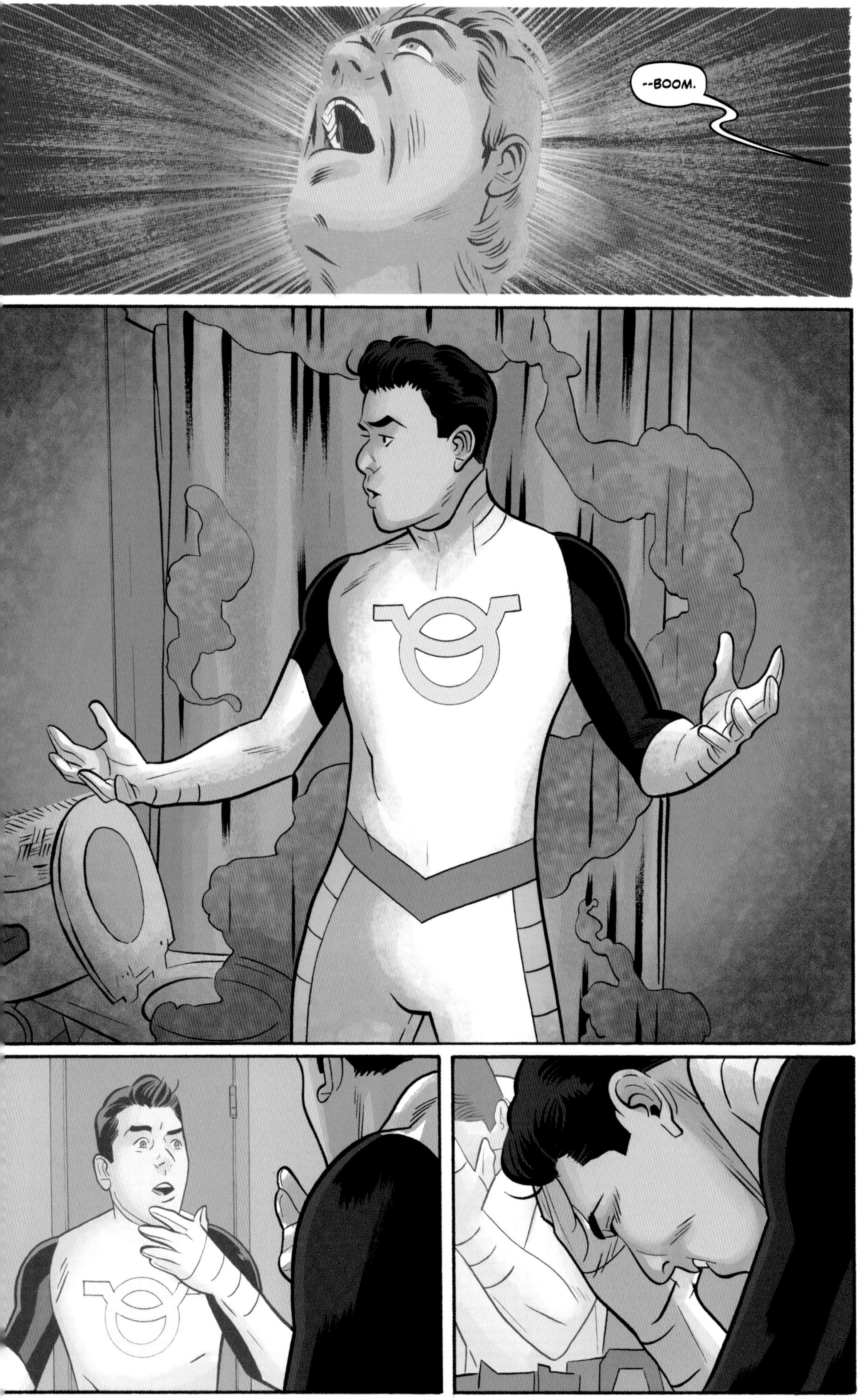
--BOOM.

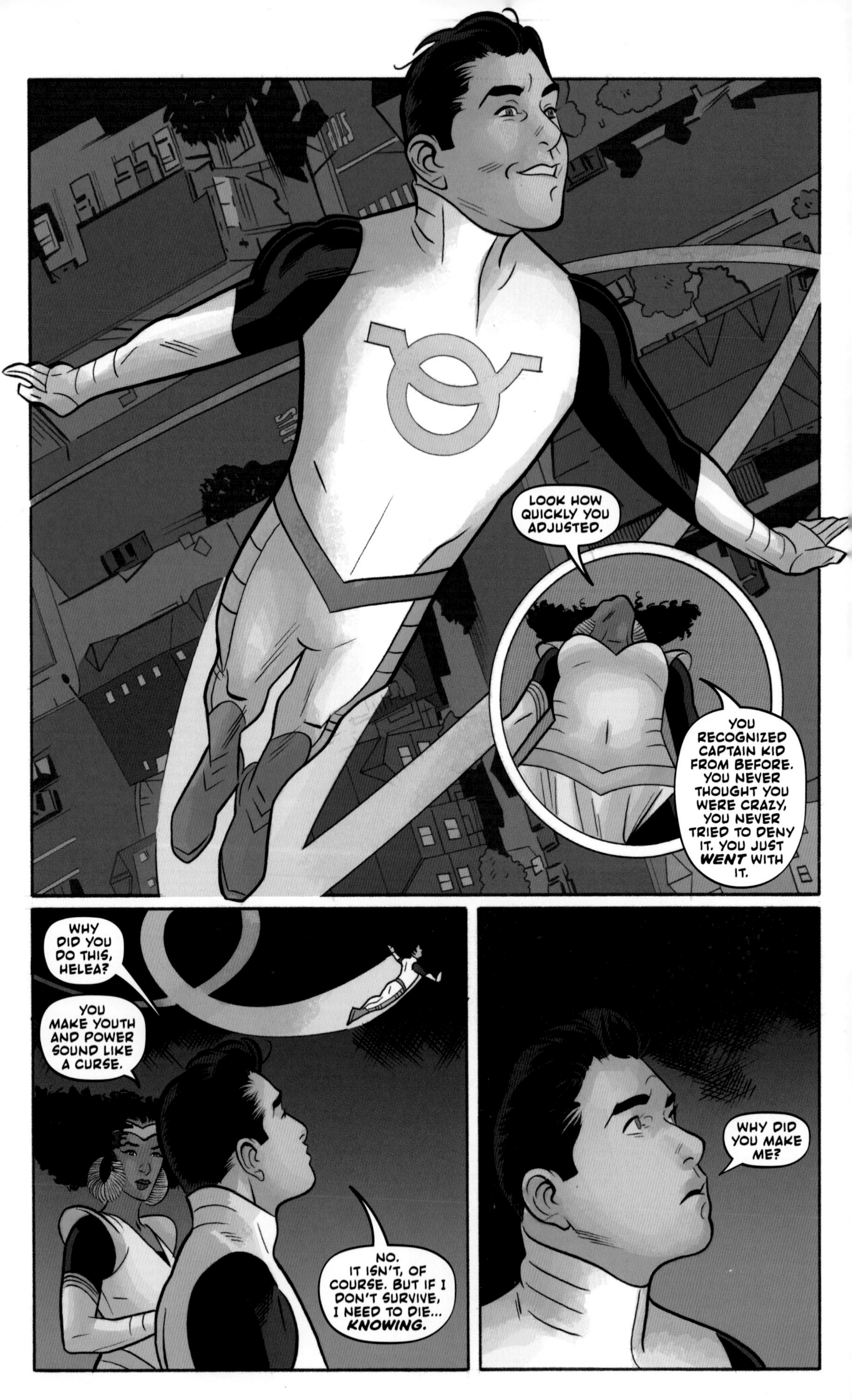
LOOK HOW QUICKLY YOU ADJUSTED.
YOU RECOGNIZED CAPTAIN KID FROM BEFORE. YOU NEVER THOUGHT YOU WERE CRAZY, YOU NEVER TRIED TO DENY IT. YOU JUST WENT WITH IT.
WHY DID YOU DO THIS, HELEA?
YOU MAKE YOUTH AND POWER SOUND LIKE A CURSE.
NO. IT ISN'T, OF COURSE. BUT IF I DON'T SURVIVE, I NEED TO DIE... KNOWING.
WHY DID YOU MAKE ME?

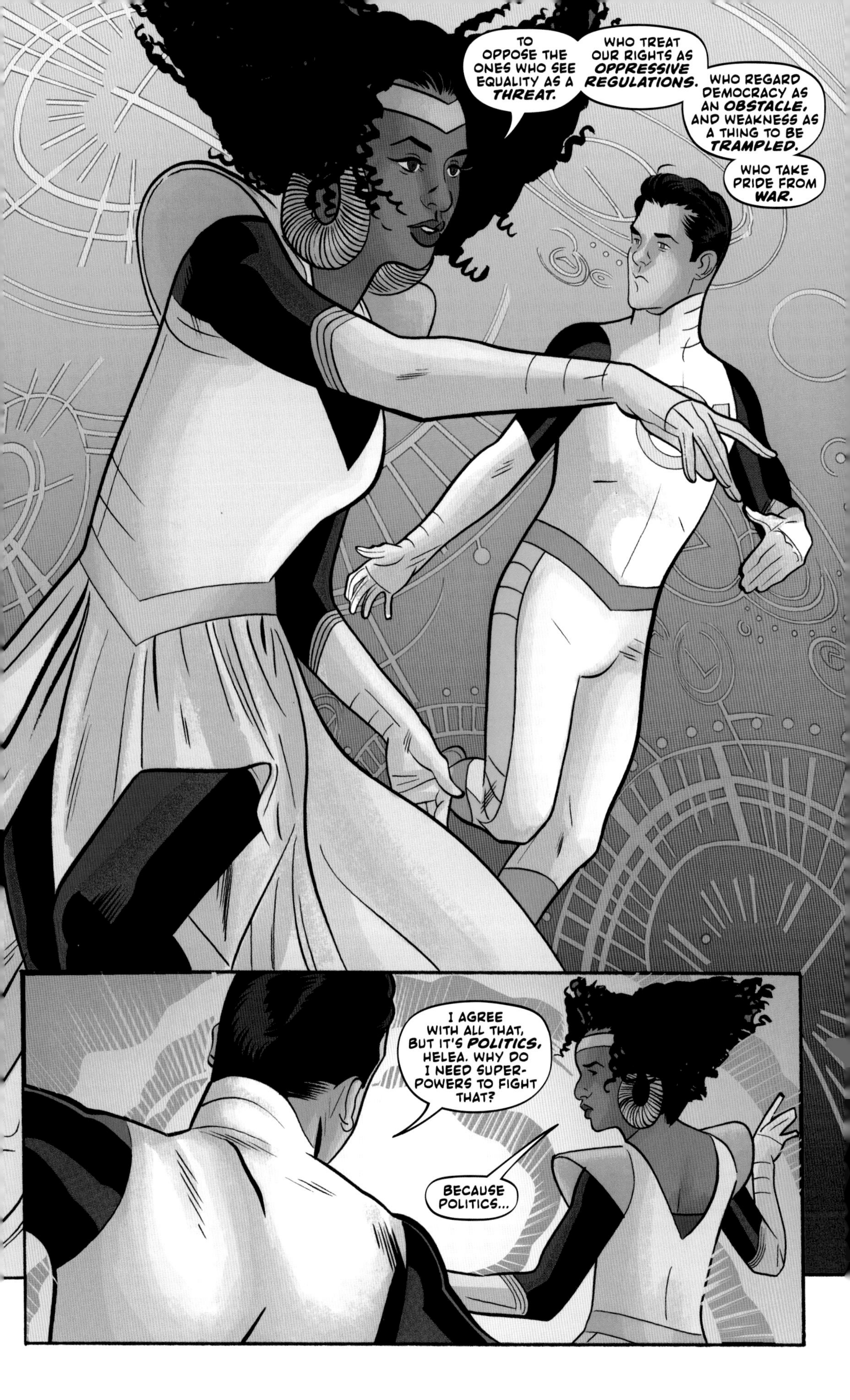
TO OPPOSE THE ONES WHO SEE EQUALITY AS A *THREAT.*
WHO TREAT OUR RIGHTS AS *OPPRESSIVE REGULATIONS.*
WHO REGARD DEMOCRACY AS AN *OBSTACLE,* AND WEAKNESS AS A THING TO BE *TRAMPLED.*
WHO TAKE PRIDE FROM *WAR.*
I AGREE WITH ALL THAT, BUT IT'S *POLITICS,* HELEA. WHY DO I NEED SUPER-POWERS TO FIGHT THAT?
BECAUSE POLITICS...

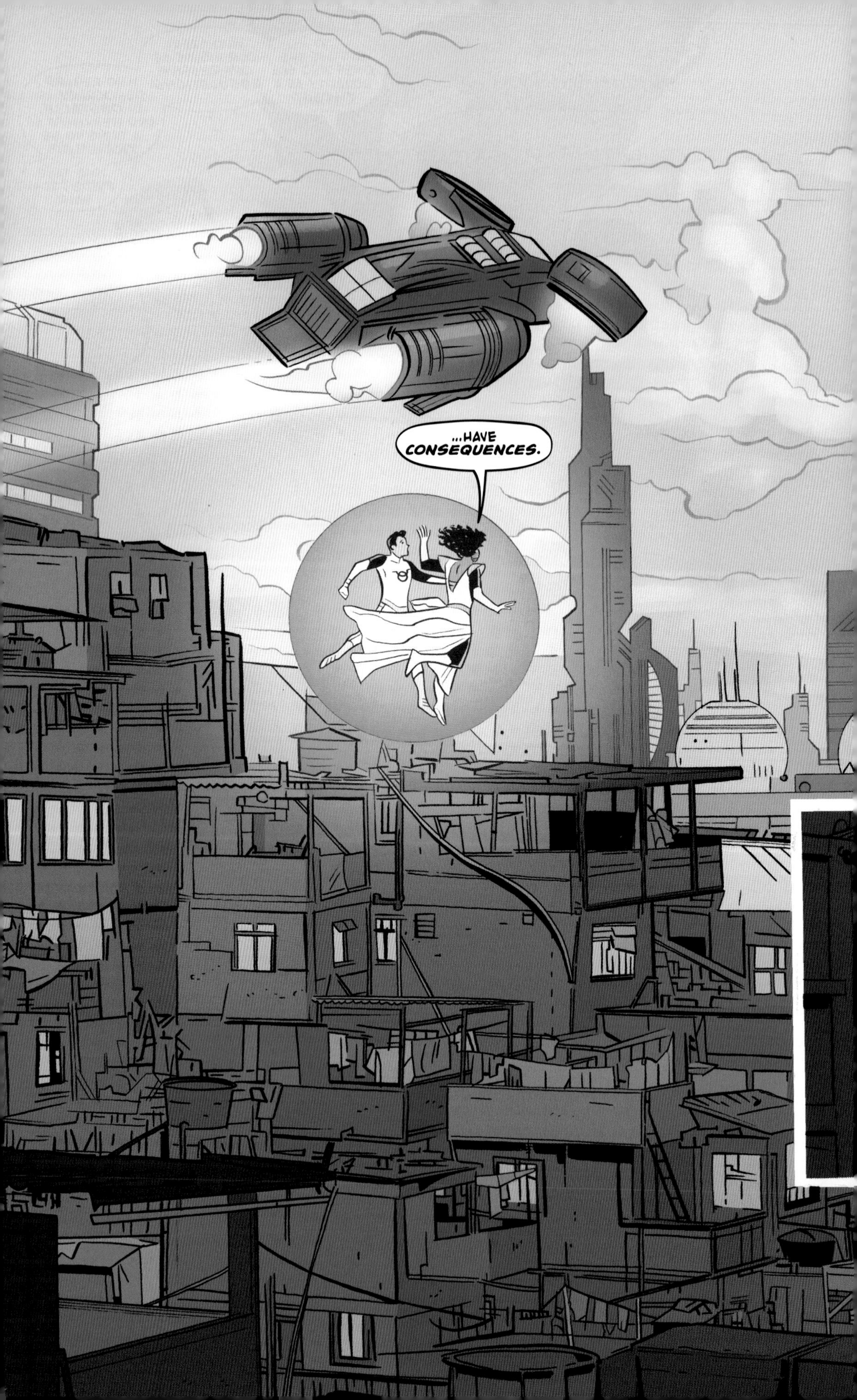
...HAVE CONSEQUENCES.

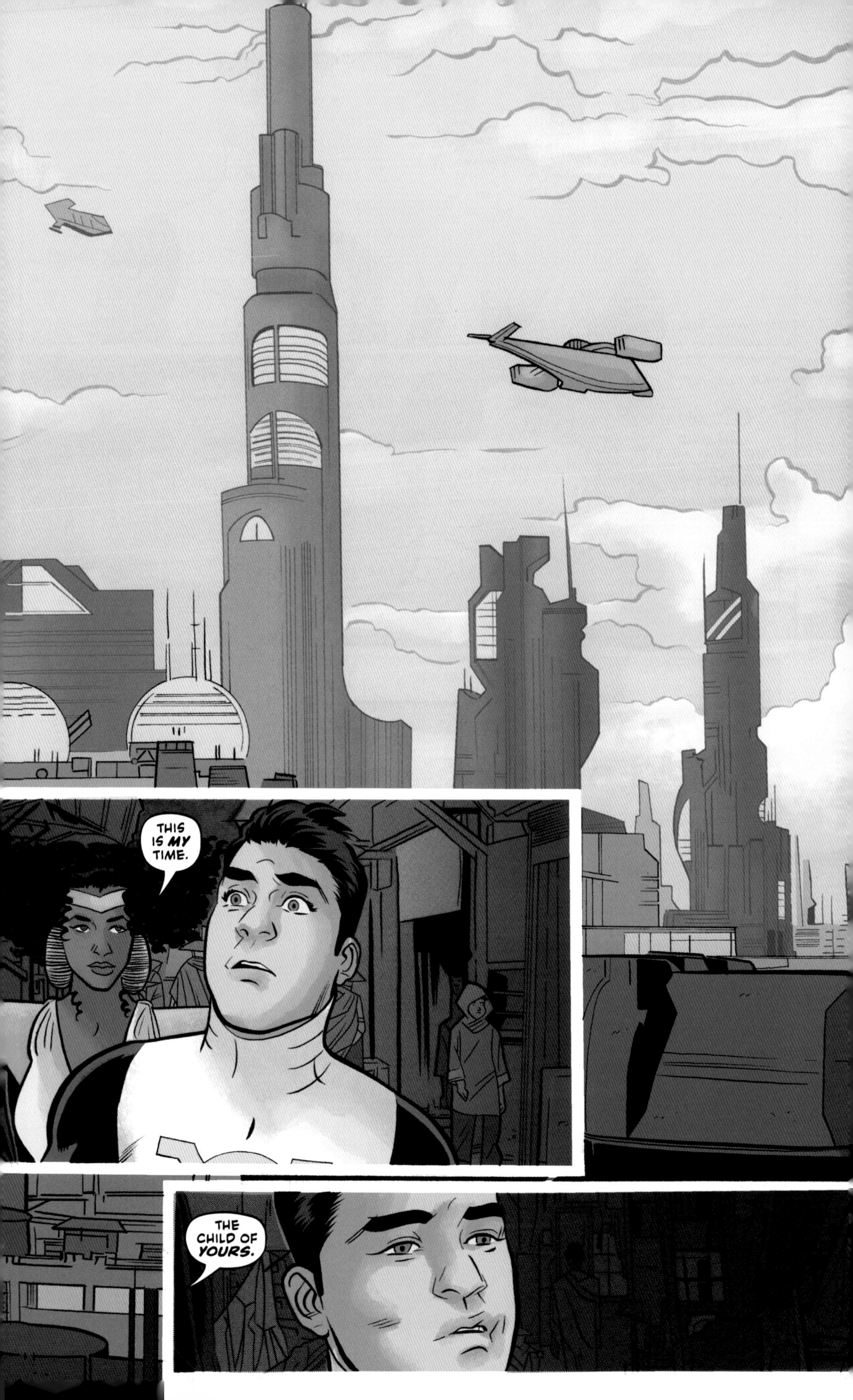
THIS IS MY TIME.
THE CHILD OF YOURS.

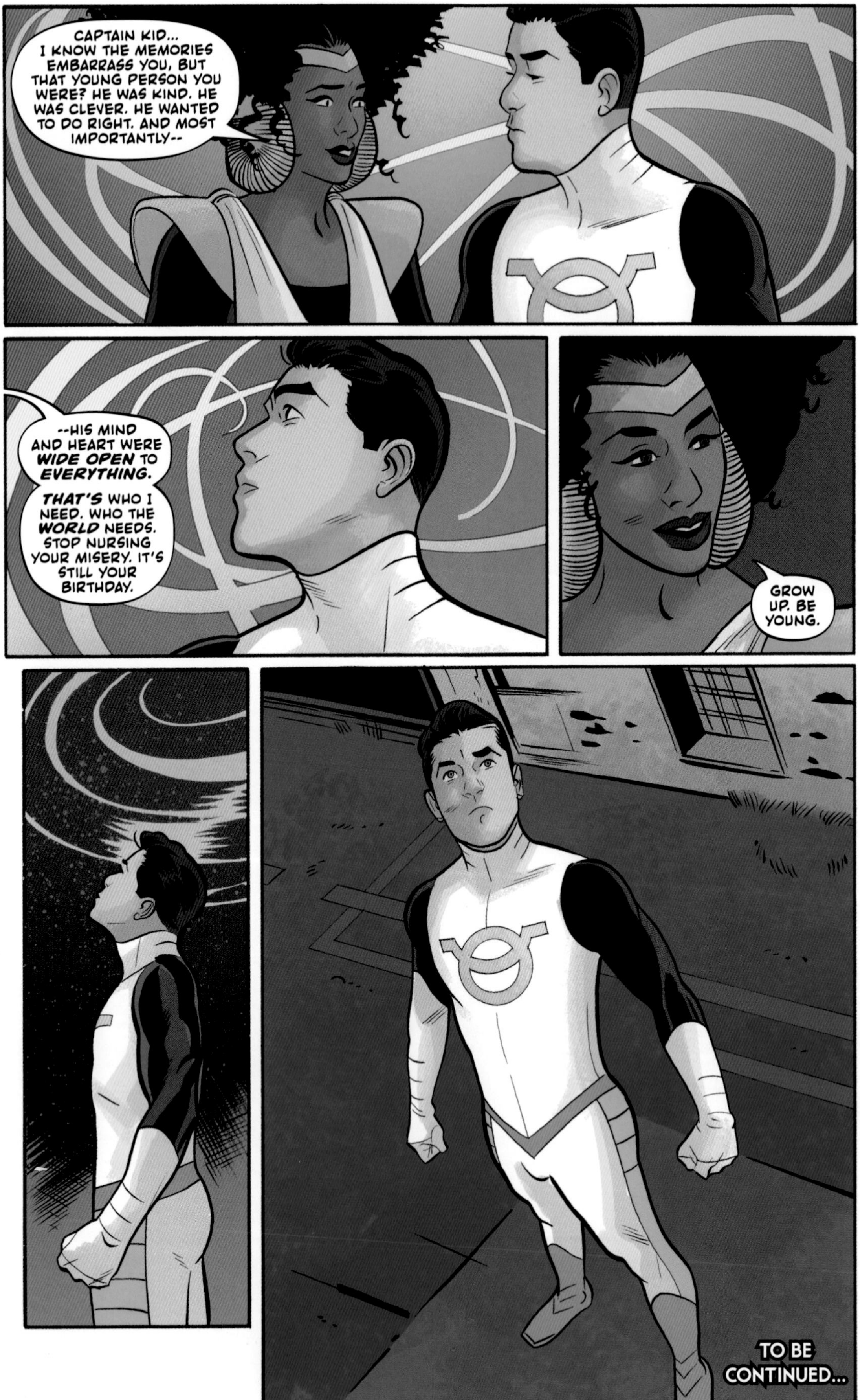
CAPTAIN KID... I KNOW THE MEMORIES EMBARRASS YOU, BUT THAT YOUNG PERSON YOU WERE? HE WAS KIND. HE WAS CLEVER. HE WANTED TO DO RIGHT. AND MOST IMPORTANTLY--
--HIS MIND AND HEART WERE WIDE OPEN TO EVERYTHING.
THAT'S WHO I NEED. WHO THE WORLD NEEDS. STOP NURSING YOUR MISERY. IT'S STILL YOUR BIRTHDAY.
GROW UP. BE YOUNG.
TO BE CONTINUED...

"HE'LL LIVE"

4

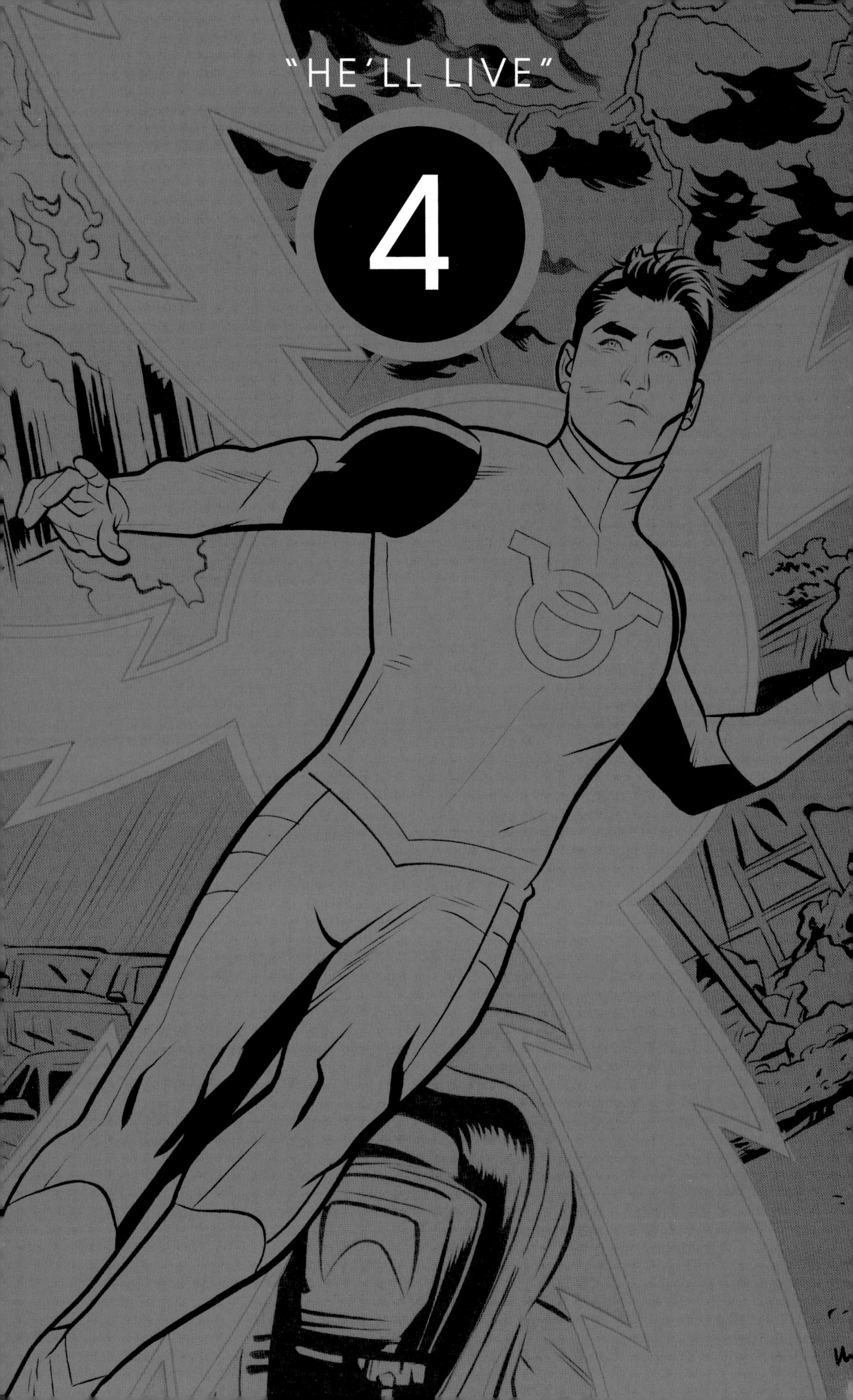

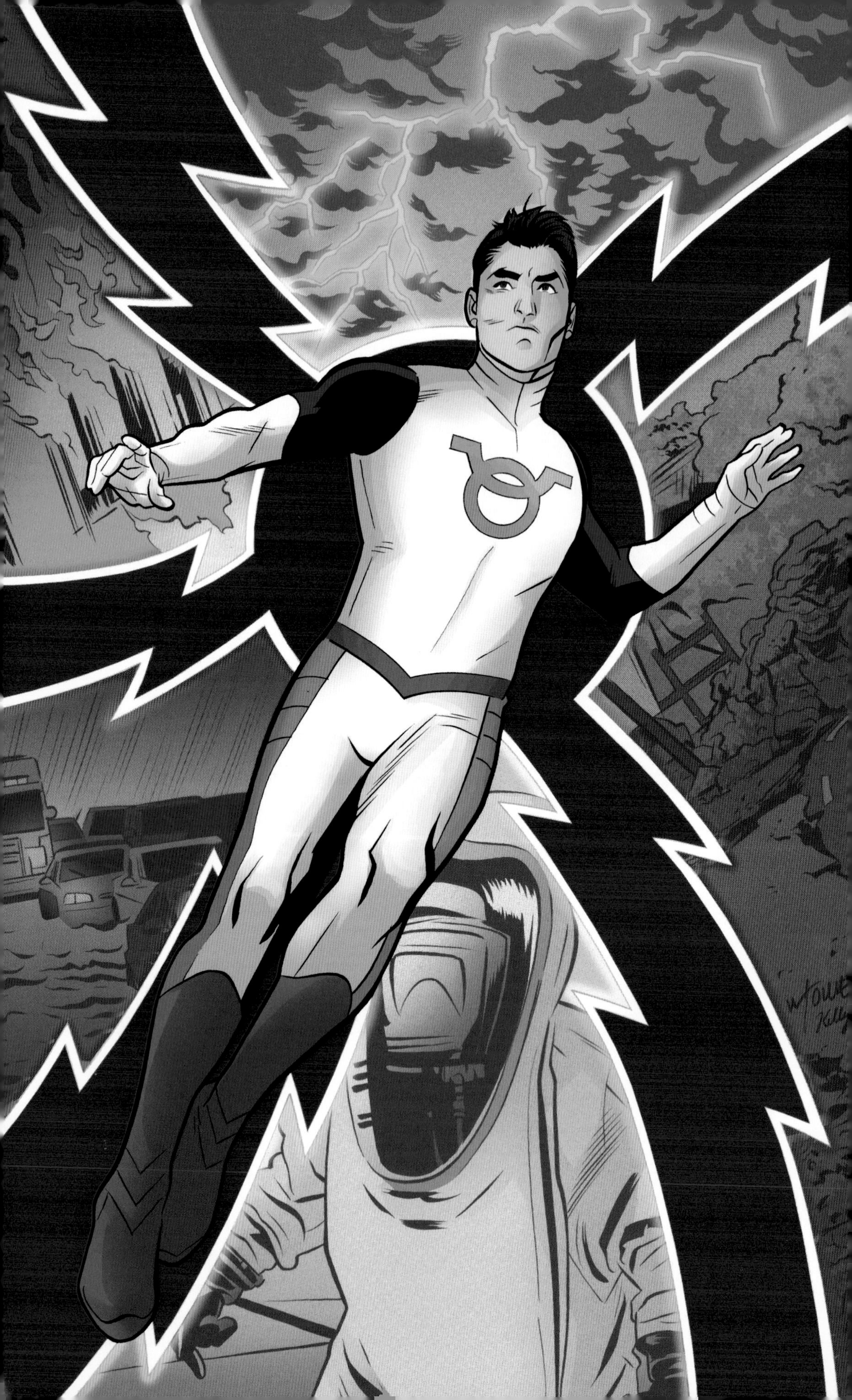

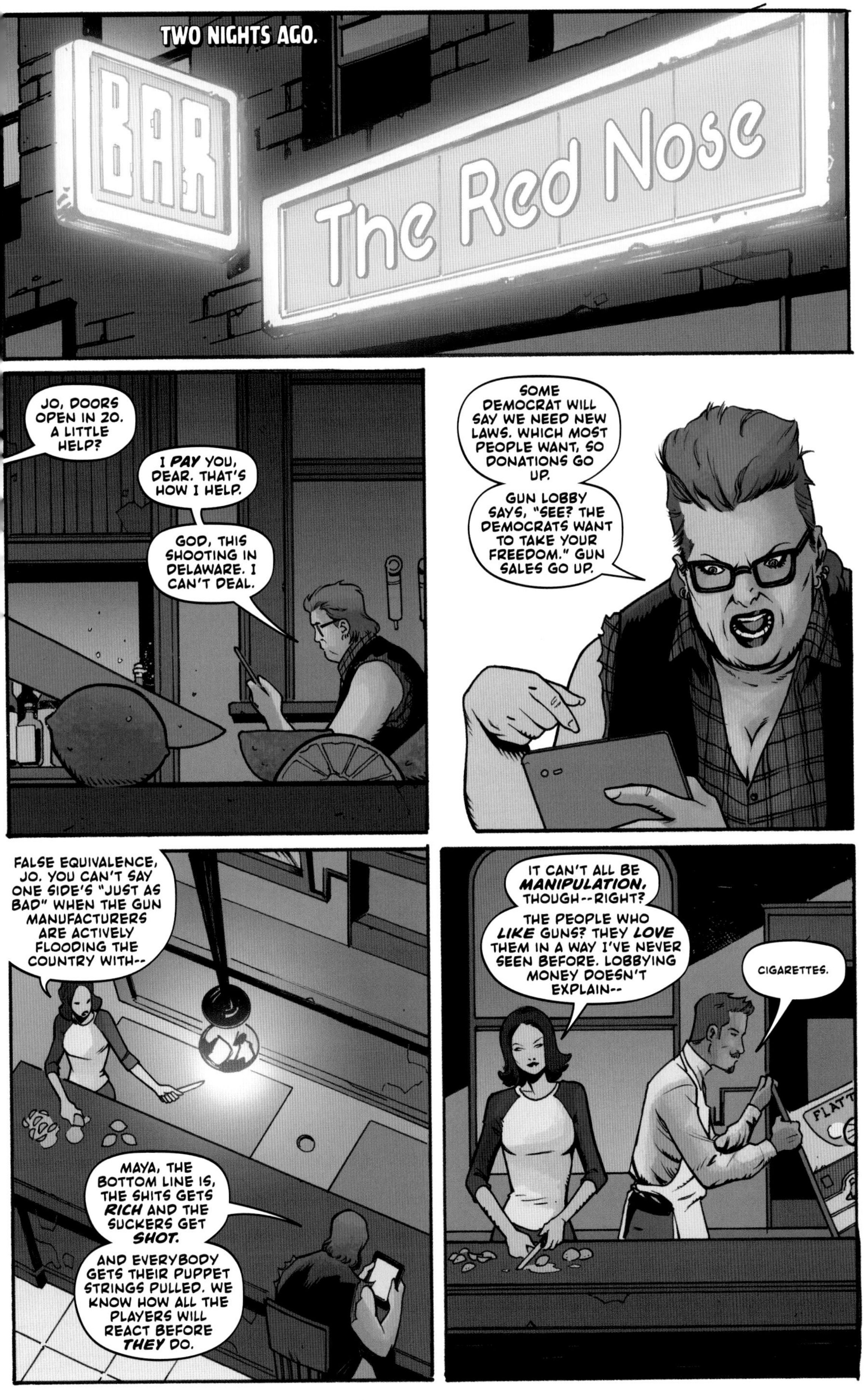
TWO NIGHTS AGO.
BAR
The Red Nose
JO, DOORS OPEN IN 20. A LITTLE HELP?
I PAY YOU, DEAR. THAT'S HOW I HELP.
GOD, THIS SHOOTING IN DELAWARE. I CAN'T DEAL.
SOME DEMOCRAT WILL SAY WE NEED NEW LAWS. WHICH MOST PEOPLE WANT, SO DONATIONS GO UP.
GUN LOBBY SAYS, "SEE? THE DEMOCRATS WANT TO TAKE YOUR FREEDOM." GUN SALES GO UP.
FALSE EQUIVALENCE, JO. YOU CAN'T SAY ONE SIDE'S "JUST AS BAD" WHEN THE GUN MANUFACTURERS ARE ACTIVELY FLOODING THE COUNTRY WITH--
MAYA, THE BOTTOM LINE IS, THE SHITS GETS RICH AND THE SUCKERS GET SHOT.
AND EVERYBODY GETS THEIR PUPPET STRINGS PULLED. WE KNOW HOW ALL THE PLAYERS WILL REACT BEFORE THEY DO.
IT CAN'T ALL BE MANIPULATION, THOUGH--RIGHT?
THE PEOPLE WHO LIKE GUNS? THEY LOVE THEM IN A WAY I'VE NEVER SEEN BEFORE. LOBBYING MONEY DOESN'T EXPLAIN--
CIGARETTES.

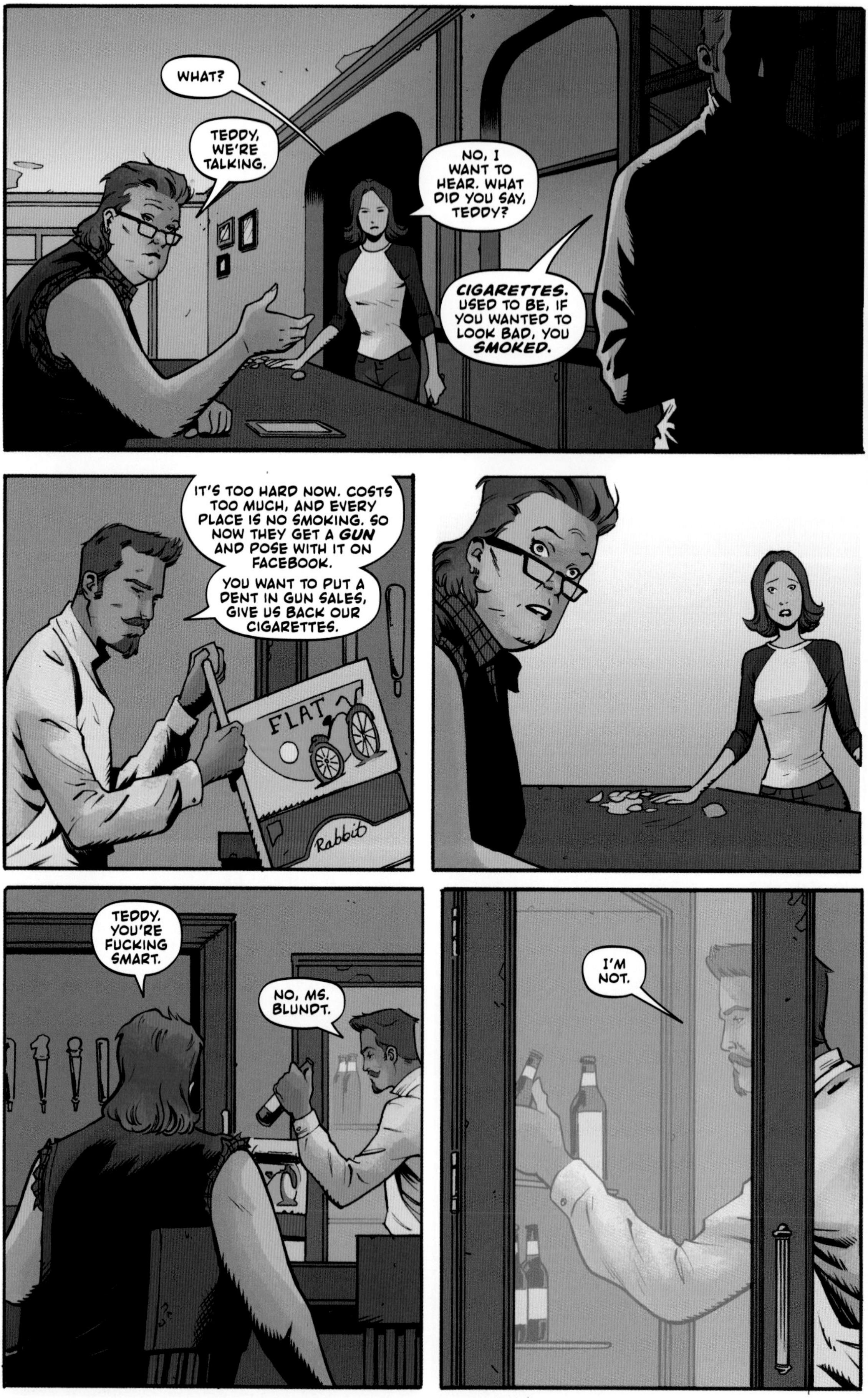
WHAT?
TEDDY, WE'RE TALKING.
NO, I WANT TO HEAR. WHAT DID YOU SAY, TEDDY?
CIGARETTES. USED TO BE, IF YOU WANTED TO LOOK BAD, YOU SMOKED.
IT'S TOO HARD NOW. COSTS TOO MUCH, AND EVERY PLACE IS NO SMOKING. SO NOW THEY GET A GUN AND POSE WITH IT ON FACEBOOK.
YOU WANT TO PUT A DENT IN GUN SALES, GIVE US BACK OUR CIGARETTES.
FLAT
Rabbit
TEDDY. YOU'RE FUCKING SMART.
NO, MS. BLUNDT.
I'M NOT.

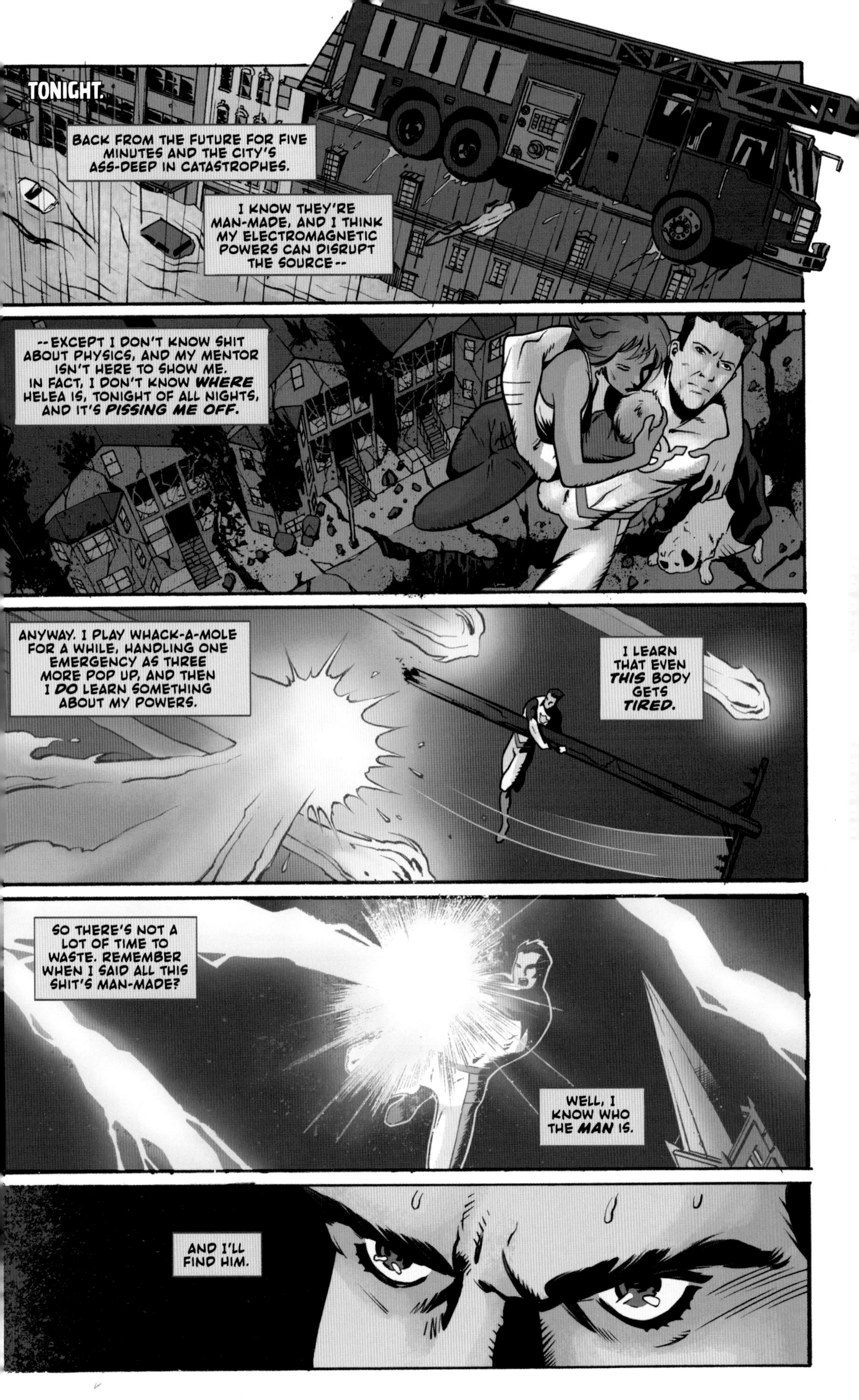
TONIGHT.
BACK FROM THE FUTURE FOR FIVE MINUTES AND THE CITY'S ASS-DEEP IN CATASTROPHES.
I KNOW THEY'RE MAN-MADE, AND I THINK MY ELECTROMAGNETIC POWERS CAN DISRUPT THE SOURCE--
--EXCEPT I DON'T KNOW SHIT ABOUT PHYSICS, AND MY MENTOR ISN'T HERE TO SHOW ME. IN FACT, I DON'T KNOW *WHERE* HELEA IS, TONIGHT OF ALL NIGHTS, AND IT'S *PISSING ME OFF.*
ANYWAY. I PLAY WHACK-A-MOLE FOR A WHILE, HANDLING ONE EMERGENCY AS THREE MORE POP UP, AND THEN I *DO* LEARN SOMETHING ABOUT MY POWERS.
I LEARN THAT EVEN *THIS* BODY GETS *TIRED.*
SO THERE'S NOT A LOT OF TIME TO WASTE. REMEMBER WHEN I SAID ALL THIS SHIT'S MAN-MADE?
WELL, I KNOW WHO THE *MAN* IS.
AND I'LL FIND HIM.

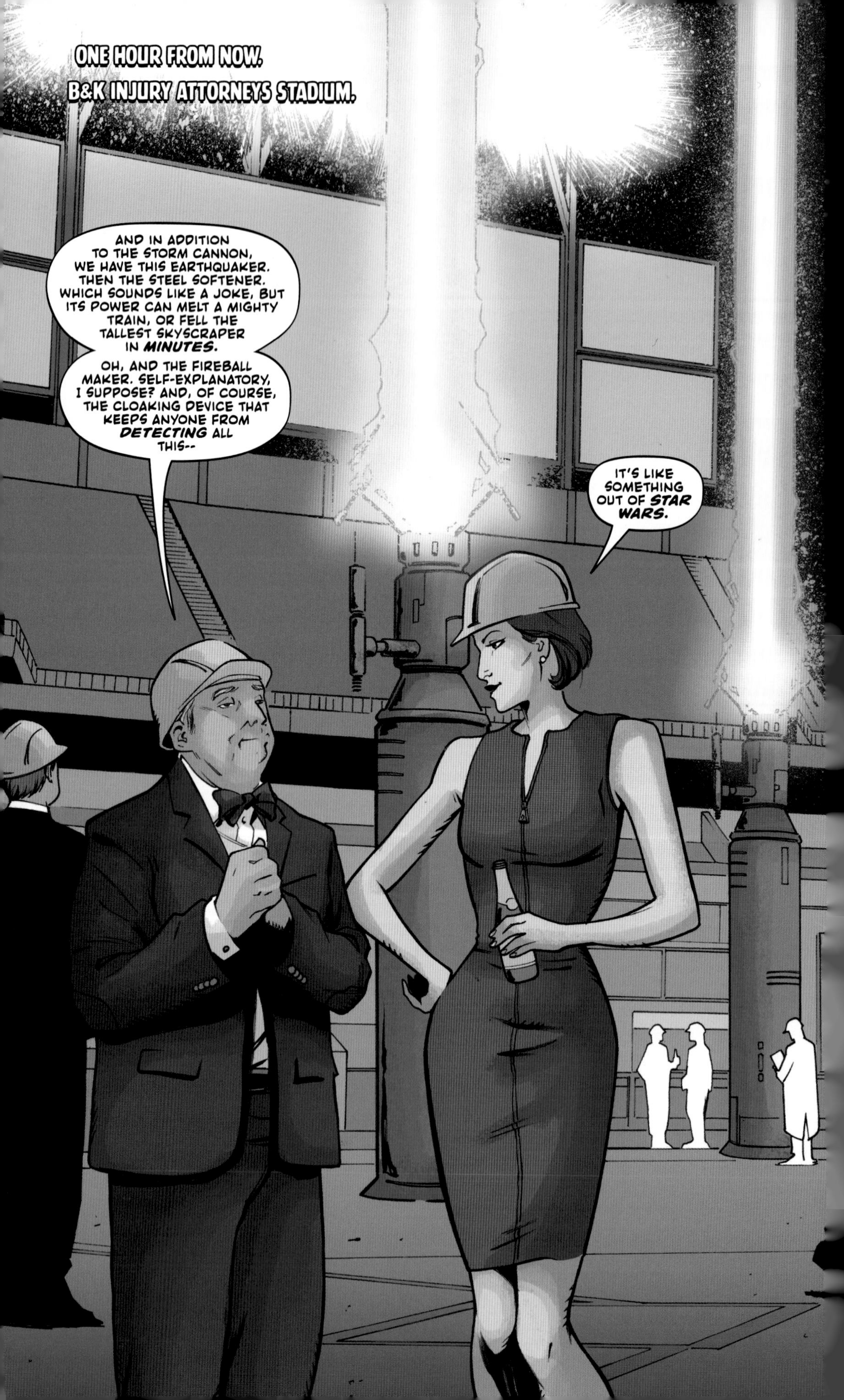
ONE HOUR FROM NOW.
B&K INJURY ATTORNEYS STADIUM.
AND IN ADDITION TO THE STORM CANNON, WE HAVE THIS EARTHQUAKER. THEN THE STEEL SOFTENER. WHICH SOUNDS LIKE A JOKE, BUT ITS POWER CAN MELT A MIGHTY TRAIN, OR FELL THE TALLEST SKYSCRAPER IN *MINUTES.*
OH, AND THE FIREBALL MAKER. SELF-EXPLANATORY, I SUPPOSE? AND, OF COURSE, THE CLOAKING DEVICE THAT KEEPS ANYONE FROM *DETECTING* ALL THIS--
IT'S LIKE SOMETHING OUT OF *STAR WARS.*

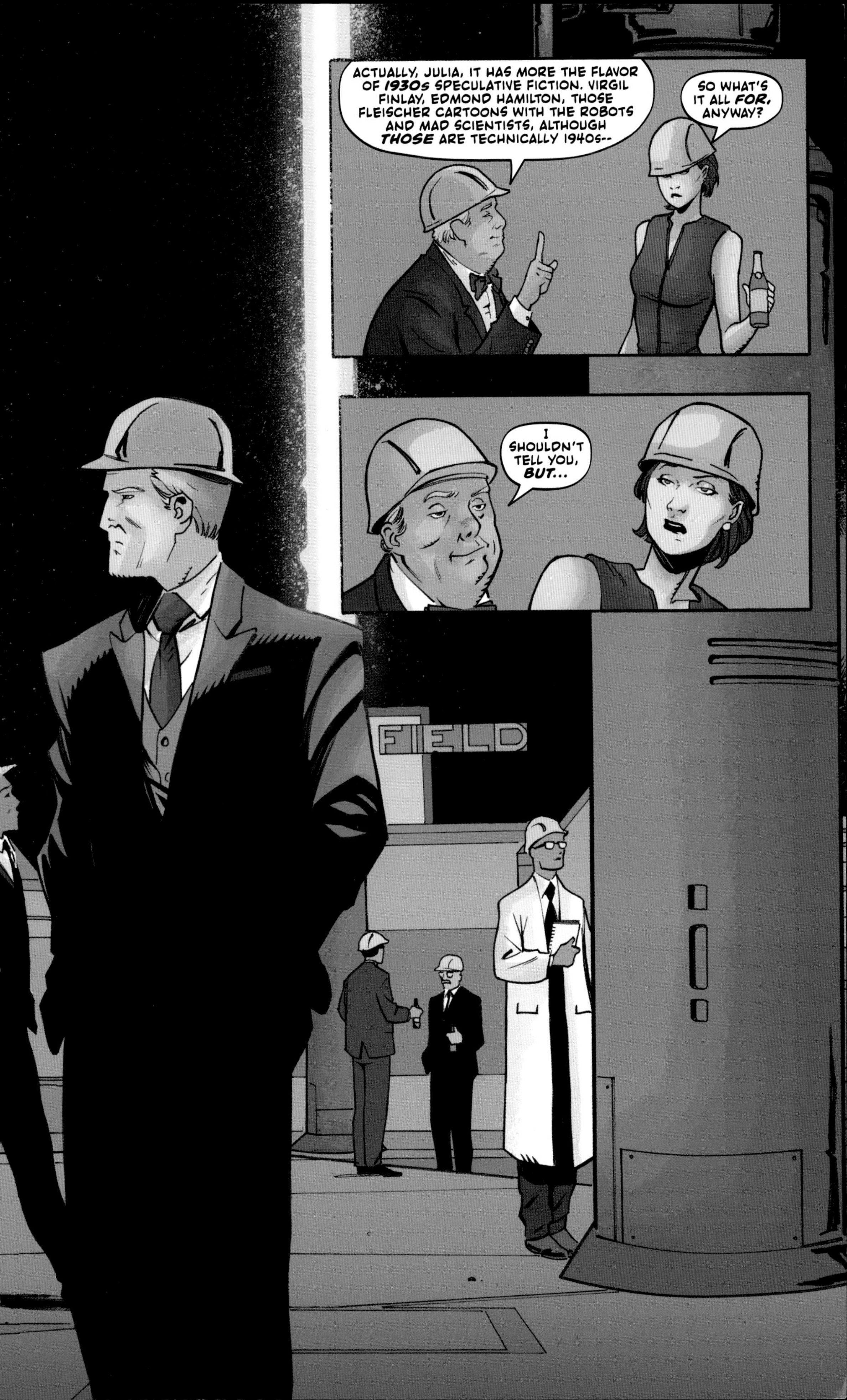
ACTUALLY, JULIA, IT HAS MORE THE FLAVOR OF *1930s* SPECULATIVE FICTION. VIRGIL FINLAY, EDMOND HAMILTON, THOSE FLEISCHER CARTOONS WITH THE ROBOTS AND MAD SCIENTISTS, ALTHOUGH *THOSE* ARE TECHNICALLY 1940s--
SO WHAT'S IT ALL *FOR,* ANYWAY?
I SHOULDN'T TELL YOU, *BUT...*
FIELD

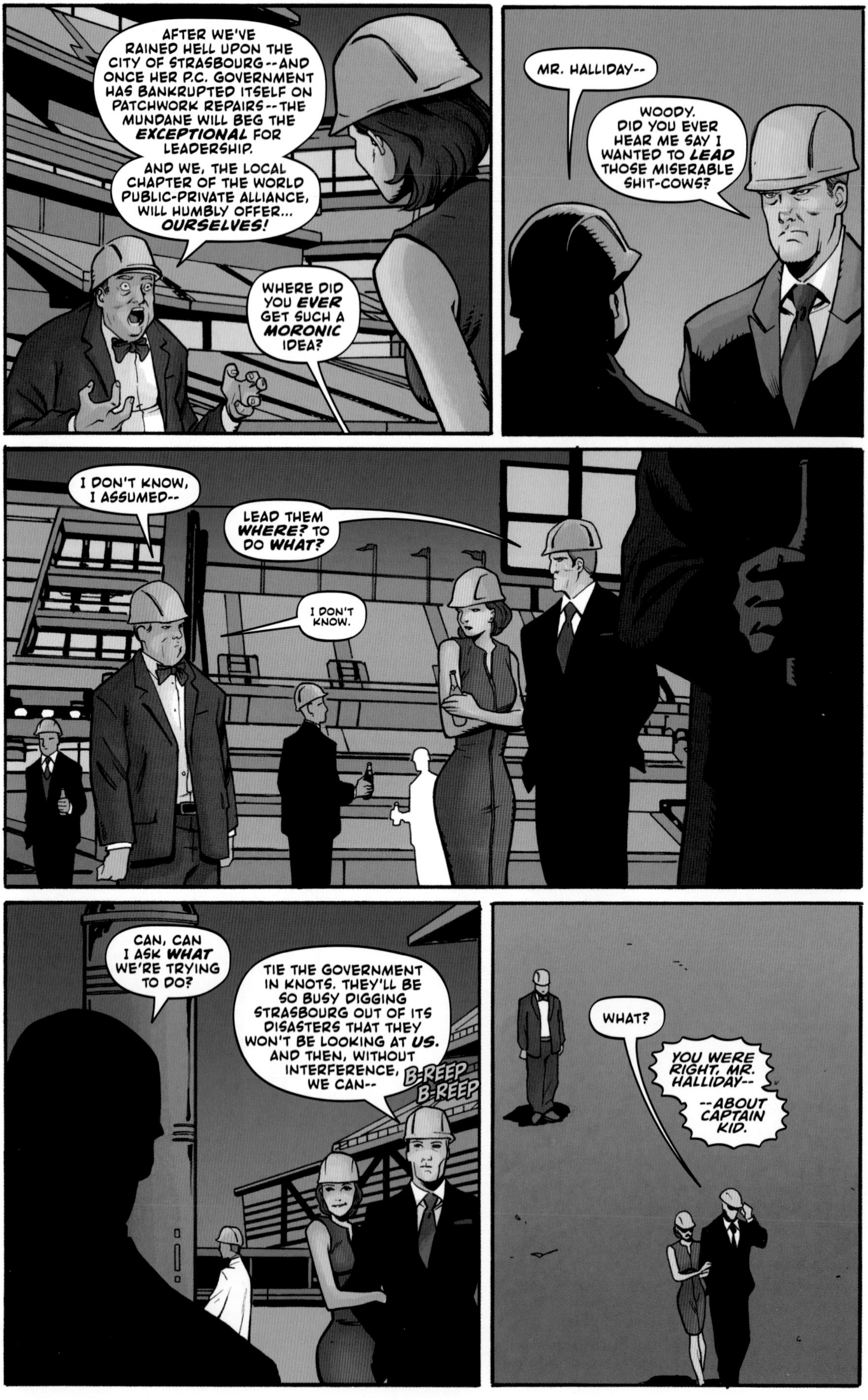
AFTER WE'VE RAINED HELL UPON THE CITY OF STRASBOURG--AND ONCE HER P.C. GOVERNMENT HAS BANKRUPTED ITSELF ON PATCHWORK REPAIRS--THE MUNDANE WILL BEG THE EXCEPTIONAL FOR LEADERSHIP.
AND WE, THE LOCAL CHAPTER OF THE WORLD PUBLIC-PRIVATE ALLIANCE, WILL HUMBLY OFFER... OURSELVES!
WHERE DID YOU EVER GET SUCH A MORONIC IDEA?
MR. HALLIDAY--
WOODY. DID YOU EVER HEAR ME SAY I WANTED TO LEAD THOSE MISERABLE SHIT-COWS?
I DON'T KNOW, I ASSUMED--
LEAD THEM WHERE? TO DO WHAT?
I DON'T KNOW.
CAN, CAN I ASK WHAT WE'RE TRYING TO DO?
TIE THE GOVERNMENT IN KNOTS. THEY'LL BE SO BUSY DIGGING STRASBOURG OUT OF ITS DISASTERS THAT THEY WON'T BE LOOKING AT US. AND THEN, WITHOUT INTERFERENCE, WE CAN--
B-REEP
B-REEP
WHAT?
YOU WERE RIGHT, MR. HALLIDAY--
--ABOUT CAPTAIN KID.

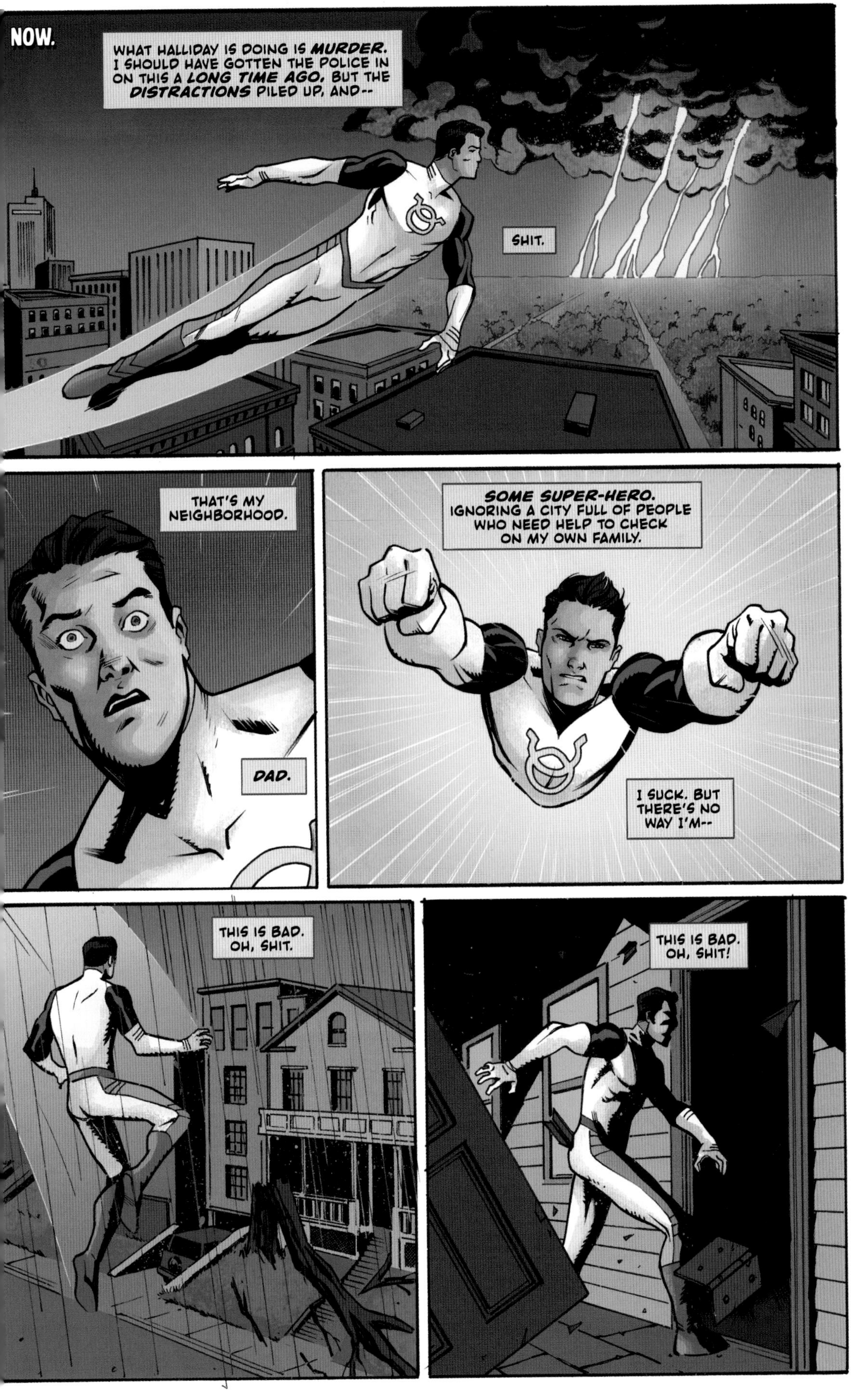
NOW.
WHAT HALLIDAY IS DOING IS MURDER. I SHOULD HAVE GOTTEN THE POLICE IN ON THIS A LONG TIME AGO. BUT THE DISTRACTIONS PILED UP, AND--
SHIT.
THAT'S MY NEIGHBORHOOD.
DAD.
SOME SUPER-HERO. IGNORING A CITY FULL OF PEOPLE WHO NEED HELP TO CHECK ON MY OWN FAMILY.
I SUCK. BUT THERE'S NO WAY I'M--
THIS IS BAD. OH, SHIT.
THIS IS BAD. OH, SHIT!

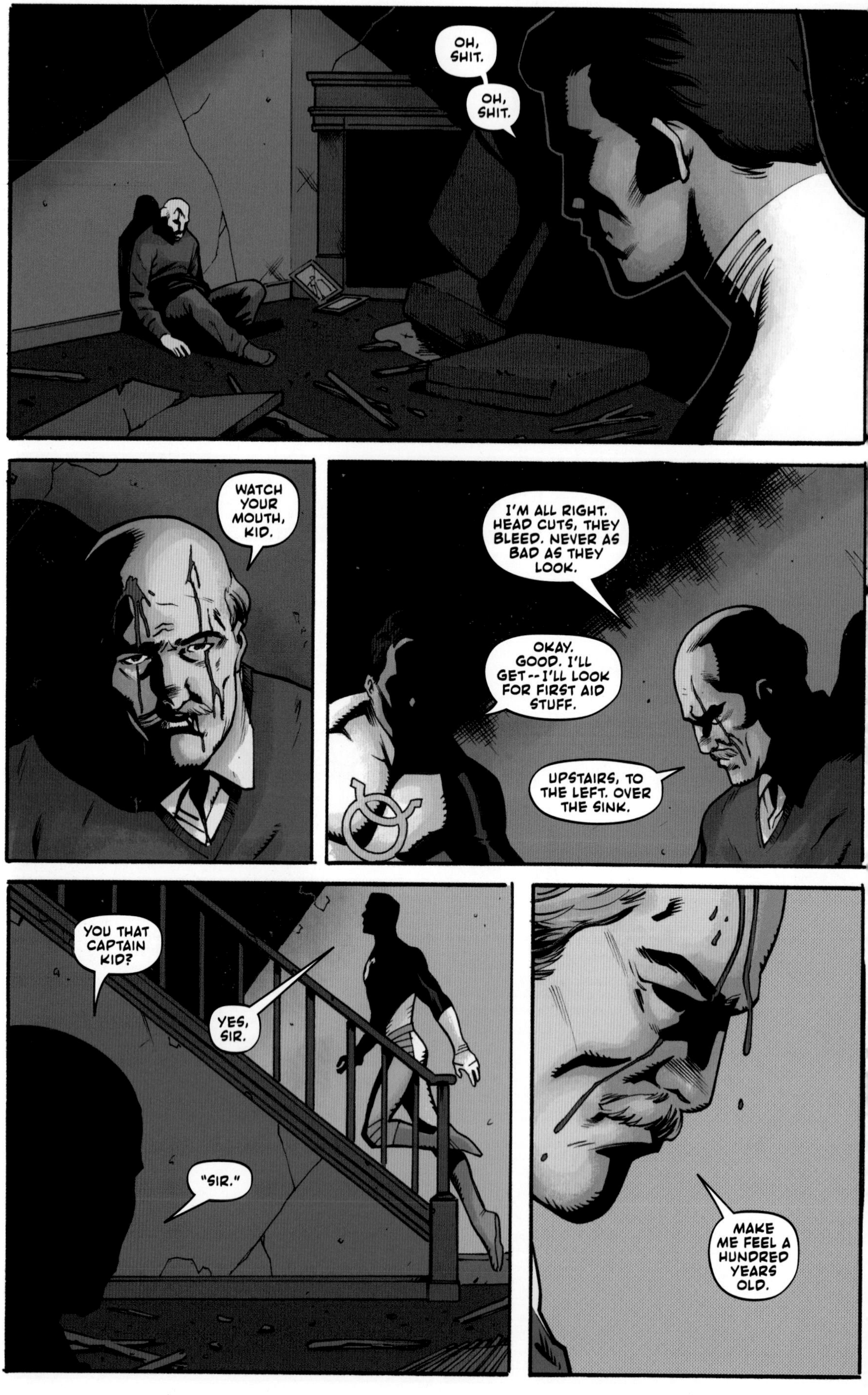
OH, SHIT.
OH, SHIT.
WATCH YOUR MOUTH, KID.
I'M ALL RIGHT. HEAD CUTS, THEY BLEED. NEVER AS BAD AS THEY LOOK.
OKAY. GOOD. I'LL GET--I'LL LOOK FOR FIRST AID STUFF.
UPSTAIRS, TO THE LEFT. OVER THE SINK.
YOU THAT CAPTAIN KID?
YES, SIR.
"SIR."
MAKE ME FEEL A HUNDRED YEARS OLD.

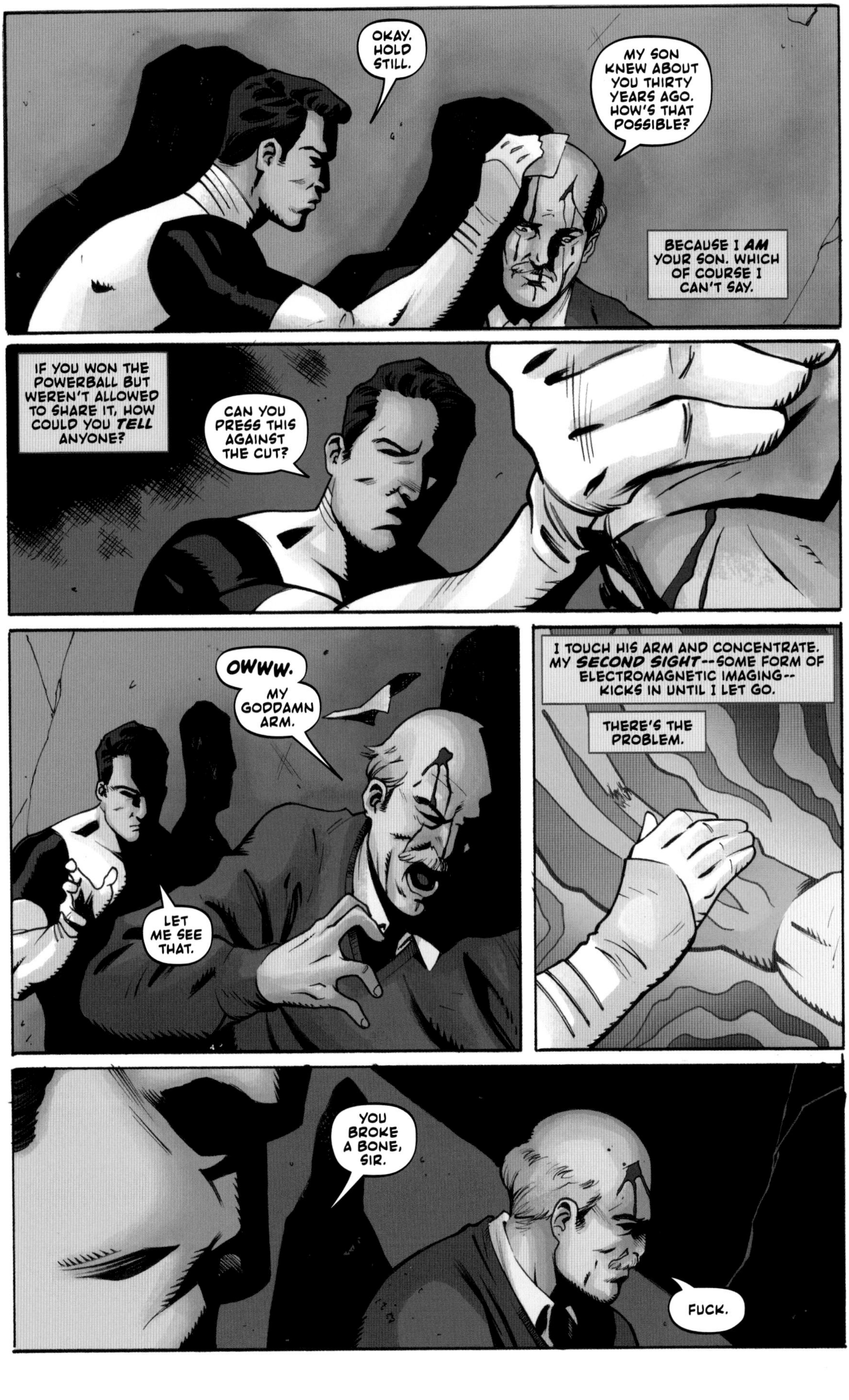
OKAY. HOLD STILL.
MY SON KNEW ABOUT YOU THIRTY YEARS AGO. HOW'S THAT POSSIBLE?
BECAUSE I **AM** YOUR SON. WHICH OF COURSE I CAN'T SAY.
IF YOU WON THE POWERBALL BUT WEREN'T ALLOWED TO SHARE IT, HOW COULD YOU **TELL** ANYONE?
CAN YOU PRESS THIS AGAINST THE CUT?
OWWW. MY GODDAMN ARM.
LET ME SEE THAT.
I TOUCH HIS ARM AND CONCENTRATE. MY **SECOND SIGHT**--SOME FORM OF ELECTROMAGNETIC IMAGING--KICKS IN UNTIL I LET GO.
THERE'S THE PROBLEM.
YOU BROKE A BONE, SIR.
FUCK.

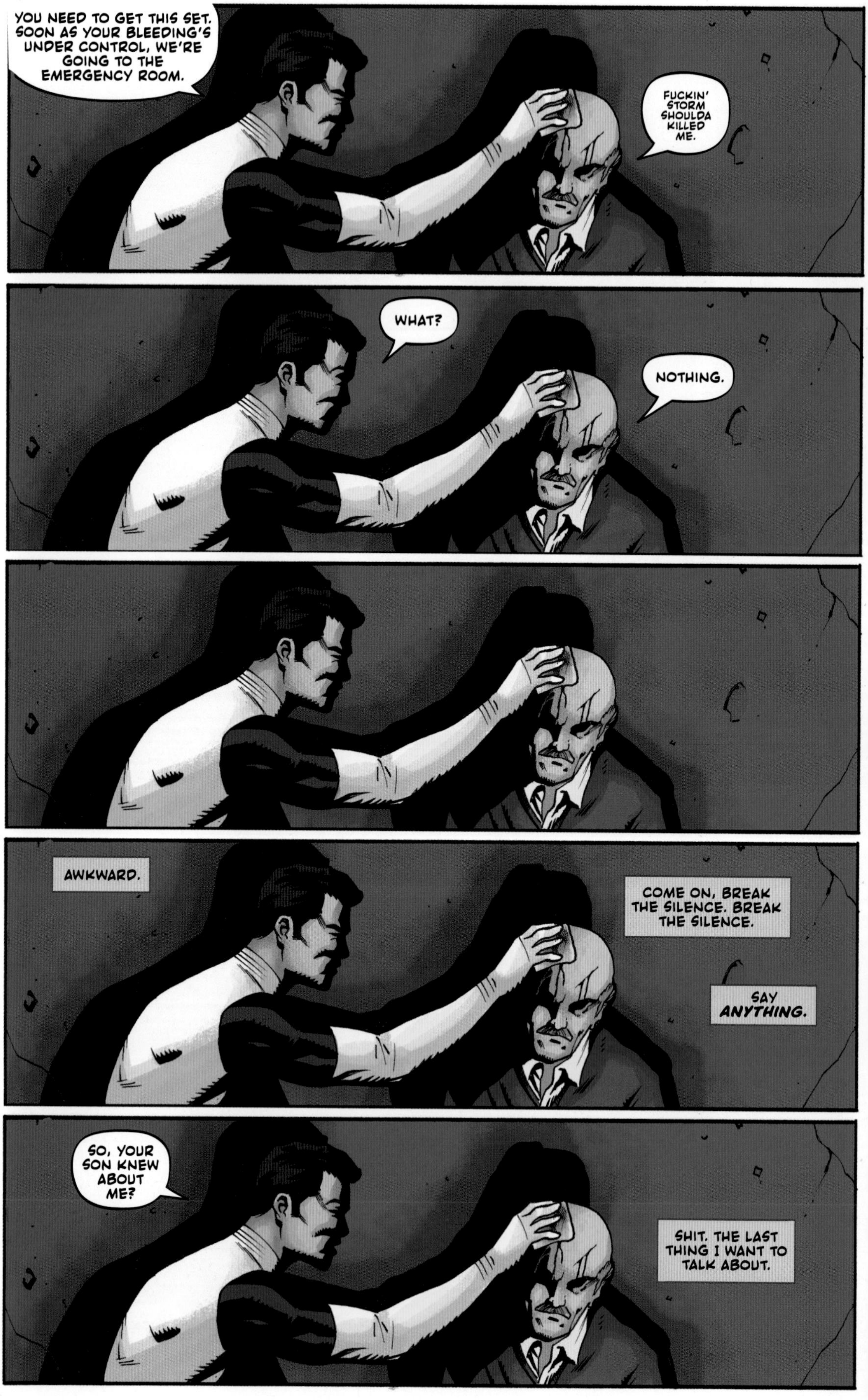
YOU NEED TO GET THIS SET. SOON AS YOUR BLEEDING'S UNDER CONTROL, WE'RE GOING TO THE EMERGENCY ROOM.
FUCKIN' STORM SHOULDA KILLED ME.
WHAT?
NOTHING.
AWKWARD.
COME ON, BREAK THE SILENCE. BREAK THE SILENCE.
SAY *ANYTHING.*
SO, YOUR SON KNEW ABOUT ME?
SHIT. THE LAST THING I WANT TO TALK ABOUT.

WHEN HE WAS ABOUT YOUR AGE, HE USED TO DRAW PICTURES OF YOU ALL THE TIME. HE THOUGHT HE MADE YOU UP. HAD TO BE, WHAT? 1986.

LIKE YOU SAID...HOW IS THAT POSSIBLE?

MAYBE YOU'RE OLDER THAN YOU LOOK.

WE'LL NEVER GET AN AMBULANCE TONIGHT. I'M GOING TO HAVE TO FLY YOU.

WHAT? NO.

RIGHT. HE'S *TERRIFIED* OF HEIGHTS.

I REMEMBER WHEN HE TRIED TO CLIMB UP ON THE GARAGE ROOF TO GET MY FRISBEE. ONLY WHAT, TEN FEET UP? PANIC ATTACK.

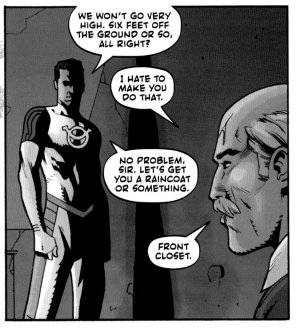

WE WON'T GO VERY HIGH. SIX FEET OFF THE GROUND OR SO, ALL RIGHT?

I HATE TO MAKE YOU DO THAT.

NO PROBLEM, SIR. LET'S GET YOU A RAINCOAT OR SOMETHING.

FRONT CLOSET.

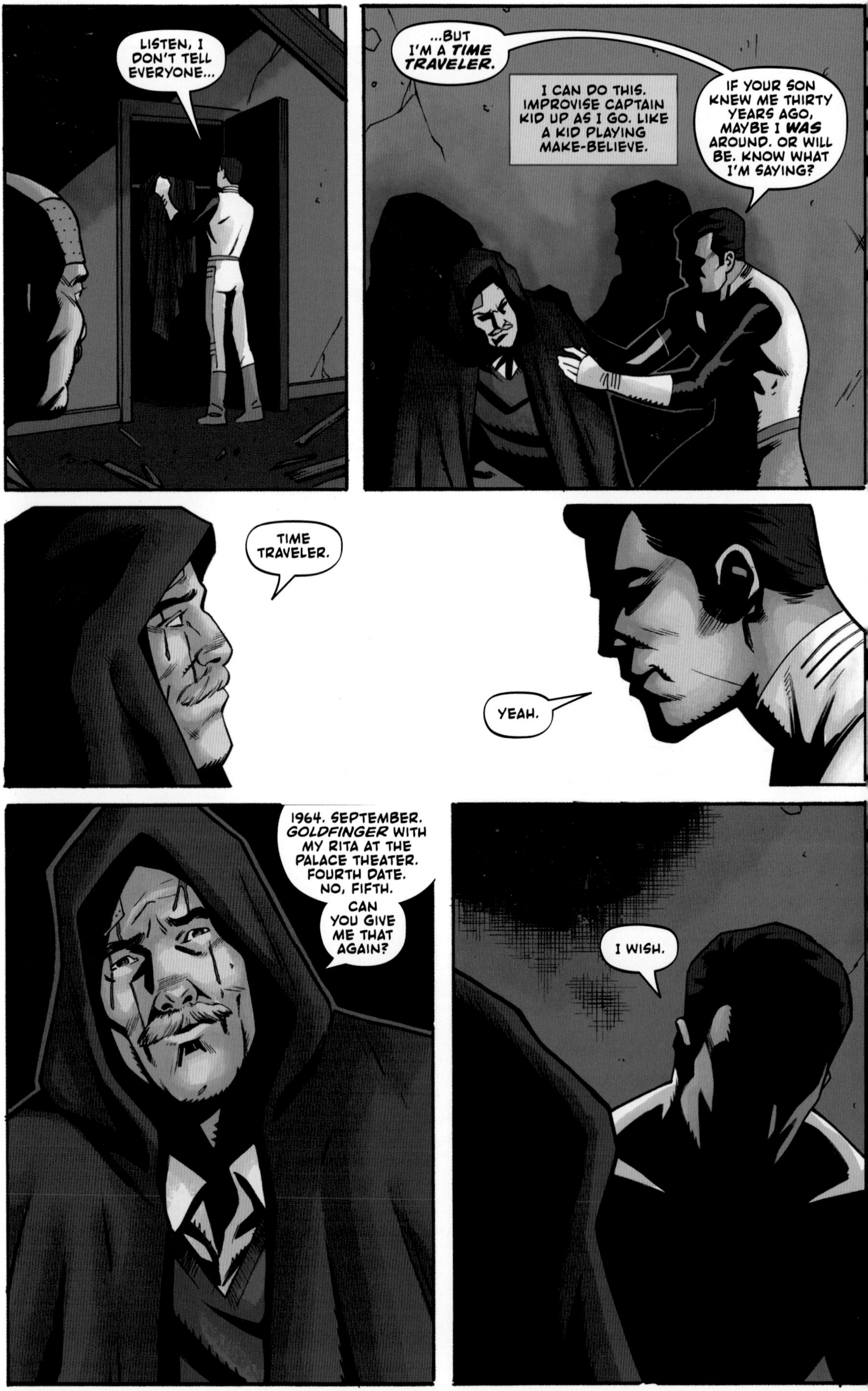
LISTEN, I DON'T TELL EVERYONE...
...BUT I'M A *TIME TRAVELER.*
I CAN DO THIS. IMPROVISE CAPTAIN KID UP AS I GO. LIKE A KID PLAYING MAKE-BELIEVE.
IF YOUR SON KNEW ME THIRTY YEARS AGO, MAYBE I *WAS* AROUND. OR WILL BE. KNOW WHAT I'M SAYING?
TIME TRAVELER.
YEAH.
1964. SEPTEMBER. *GOLDFINGER* WITH MY RITA AT THE PALACE THEATER. FOURTH DATE. NO, FIFTH.
CAN YOU GIVE ME THAT AGAIN?
I WISH.

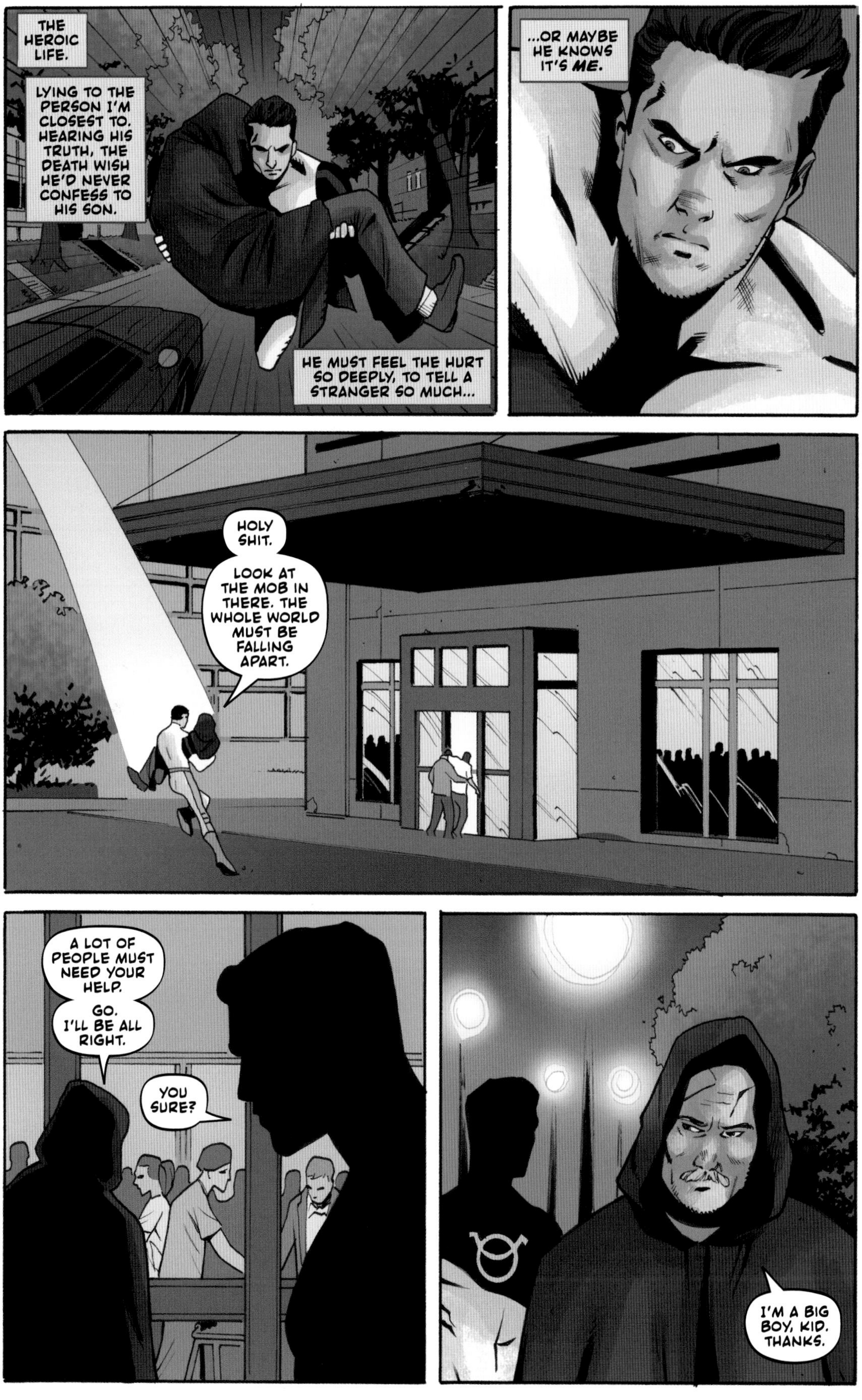
THE HEROIC LIFE.
LYING TO THE PERSON I'M CLOSEST TO. HEARING HIS TRUTH, THE DEATH WISH HE'D NEVER CONFESS TO HIS SON.
HE MUST FEEL THE HURT SO DEEPLY, TO TELL A STRANGER SO MUCH...
...OR MAYBE HE KNOWS IT'S ME.
HOLY SHIT.
LOOK AT THE MOB IN THERE. THE WHOLE WORLD MUST BE FALLING APART.
A LOT OF PEOPLE MUST NEED YOUR HELP.
GO. I'LL BE ALL RIGHT.
YOU SURE?
I'M A BIG BOY, KID. THANKS.

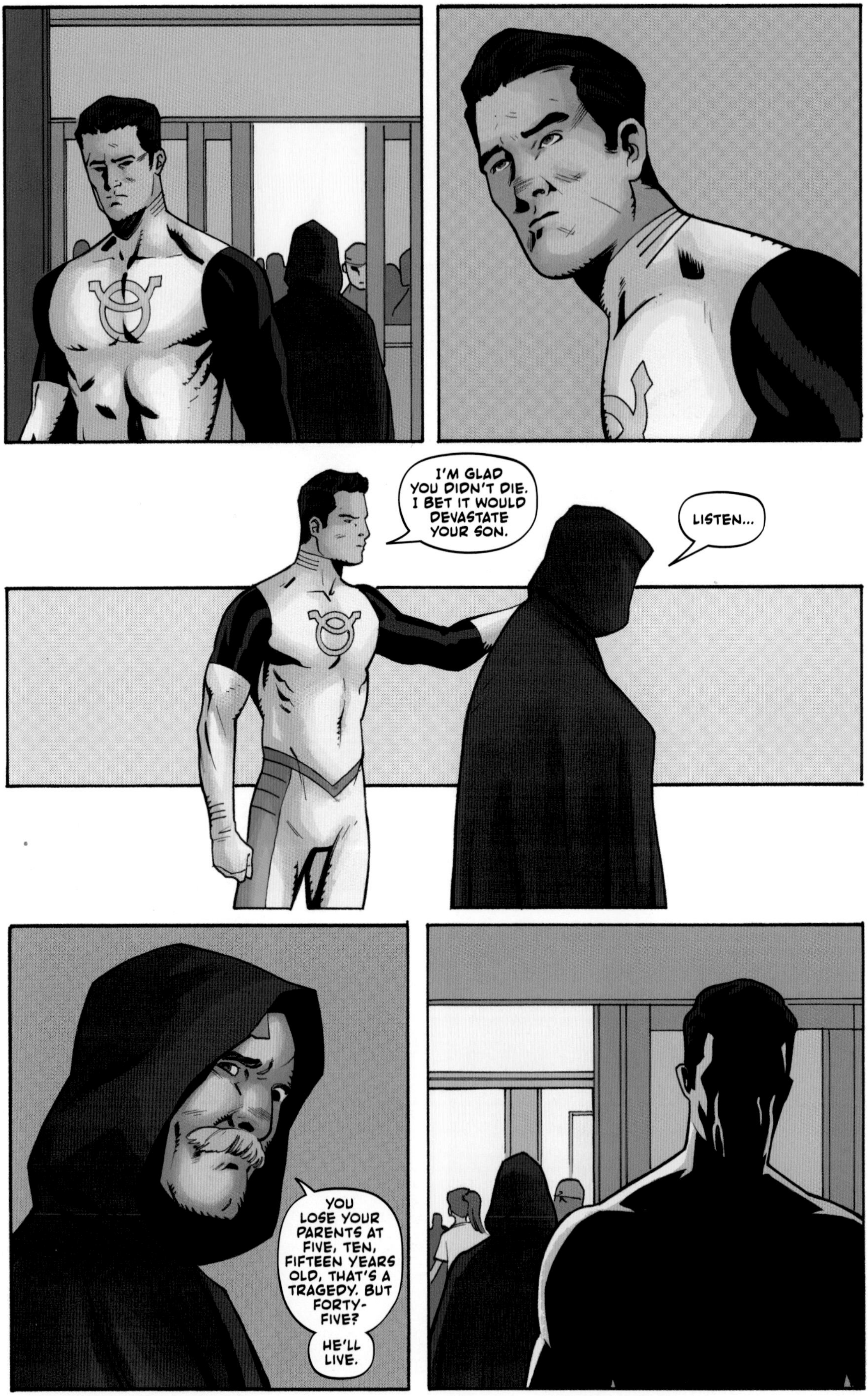
I'M GLAD YOU DIDN'T DIE. I BET IT WOULD DEVASTATE YOUR SON.
LISTEN...
YOU LOSE YOUR PARENTS AT FIVE, TEN, FIFTEEN YEARS OLD, THAT'S A TRAGEDY. BUT FORTY-FIVE?
HE'LL LIVE.

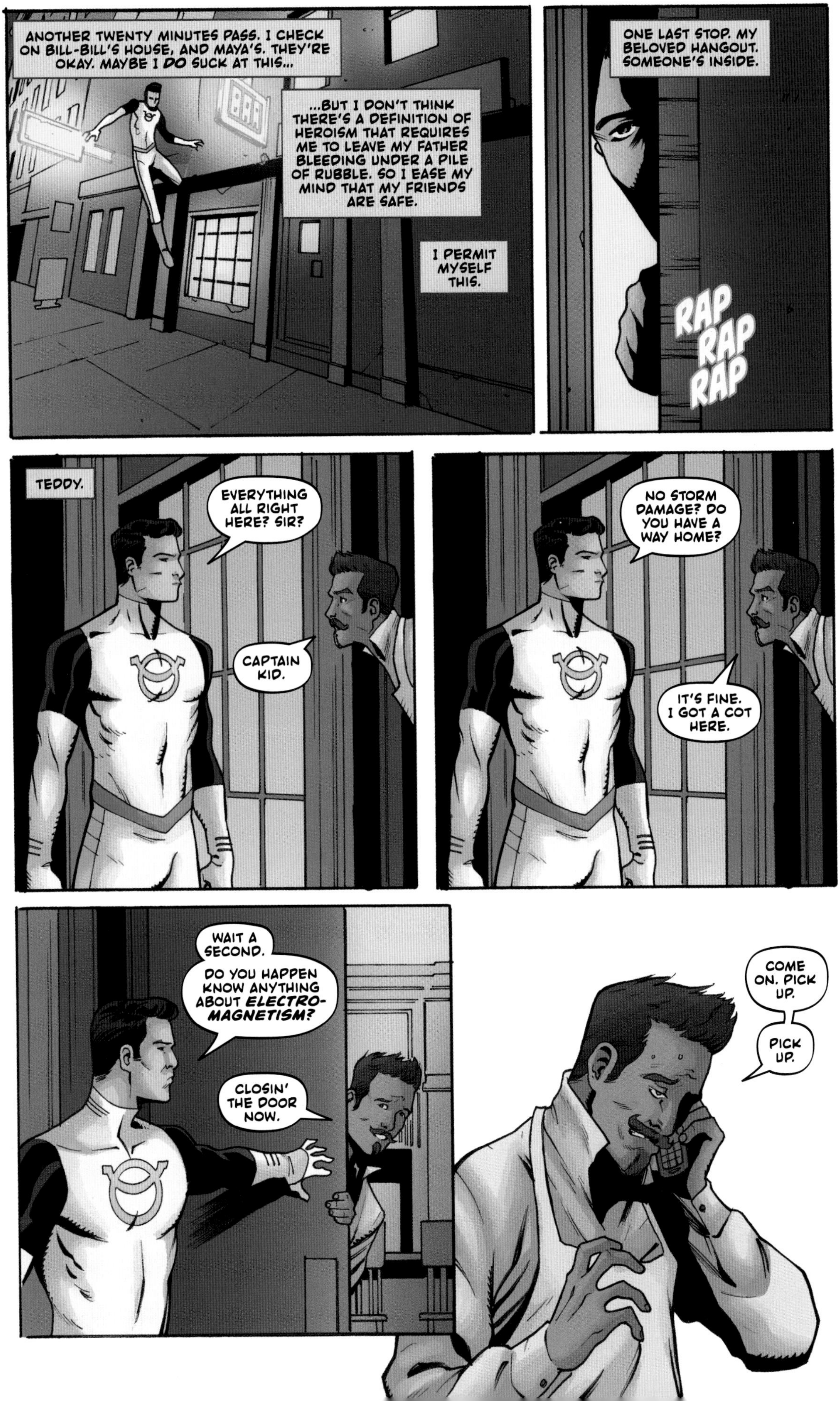
ANOTHER TWENTY MINUTES PASS. I CHECK ON BILL-BILL'S HOUSE, AND MAYA'S. THEY'RE OKAY. MAYBE I *DO* SUCK AT THIS...
...BUT I DON'T THINK THERE'S A DEFINITION OF HEROISM THAT REQUIRES ME TO LEAVE MY FATHER BLEEDING UNDER A PILE OF RUBBLE. SO I EASE MY MIND THAT MY FRIENDS ARE SAFE.
I PERMIT MYSELF THIS.
ONE LAST STOP. MY BELOVED HANGOUT. SOMEONE'S INSIDE.
RAP RAP RAP
TEDDY.
EVERYTHING ALL RIGHT HERE? SIR?
CAPTAIN KID.
NO STORM DAMAGE? DO YOU HAVE A WAY HOME?
IT'S FINE. I GOT A COT HERE.
WAIT A SECOND.
DO YOU HAPPEN KNOW ANYTHING ABOUT *ELECTRO-MAGNETISM?*
CLOSIN' THE DOOR NOW.
COME ON. PICK UP.
PICK UP.

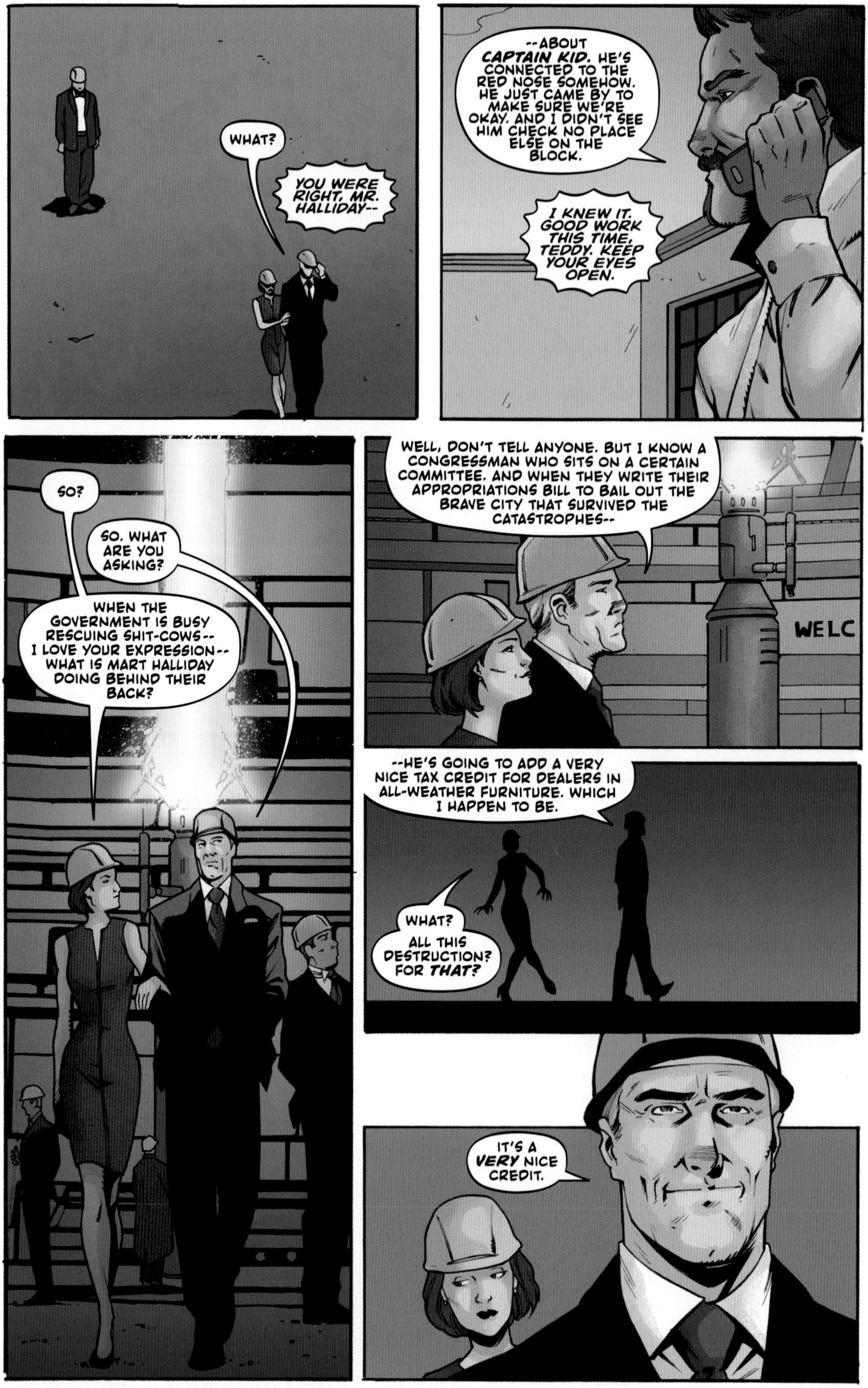
WHAT?
YOU WERE RIGHT, MR. HALLIDAY--
--ABOUT CAPTAIN KID. HE'S CONNECTED TO THE RED NOSE SOMEHOW. HE JUST CAME BY TO MAKE SURE WE'RE OKAY. AND I DIDN'T SEE HIM CHECK NO PLACE ELSE ON THE BLOCK.
I KNEW IT. GOOD WORK THIS TIME, TEDDY. KEEP YOUR EYES OPEN.
SO?
SO. WHAT ARE YOU ASKING?
WHEN THE GOVERNMENT IS BUSY RESCUING SHIT-COWS-- I LOVE YOUR EXPRESSION-- WHAT IS MART HALLIDAY DOING BEHIND THEIR BACK?
WELL, DON'T TELL ANYONE. BUT I KNOW A CONGRESSMAN WHO SITS ON A CERTAIN COMMITTEE. AND WHEN THEY WRITE THEIR APPROPRIATIONS BILL TO BAIL OUT THE BRAVE CITY THAT SURVIVED THE CATASTROPHES--
WELC
--HE'S GOING TO ADD A VERY NICE TAX CREDIT FOR DEALERS IN ALL-WEATHER FURNITURE. WHICH I HAPPEN TO BE.
WHAT? ALL THIS DESTRUCTION? FOR THAT?
IT'S A VERY NICE CREDIT.

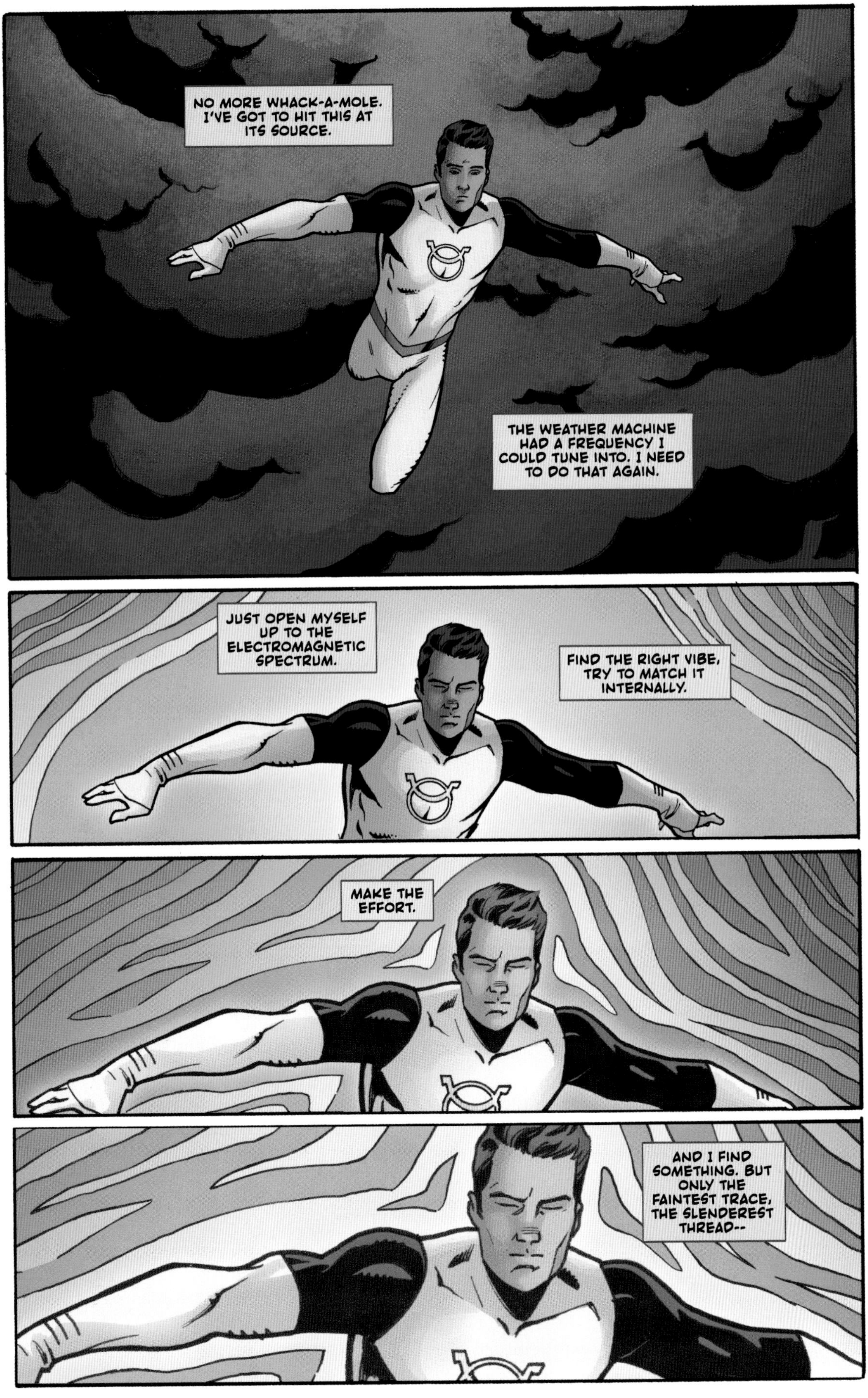
NO MORE WHACK-A-MOLE. I'VE GOT TO HIT THIS AT ITS SOURCE.
THE WEATHER MACHINE HAD A FREQUENCY I COULD TUNE INTO. I NEED TO DO THAT AGAIN.
JUST OPEN MYSELF UP TO THE ELECTROMAGNETIC SPECTRUM.
FIND THE RIGHT VIBE, TRY TO MATCH IT INTERNALLY.
MAKE THE EFFORT.
AND I FIND SOMETHING. BUT ONLY THE FAINTEST TRACE, THE SLENDEREST THREAD--

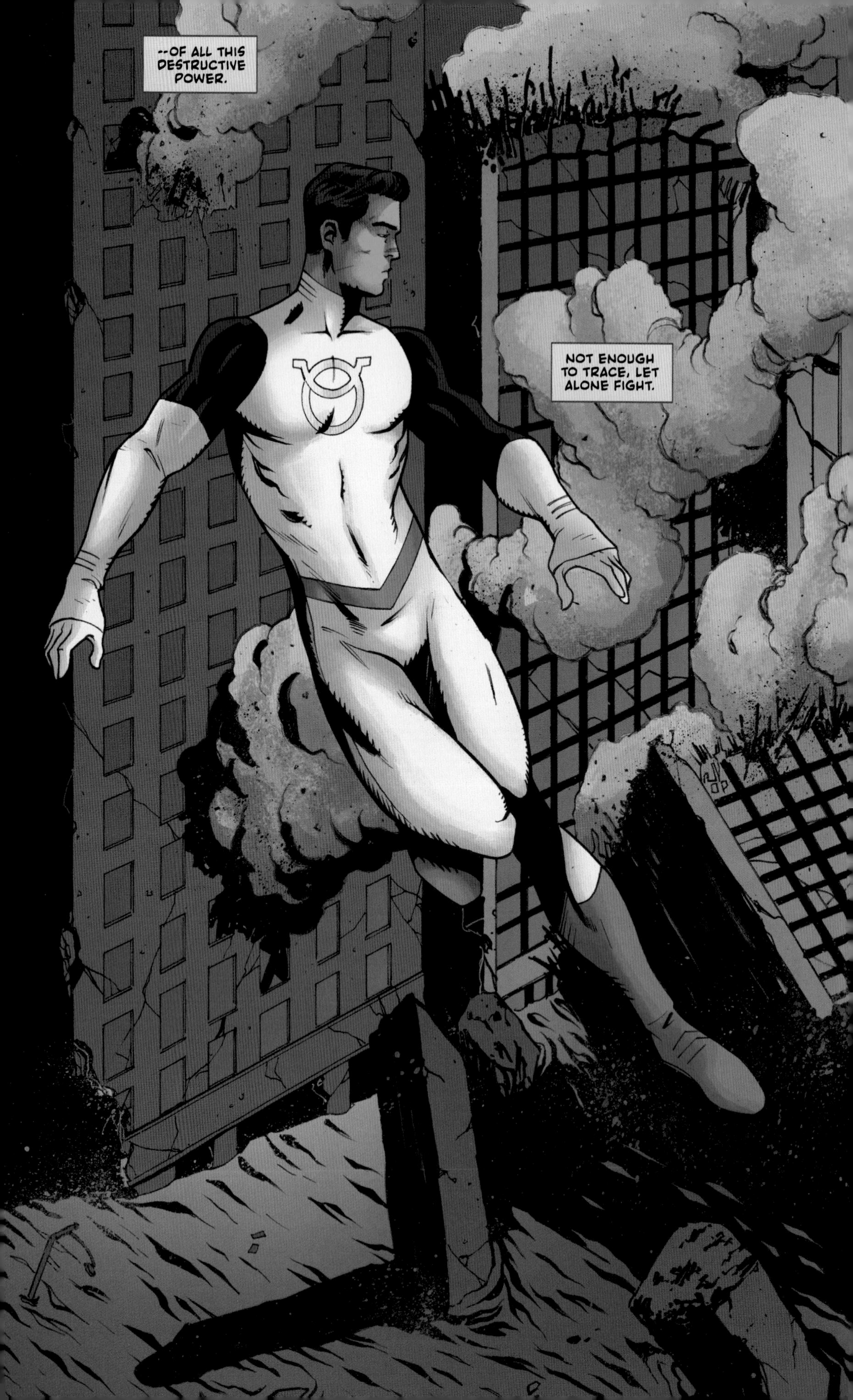
--OF ALL THIS DESTRUCTIVE POWER.
NOT ENOUGH TO TRACE, LET ALONE FIGHT.

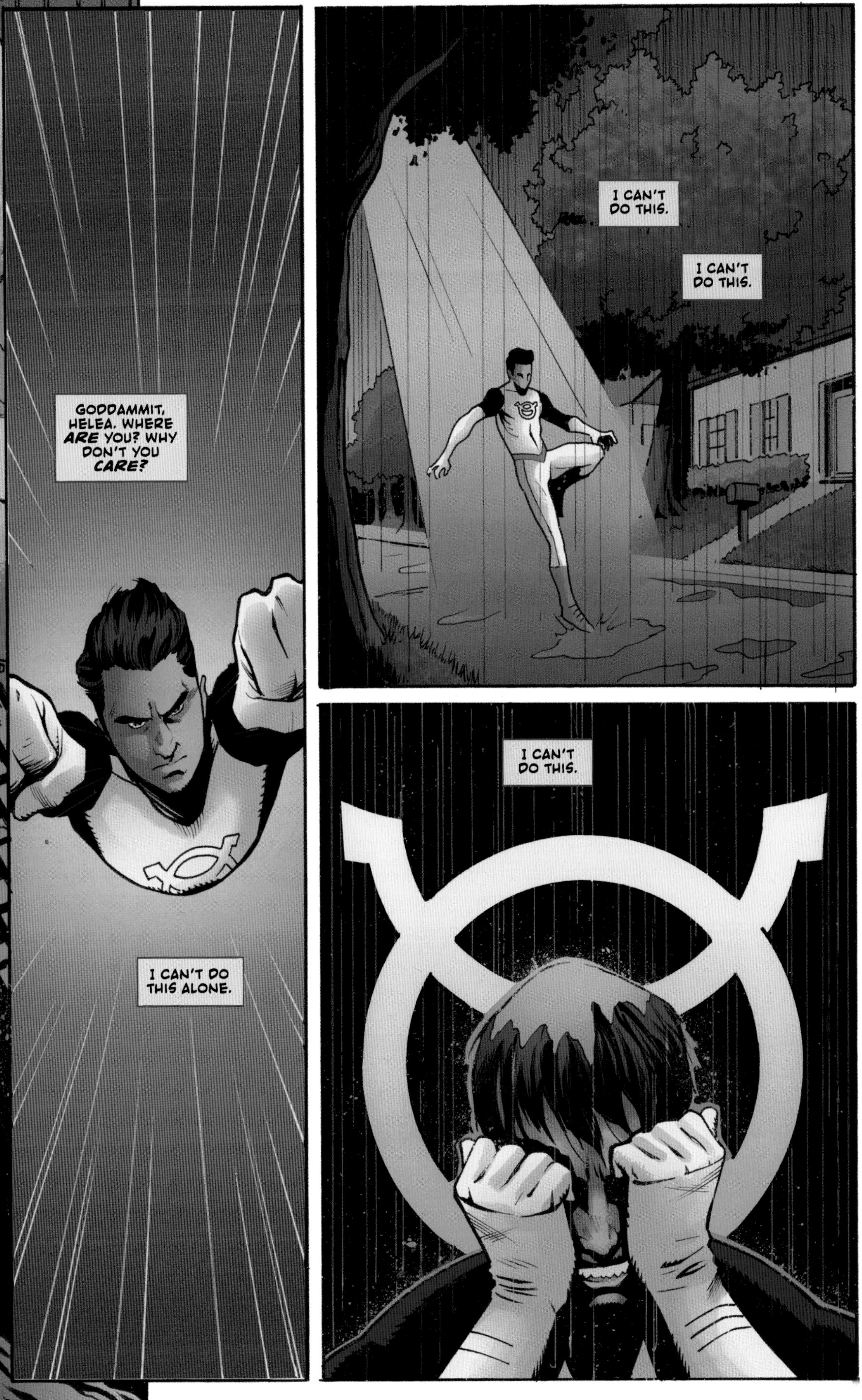
GODDAMMIT, HELEA. WHERE ARE YOU? WHY DON'T YOU CARE?
I CAN'T DO THIS ALONE.
I CAN'T DO THIS.
I CAN'T DO THIS.
I CAN'T DO THIS.

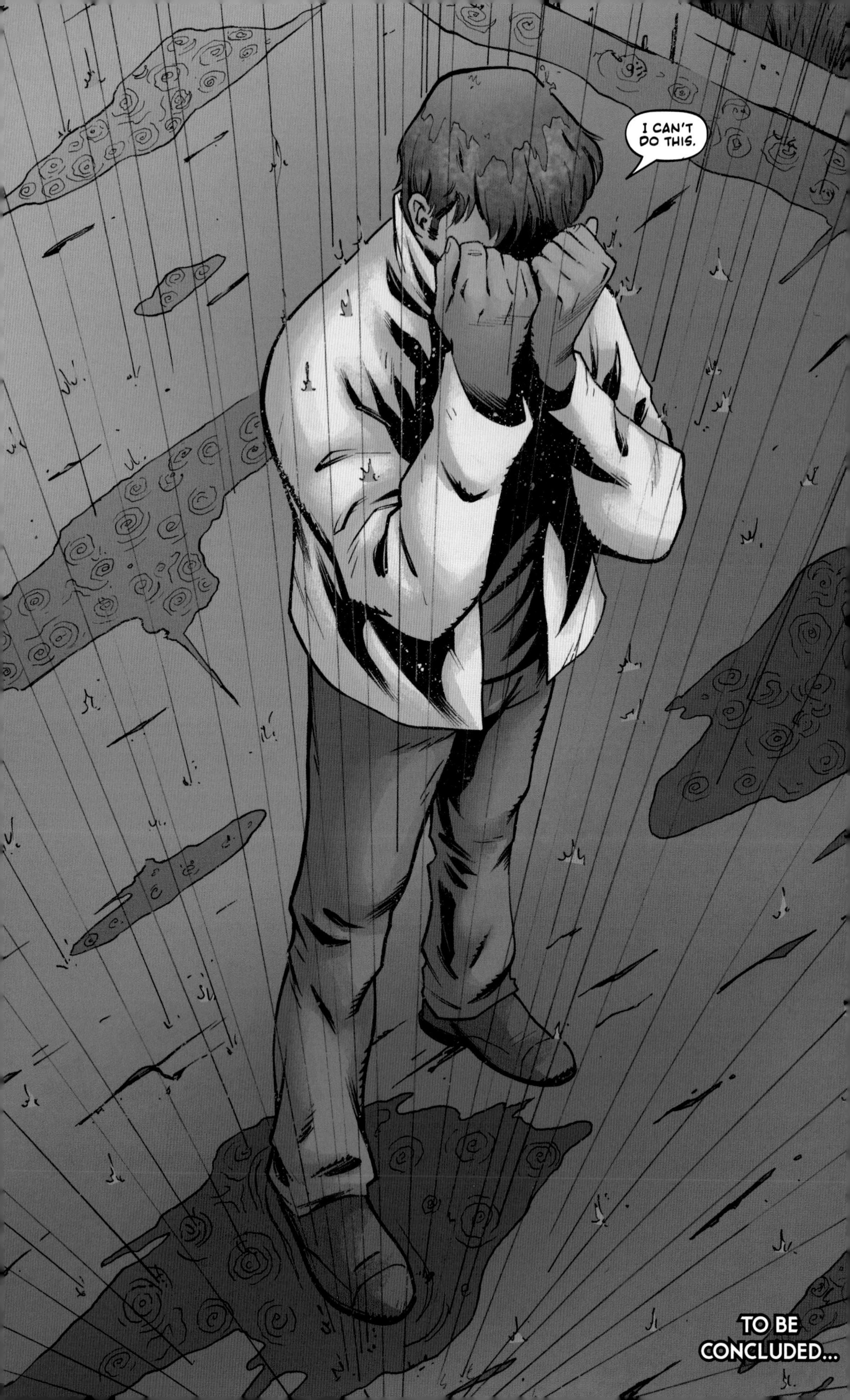
I CAN'T DO THIS.
TO BE CONCLUDED...

5

"THE GOOD NEWS"

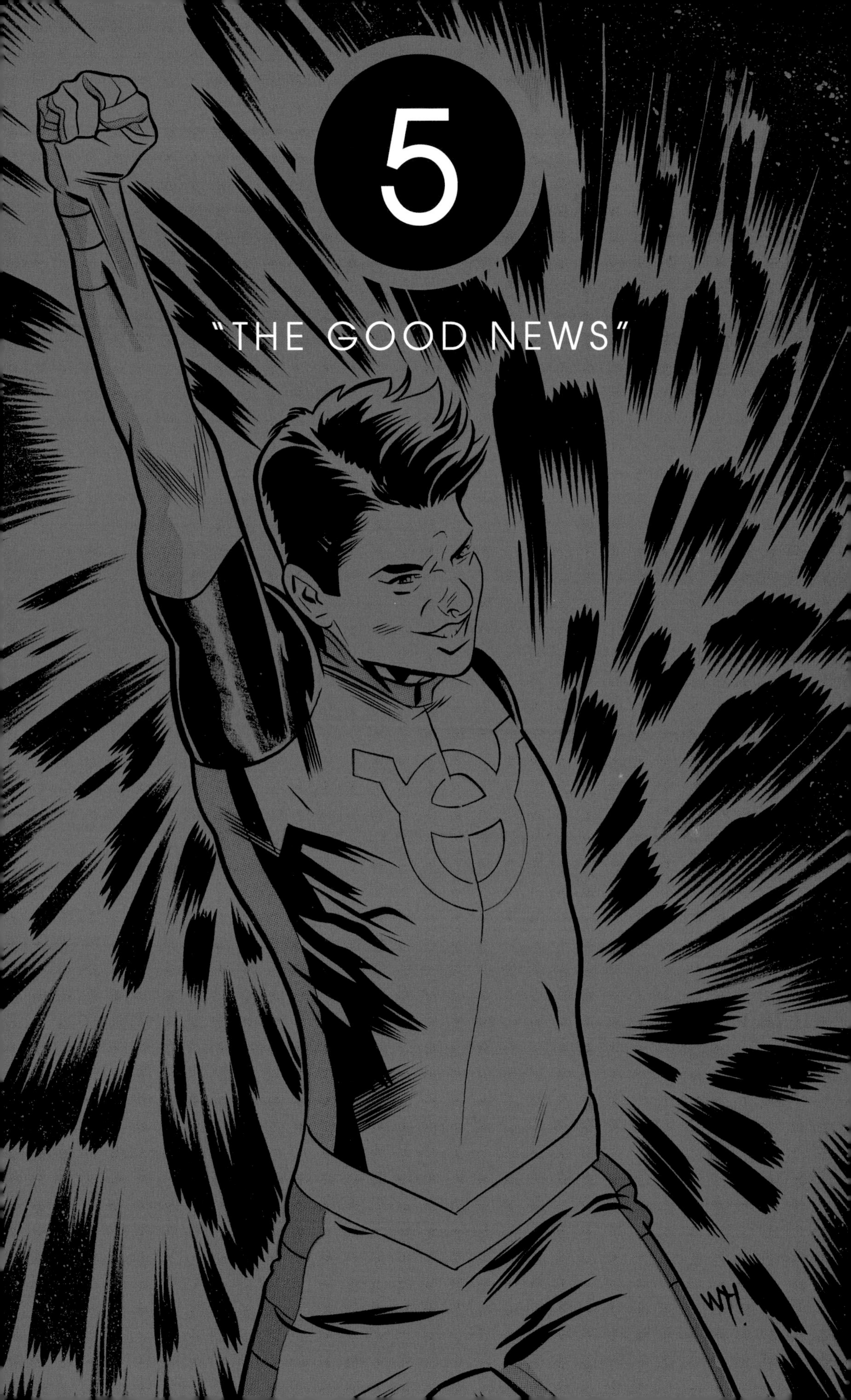

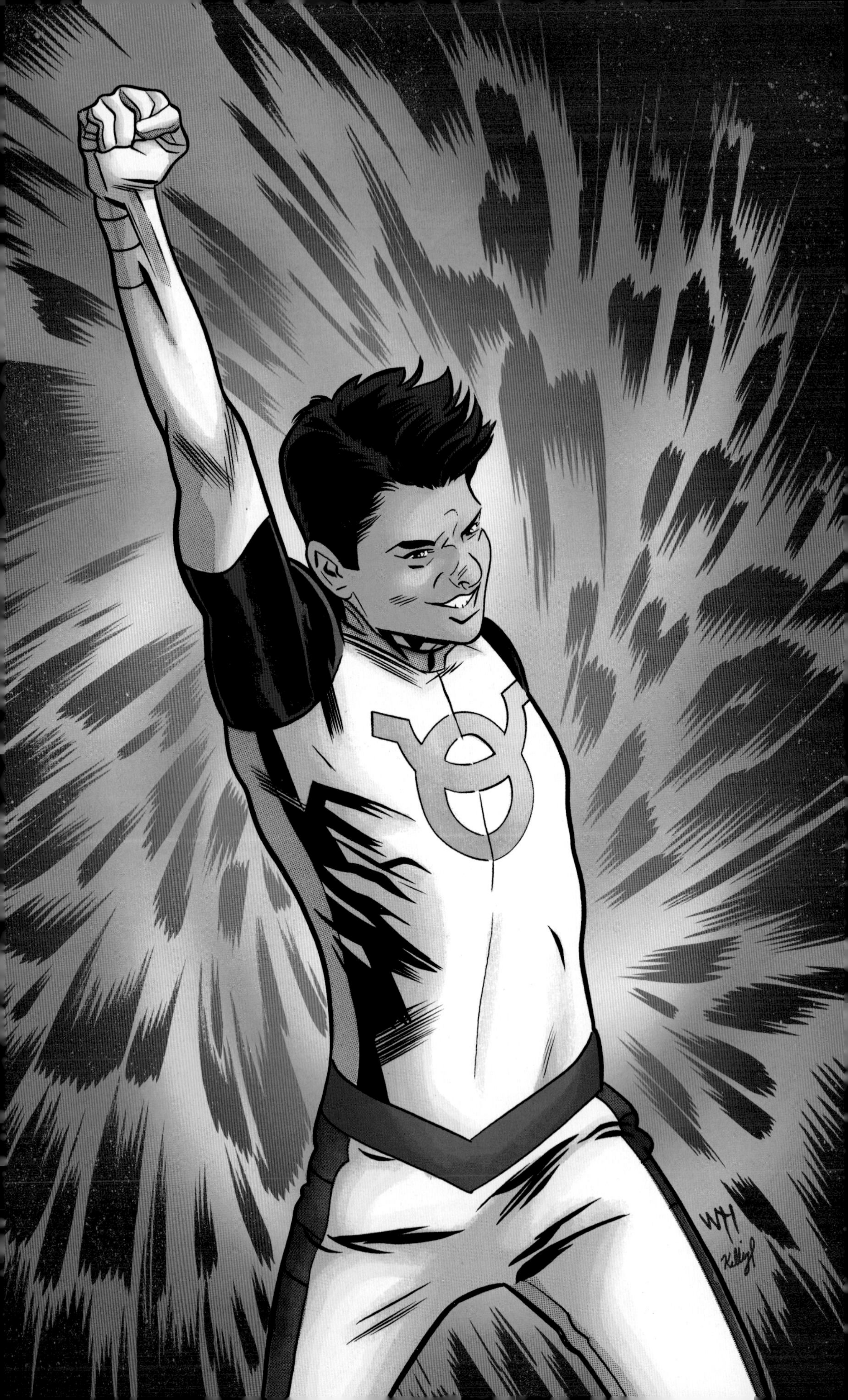

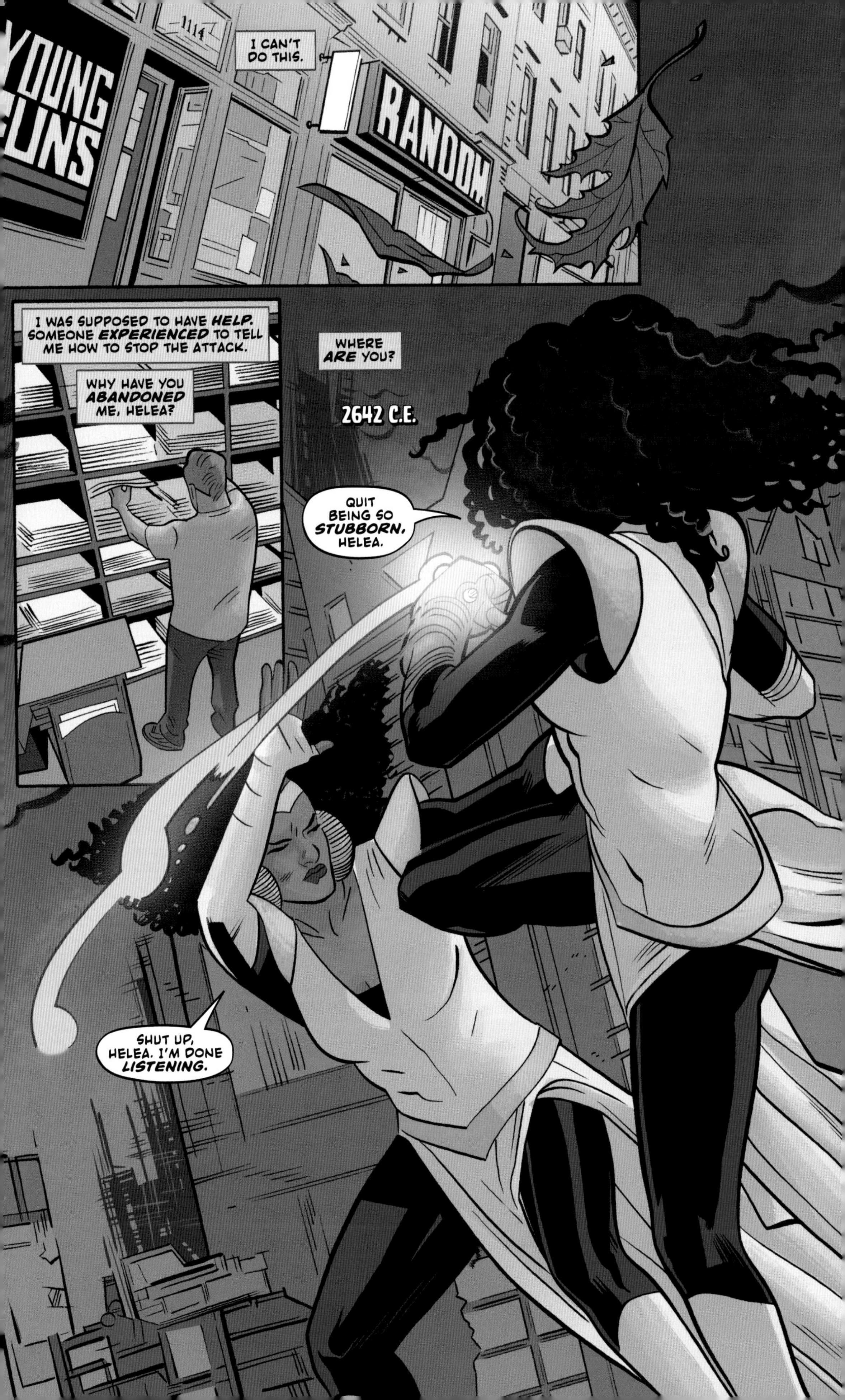

YOUNG GUNS
1114
RANDOM
I CAN'T DO THIS.
I WAS SUPPOSED TO HAVE HELP. SOMEONE EXPERIENCED TO TELL ME HOW TO STOP THE ATTACK.
WHY HAVE YOU ABANDONED ME, HELEA?
WHERE ARE YOU?
2642 C.E.
QUIT BEING SO STUBBORN, HELEA.
SHUT UP, HELEA. I'M DONE LISTENING.

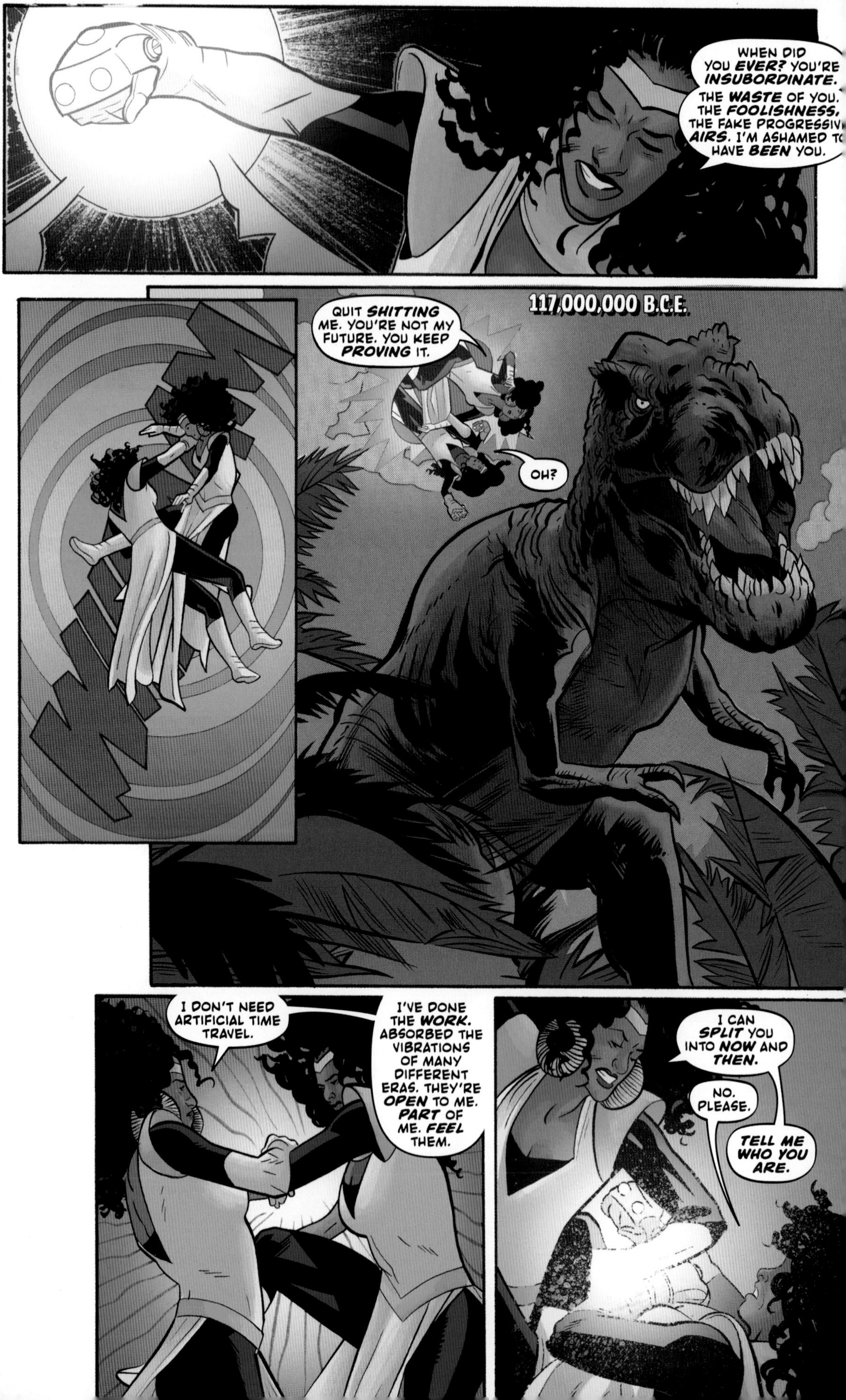
WHEN DID YOU EVER? YOU'RE INSUBORDINATE.
THE WASTE OF YOU. THE FOOLISHNESS. THE FAKE PROGRESSIVE AIRS. I'M ASHAMED TO HAVE BEEN YOU.
117,000,000 B.C.E.
QUIT SHITTING ME. YOU'RE NOT MY FUTURE. YOU KEEP PROVING IT.
OH?
I DON'T NEED ARTIFICIAL TIME TRAVEL.
I'VE DONE THE WORK. ABSORBED THE VIBRATIONS OF MANY DIFFERENT ERAS. THEY'RE OPEN TO ME. PART OF ME. FEEL THEM.
I CAN SPLIT YOU INTO NOW AND THEN.
NO. PLEASE.
TELL ME WHO YOU ARE.

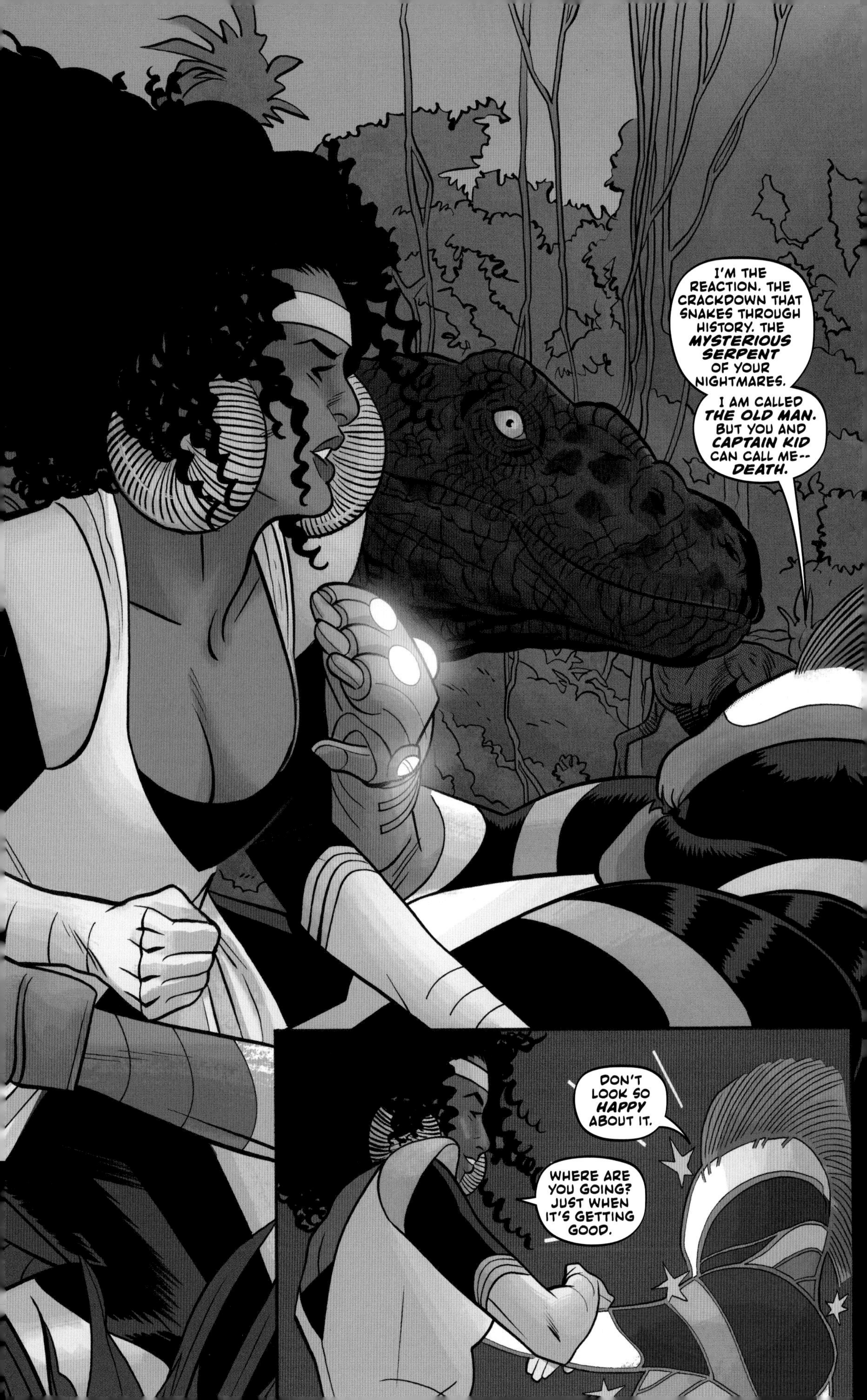
I'M THE REACTION. THE CRACKDOWN THAT SNAKES THROUGH HISTORY. THE MYSTERIOUS SERPENT OF YOUR NIGHTMARES.
I AM CALLED THE OLD MAN. BUT YOU AND CAPTAIN KID CAN CALL ME-- DEATH.
DON'T LOOK SO HAPPY ABOUT IT.
WHERE ARE YOU GOING? JUST WHEN IT'S GETTING GOOD.

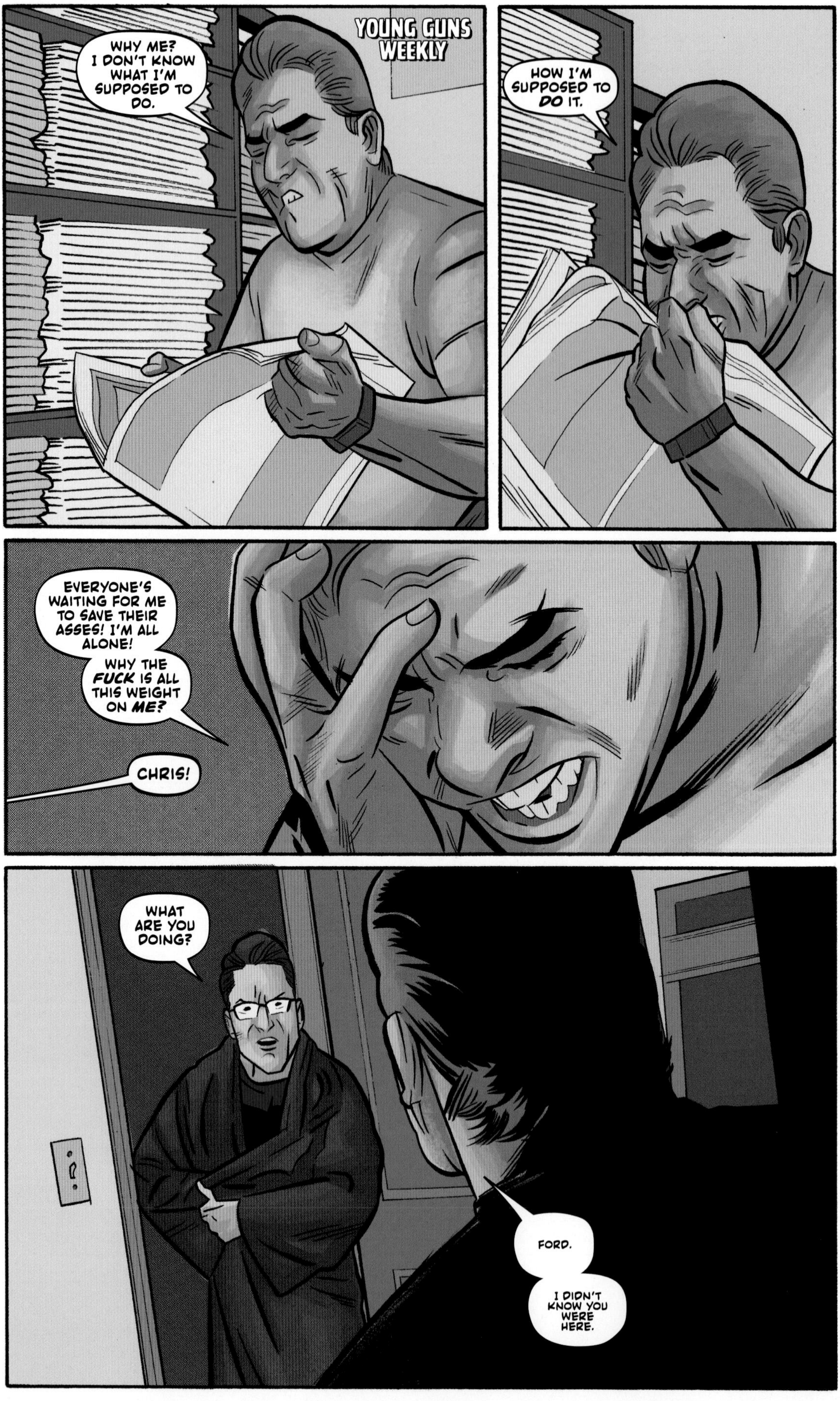
YOUNG GUNS WEEKLY
WHY ME? I DON'T KNOW WHAT I'M SUPPOSED TO DO.
HOW I'M SUPPOSED TO DO IT.
EVERYONE'S WAITING FOR ME TO SAVE THEIR ASSES! I'M ALL ALONE!
WHY THE FUCK IS ALL THIS WEIGHT ON ME?
CHRIS!
WHAT ARE YOU DOING?
FORD.
I DIDN'T KNOW YOU WERE HERE.

I COULDN'T DRIVE HOME IN THIS *TYPHOON* OR WHATEVER. HELP ME PICK THESE UP. YOU NEED TO TREAT THE ARCHIVES BETTER.

I'M TRYING TO FIND OUT ABOUT *PHYSICS*, WHICH IS A TOTAL *MYSTERY* TO ME, AND DO YOU REMEMBER THE NAME OF THAT PHYSICIST *BILL-BILL* INTERVIEWED?

BECAUSE I NEED TO *ASK* HER HOW TO SEE *WAVES*. OR AT LEAST KNOW THEY'RE THERE. I ABSORBED THEM YESTERDAY WITHOUT GETTING SICK, BUT NOW I CAN'T EVEN *TRACK* THEM--

FUCK ARE YOU *HIGH* ON? I NEVER *SAW* YOU LIKE THIS.

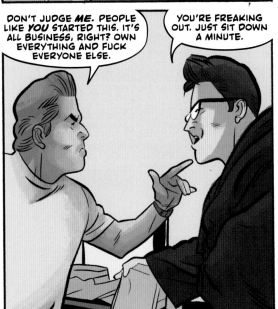

DON'T JUDGE *ME*. PEOPLE LIKE *YOU* STARTED THIS. IT'S ALL BUSINESS, RIGHT? OWN EVERYTHING AND FUCK EVERYONE ELSE.

YOU'RE FREAKING OUT. JUST SIT DOWN A MINUTE.

DON'T YOU TALK TO *ME* THAT WAY! I'M NOT--

YOU'RE FREAKING OUT BECAUSE THE WORLD'S ENDING. I GET IT.

SIT.

YOU'RE ALL WIRED. I'LL GET US A DRINK.

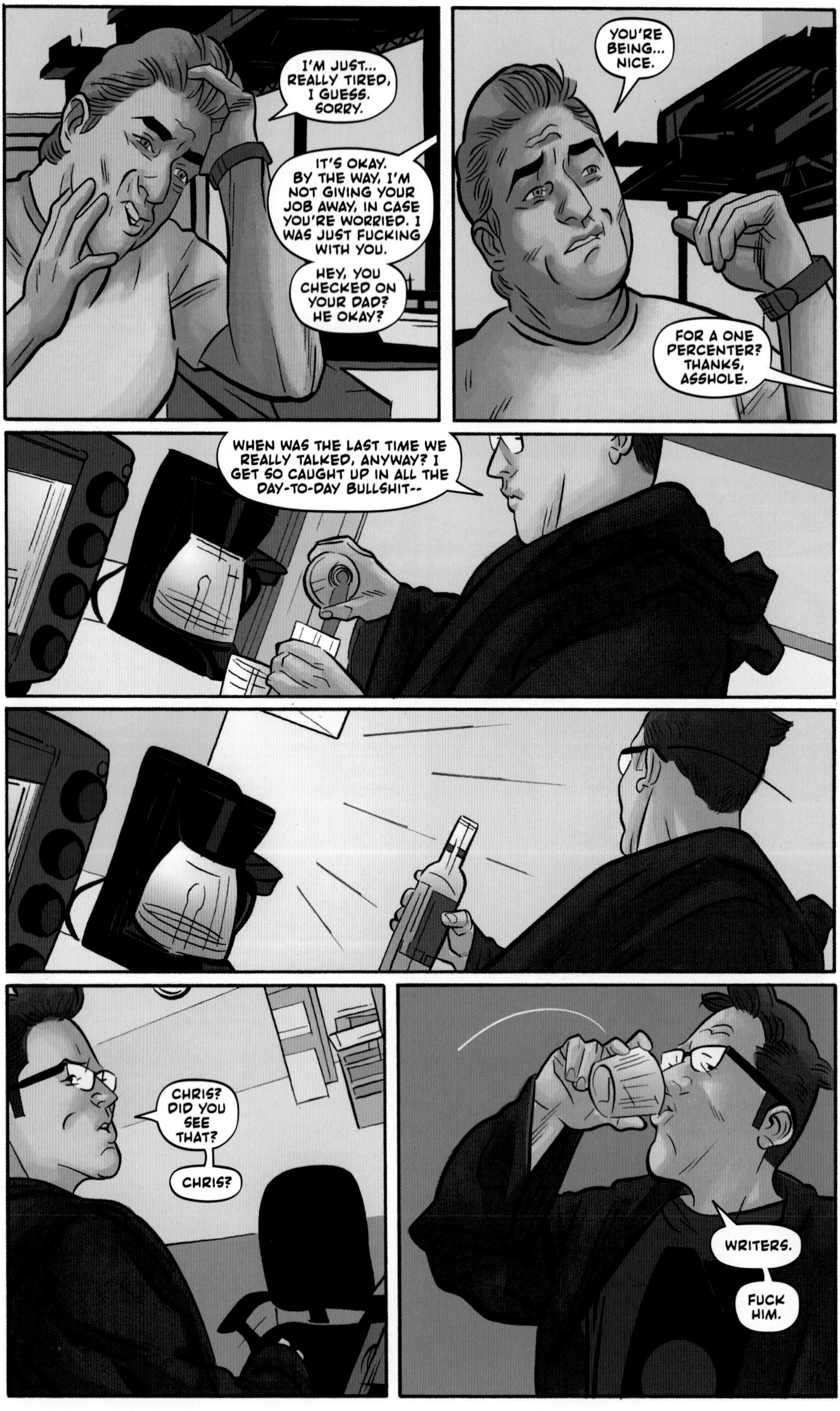
I'M JUST... REALLY TIRED, I GUESS. SORRY.
IT'S OKAY. BY THE WAY, I'M NOT GIVING YOUR JOB AWAY, IN CASE YOU'RE WORRIED. I WAS JUST FUCKING WITH YOU.
HEY, YOU CHECKED ON YOUR DAD? HE OKAY?
YOU'RE BEING... NICE.
FOR A ONE PERCENTER? THANKS, ASSHOLE.
WHEN WAS THE LAST TIME WE REALLY TALKED, ANYWAY? I GET SO CAUGHT UP IN ALL THE DAY-TO-DAY BULLSHIT--
CHRIS? DID YOU SEE THAT?
CHRIS?
WRITERS.
FUCK HIM.

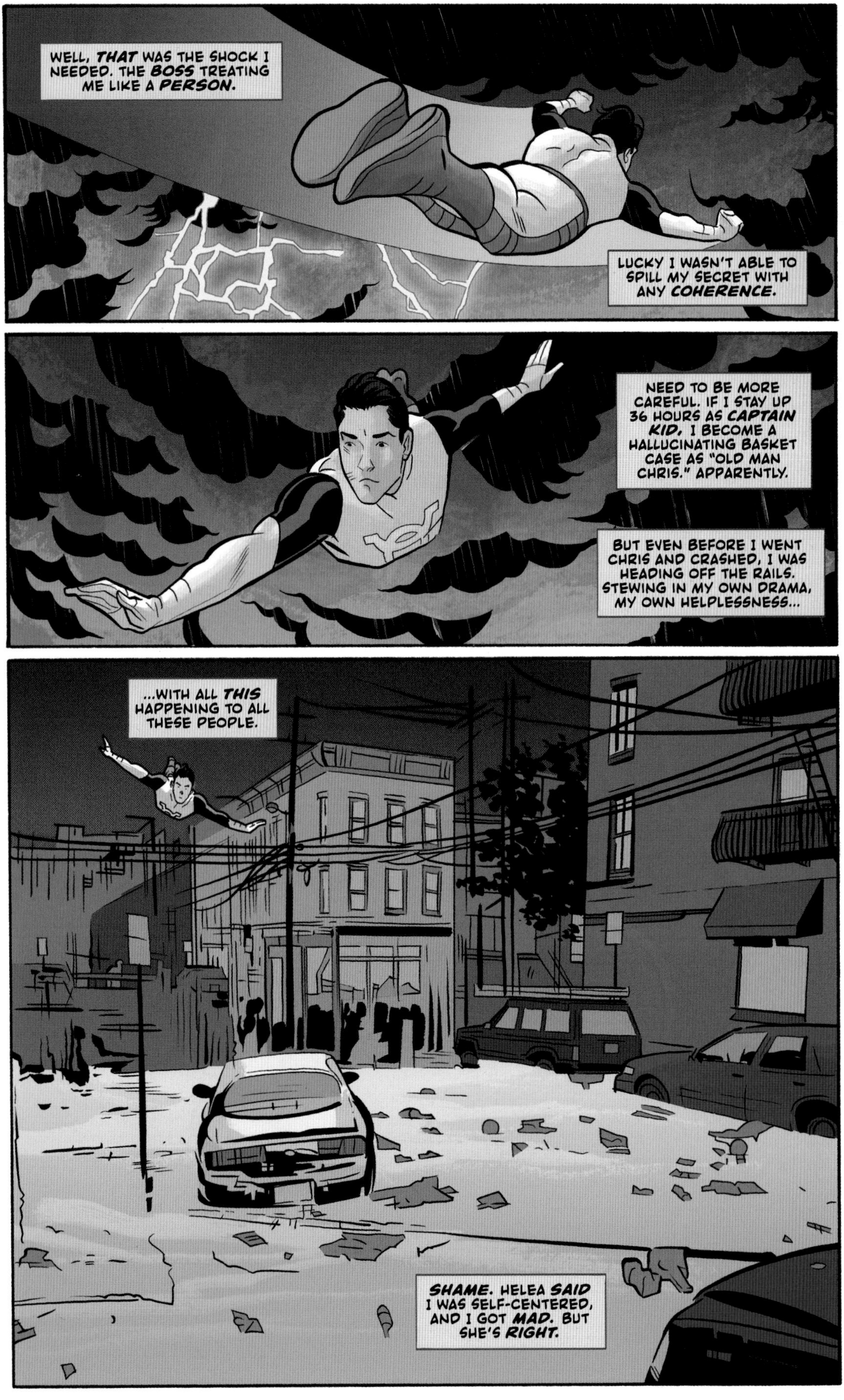
WELL, THAT WAS THE SHOCK I NEEDED. THE BOSS TREATING ME LIKE A PERSON.
LUCKY I WASN'T ABLE TO SPILL MY SECRET WITH ANY COHERENCE.
NEED TO BE MORE CAREFUL. IF I STAY UP 36 HOURS AS CAPTAIN KID, I BECOME A HALLUCINATING BASKET CASE AS "OLD MAN CHRIS." APPARENTLY.
BUT EVEN BEFORE I WENT CHRIS AND CRASHED, I WAS HEADING OFF THE RAILS. STEWING IN MY OWN DRAMA, MY OWN HELPLESSNESS...
...WITH ALL THIS HAPPENING TO ALL THESE PEOPLE.
SHAME. HELEA SAID I WAS SELF-CENTERED, AND I GOT MAD. BUT SHE'S RIGHT.

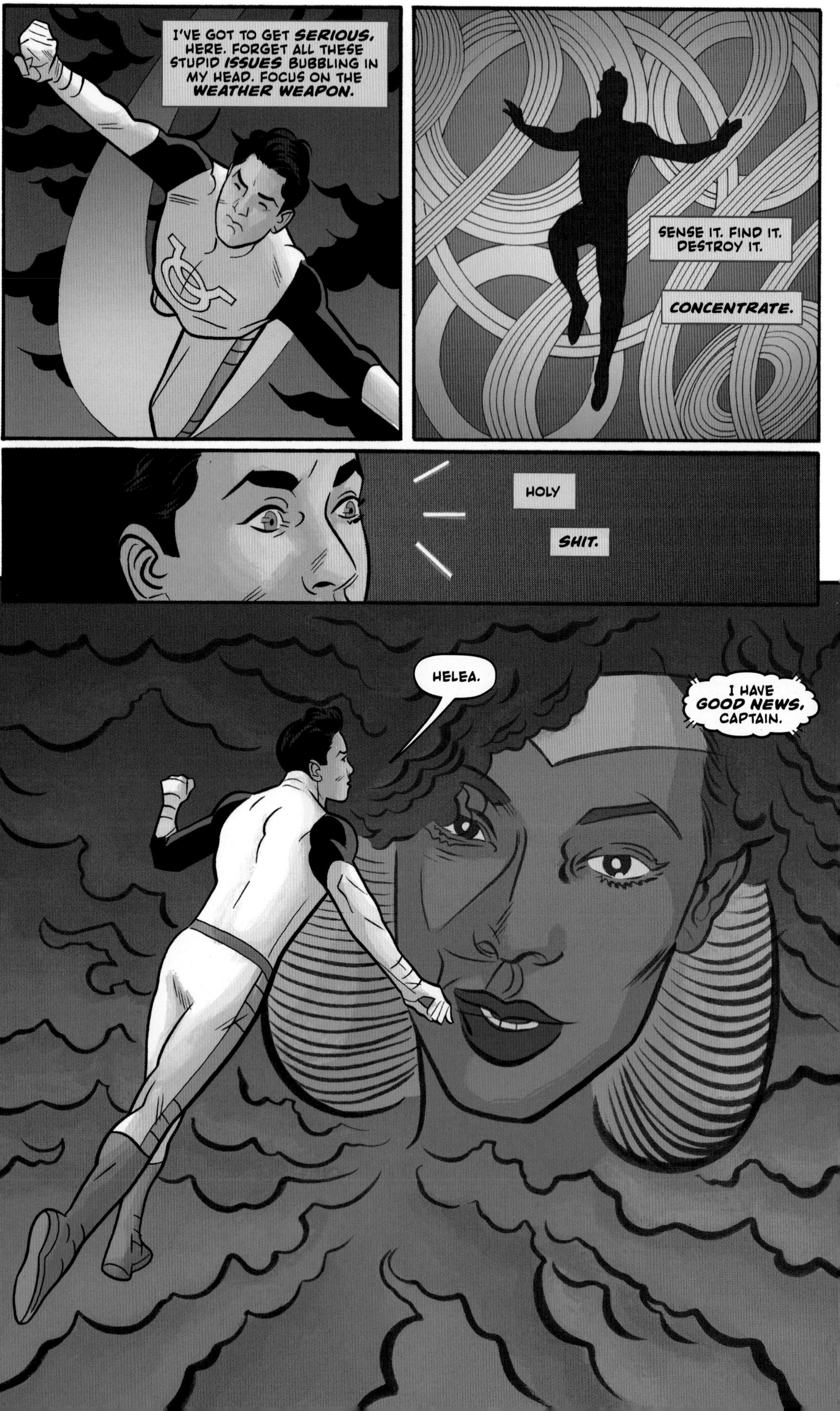
I'VE GOT TO GET SERIOUS, HERE. FORGET ALL THESE STUPID ISSUES BUBBLING IN MY HEAD. FOCUS ON THE WEATHER WEAPON.
SENSE IT. FIND IT. DESTROY IT.
CONCENTRATE.
HOLY
SHIT.
HELEA.
I HAVE GOOD NEWS, CAPTAIN.

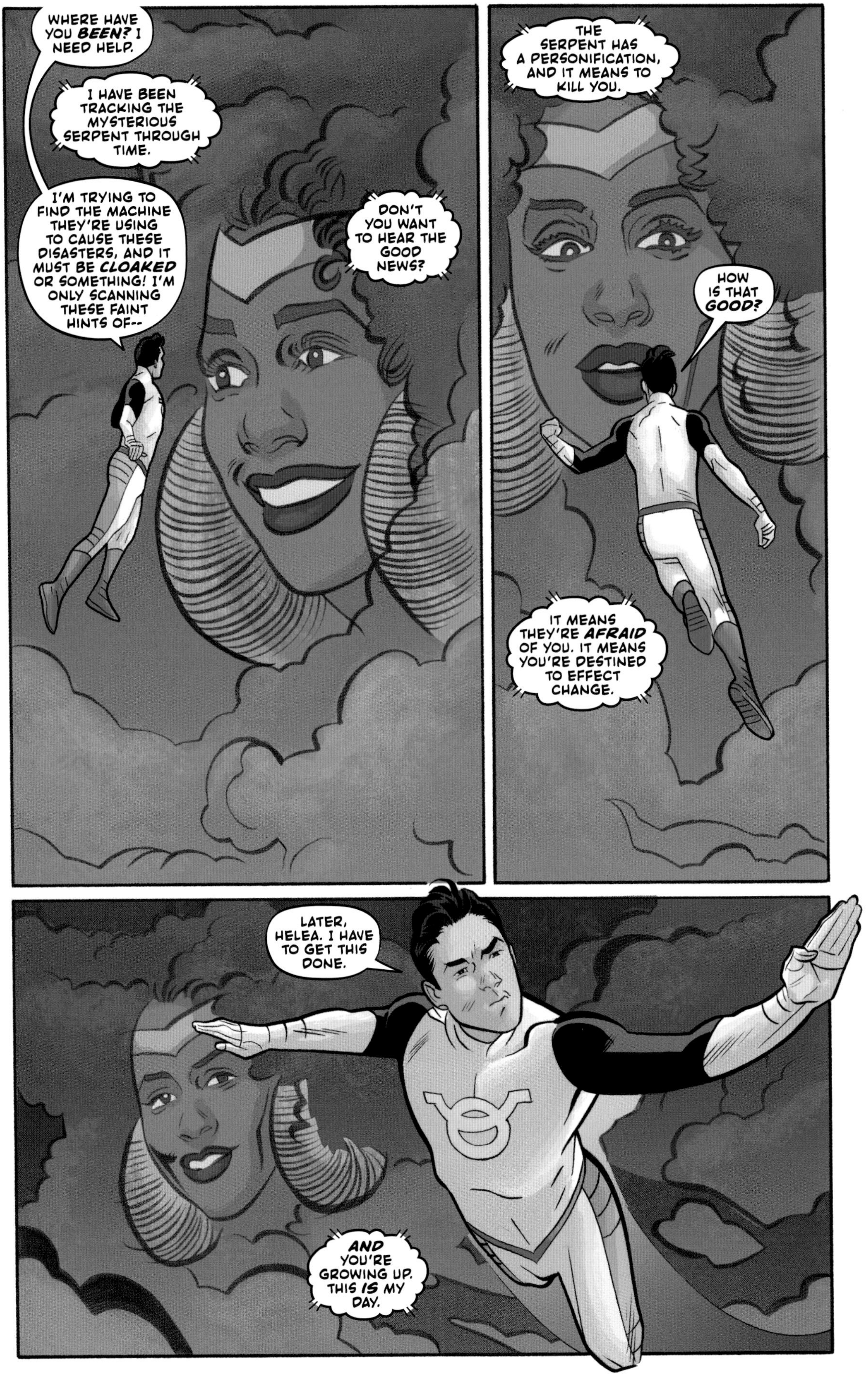
WHERE HAVE YOU BEEN? I NEED HELP.
I HAVE BEEN TRACKING THE MYSTERIOUS SERPENT THROUGH TIME.
I'M TRYING TO FIND THE MACHINE THEY'RE USING TO CAUSE THESE DISASTERS, AND IT MUST BE CLOAKED OR SOMETHING! I'M ONLY SCANNING THESE FAINT HINTS OF--
DON'T YOU WANT TO HEAR THE GOOD NEWS?
THE SERPENT HAS A PERSONIFICATION, AND IT MEANS TO KILL YOU.
HOW IS THAT GOOD?
IT MEANS THEY'RE AFRAID OF YOU. IT MEANS YOU'RE DESTINED TO EFFECT CHANGE.
LATER, HELEA. I HAVE TO GET THIS DONE.
AND YOU'RE GROWING UP. THIS IS MY DAY.

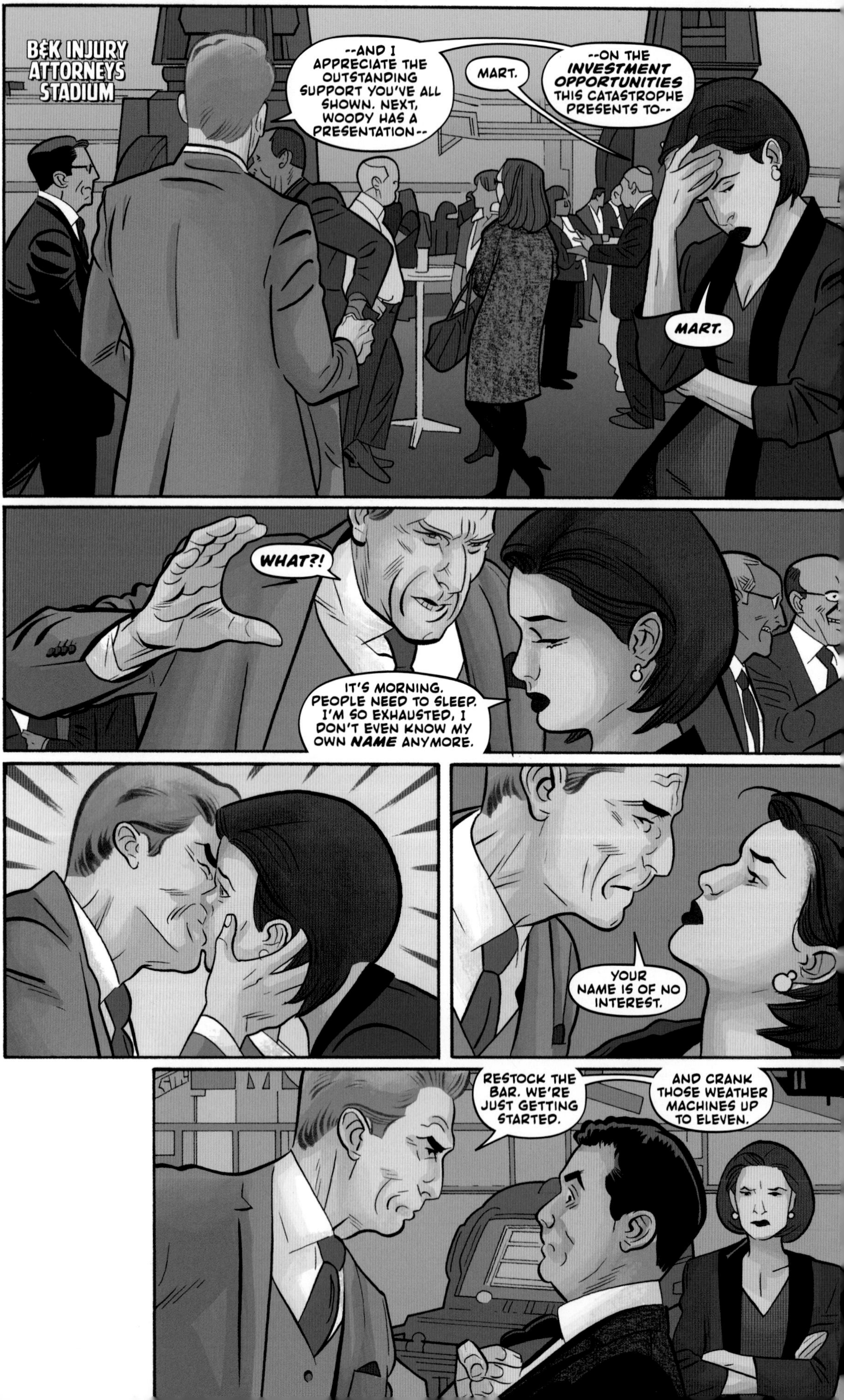
B&K INJURY ATTORNEYS STADIUM
--AND I APPRECIATE THE OUTSTANDING SUPPORT YOU'VE ALL SHOWN. NEXT, WOODY HAS A PRESENTATION--
MART.
--ON THE INVESTMENT OPPORTUNITIES THIS CATASTROPHE PRESENTS TO--
MART.
WHAT?!
IT'S MORNING. PEOPLE NEED TO SLEEP. I'M SO EXHAUSTED, I DON'T EVEN KNOW MY OWN NAME ANYMORE.
YOUR NAME IS OF NO INTEREST.
RESTOCK THE BAR. WE'RE JUST GETTING STARTED.
AND CRANK THOSE WEATHER MACHINES UP TO ELEVEN.

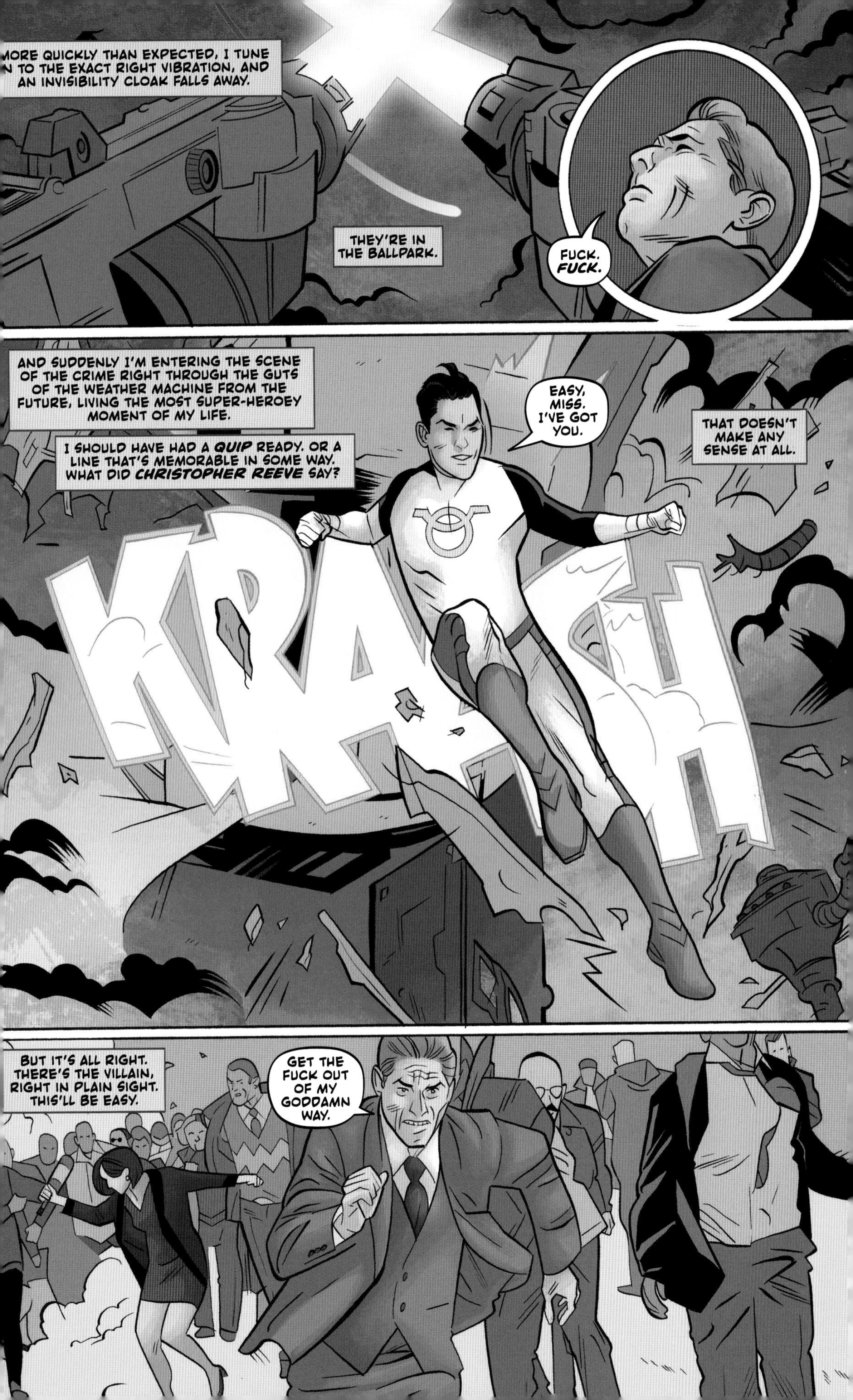

MORE QUICKLY THAN EXPECTED, I TUNE IN TO THE EXACT RIGHT VIBRATION, AND AN INVISIBILITY CLOAK FALLS AWAY.
THEY'RE IN THE BALLPARK.
FUCK. FUCK.
AND SUDDENLY I'M ENTERING THE SCENE OF THE CRIME RIGHT THROUGH THE GUTS OF THE WEATHER MACHINE FROM THE FUTURE, LIVING THE MOST SUPER-HEROEY MOMENT OF MY LIFE.
I SHOULD HAVE HAD A QUIP READY. OR A LINE THAT'S MEMORABLE IN SOME WAY. WHAT DID CHRISTOPHER REEVE SAY?
EASY, MISS. I'VE GOT YOU.
THAT DOESN'T MAKE ANY SENSE AT ALL.
KRASH
BUT IT'S ALL RIGHT. THERE'S THE VILLAIN, RIGHT IN PLAIN SIGHT. THIS'LL BE EASY.
GET THE FUCK OUT OF MY GODDAMN WAY.

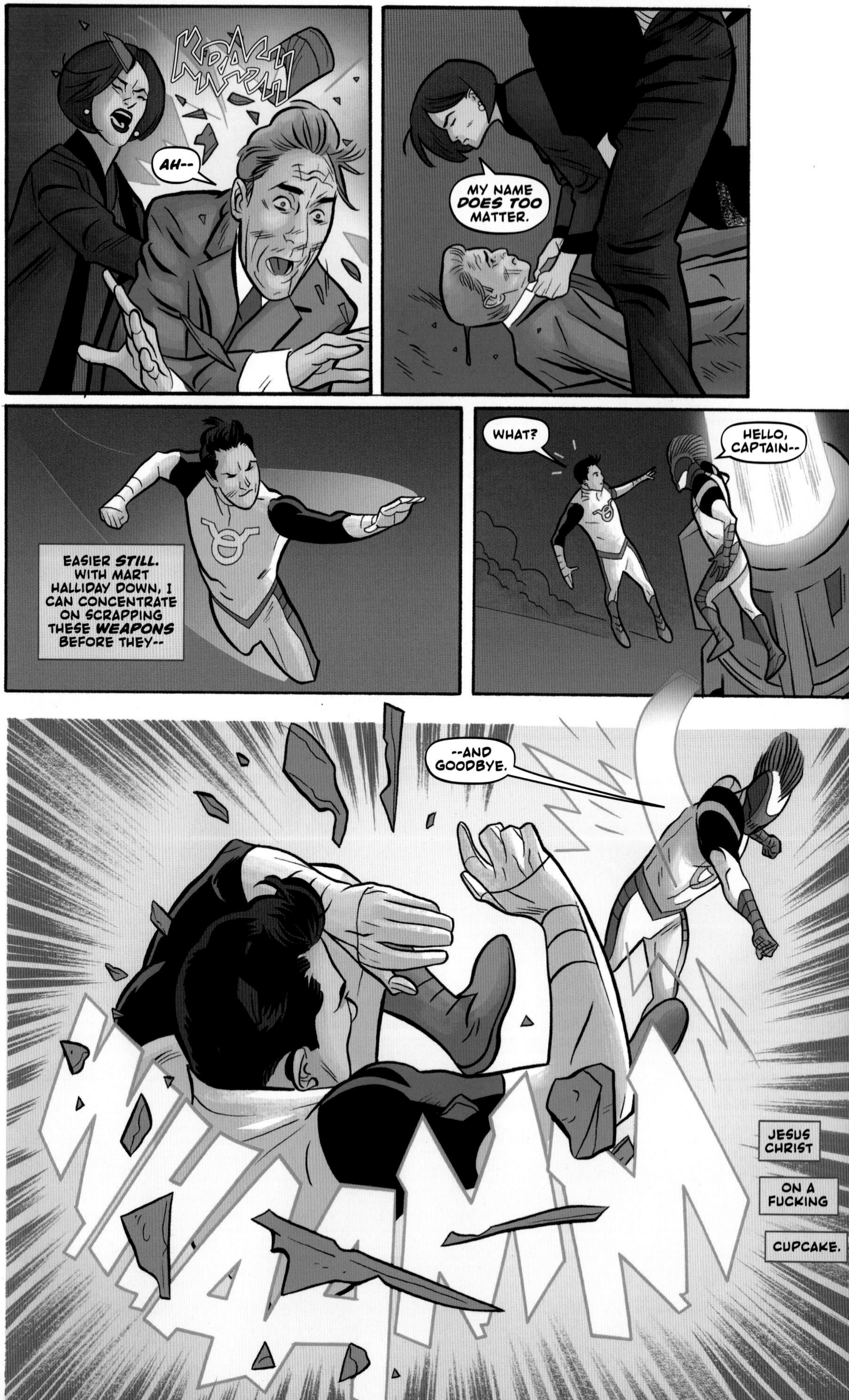
KRAAAM
AH--
MY NAME DOES TOO MATTER.
EASIER STILL. WITH MART HALLIDAY DOWN, I CAN CONCENTRATE ON SCRAPPING THESE WEAPONS BEFORE THEY--
WHAT?
HELLO, CAPTAIN--
--AND GOODBYE.
JESUS CHRIST
ON A FUCKING
CUPCAKE.

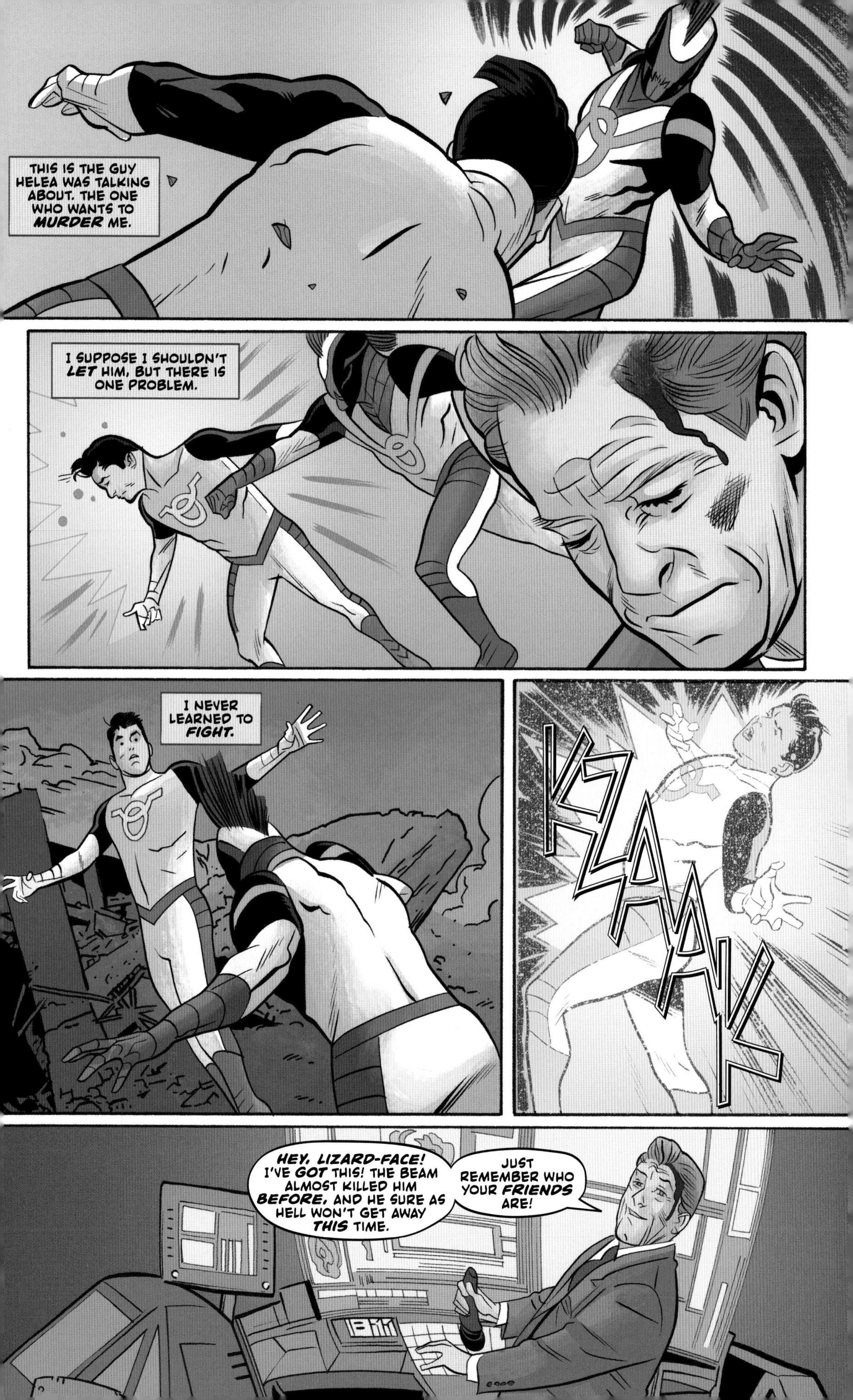
THIS IS THE GUY HELEA WAS TALKING ABOUT. THE ONE WHO WANTS TO MURDER ME.
I SUPPOSE I SHOULDN'T LET HIM, BUT THERE IS ONE PROBLEM.
I NEVER LEARNED TO FIGHT.
KSZAAAANK
HEY, LIZARD-FACE! I'VE GOT THIS! THE BEAM ALMOST KILLED HIM BEFORE, AND HE SURE AS HELL WON'T GET AWAY THIS TIME.
JUST REMEMBER WHO YOUR FRIENDS ARE!

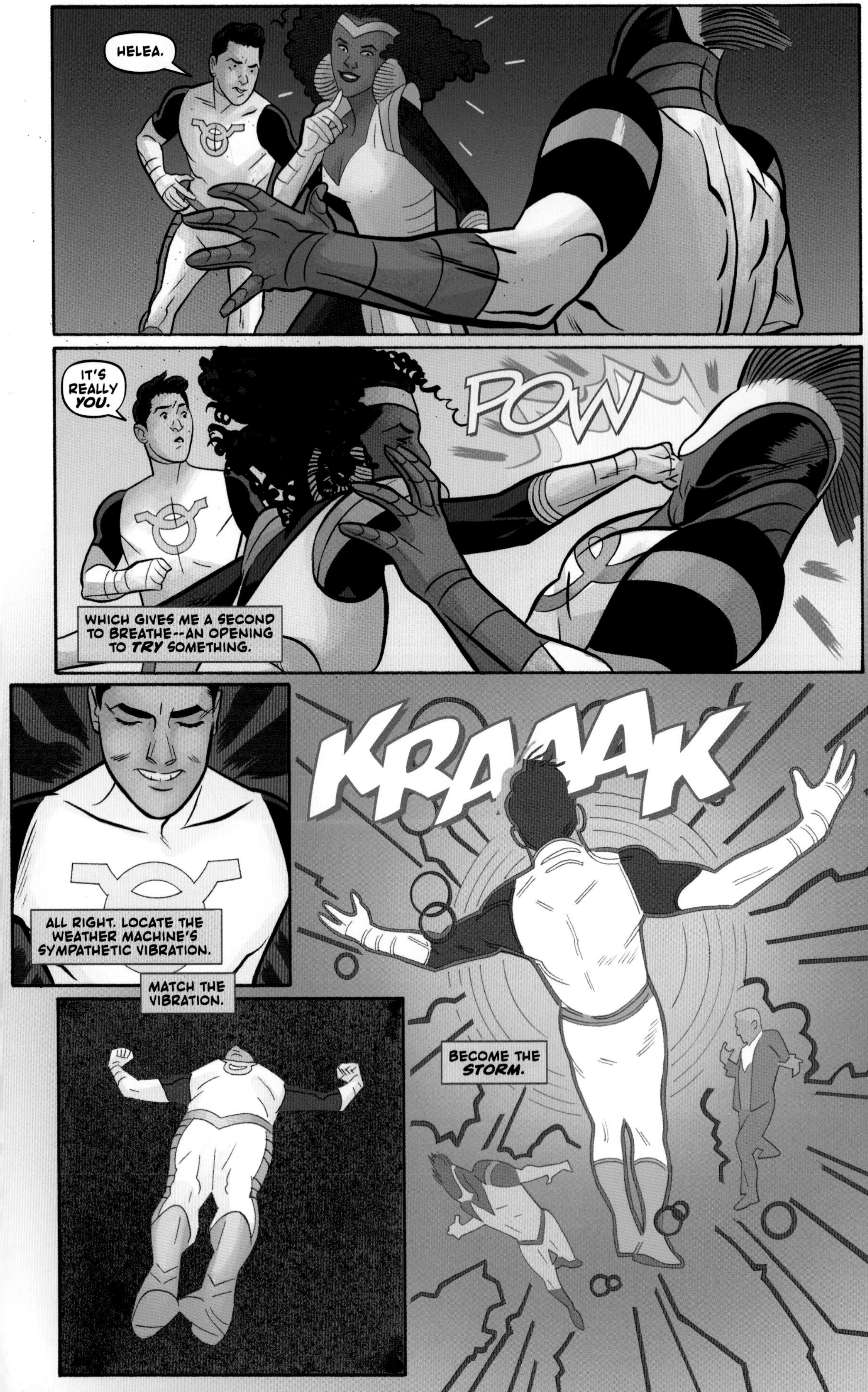

HELEA.
IT'S REALLY *YOU.*
POW
WHICH GIVES ME A SECOND TO BREATHE--AN OPENING TO *TRY* SOMETHING.
ALL RIGHT. LOCATE THE WEATHER MACHINE'S SYMPATHETIC VIBRATION.
MATCH THE VIBRATION.
KRAAAK
BECOME THE *STORM.*

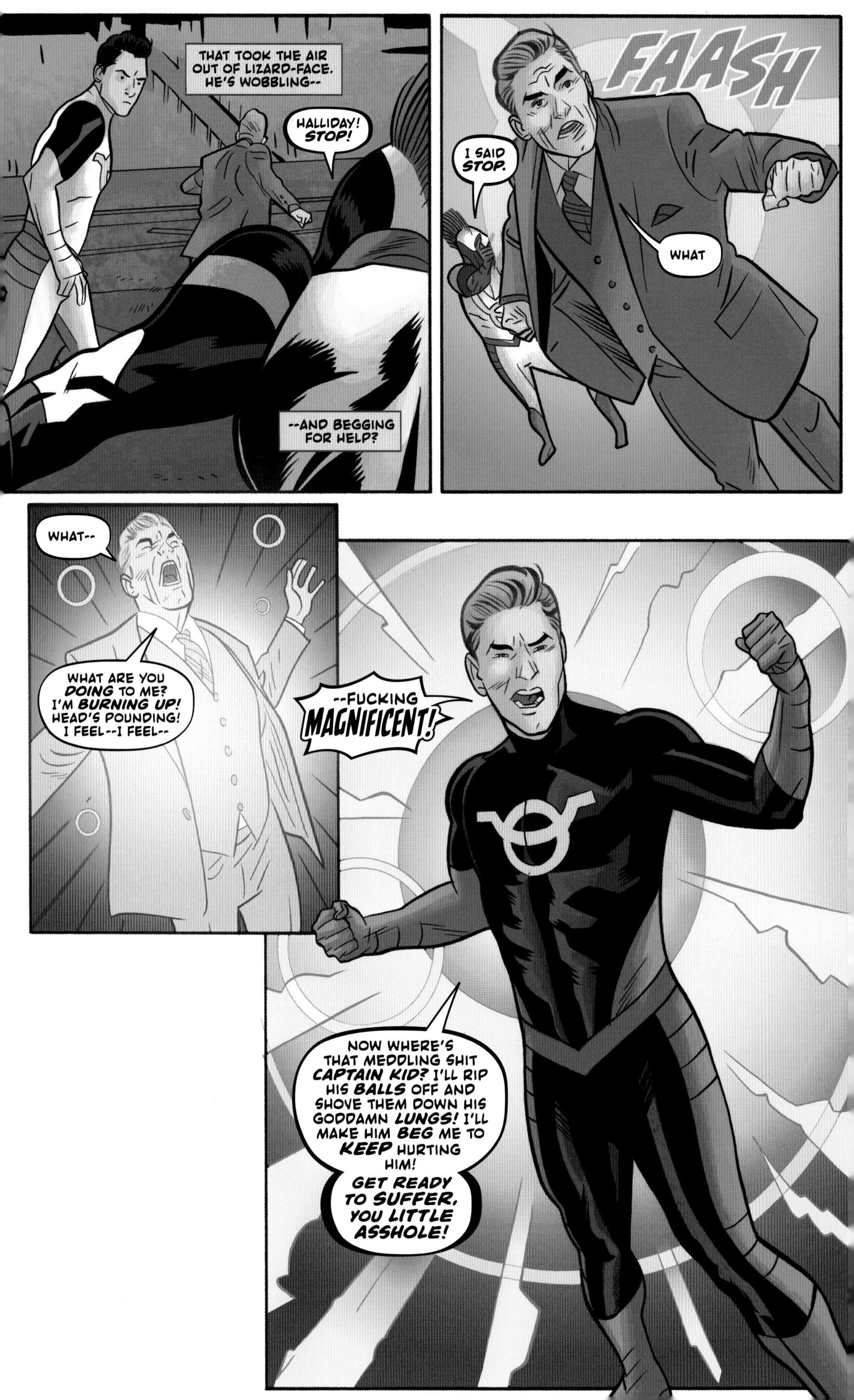
THAT TOOK THE AIR OUT OF LIZARD-FACE. HE'S WOBBLING--
HALLIDAY! STOP!
--AND BEGGING FOR HELP?
FAASH
I SAID STOP.
WHAT
WHAT--
WHAT ARE YOU DOING TO ME? I'M BURNING UP! HEAD'S POUNDING! I FEEL--I FEEL--
--FUCKING MAGNIFICENT!
NOW WHERE'S THAT MEDDLING SHIT CAPTAIN KID? I'LL RIP HIS BALLS OFF AND SHOVE THEM DOWN HIS GODDAMN LUNGS! I'LL MAKE HIM BEG ME TO KEEP HURTING HIM!
GET READY TO SUFFER, YOU LITTLE ASSHOLE!

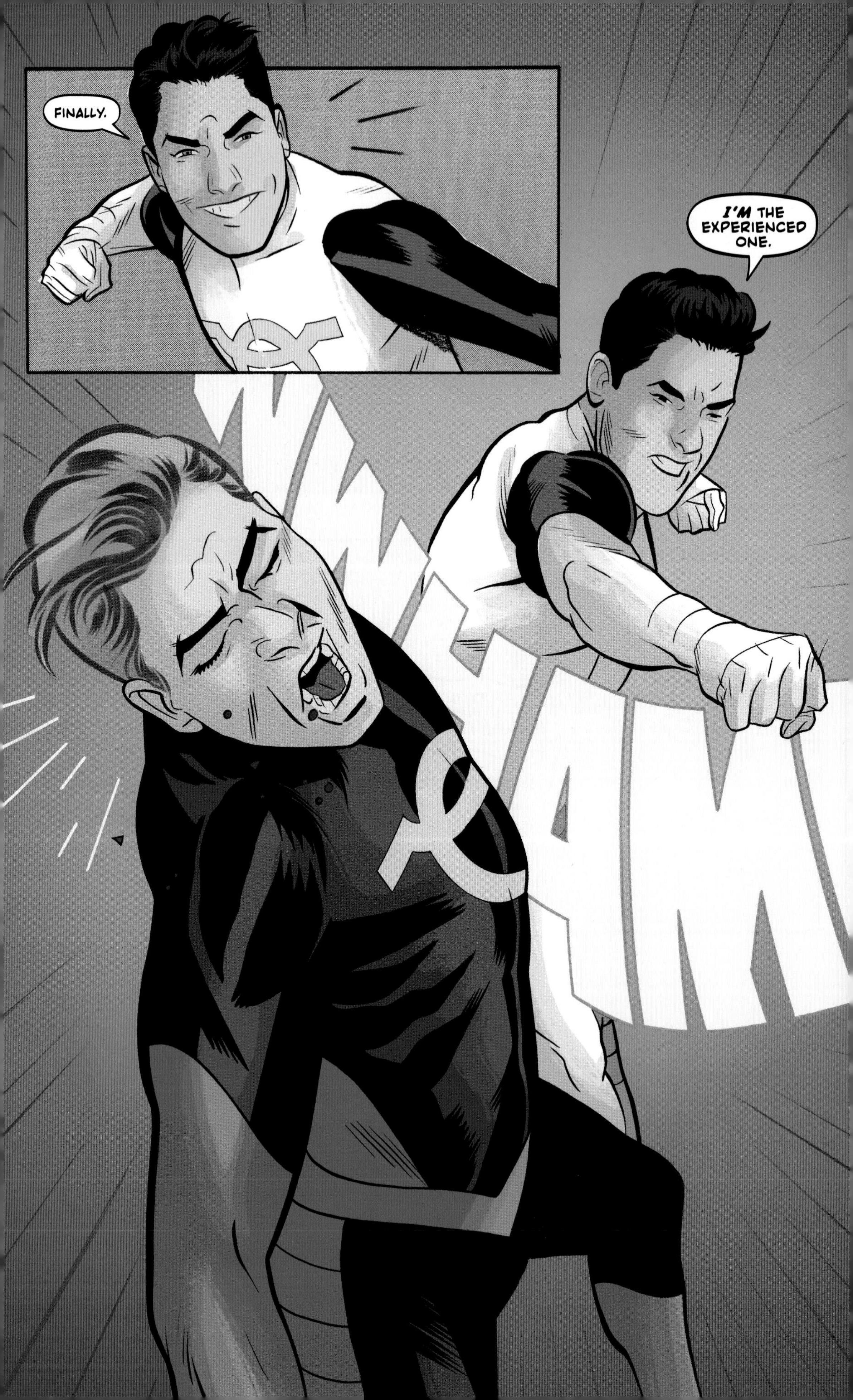
FINALLY.
I'M THE EXPERIENCED ONE.
WHAM

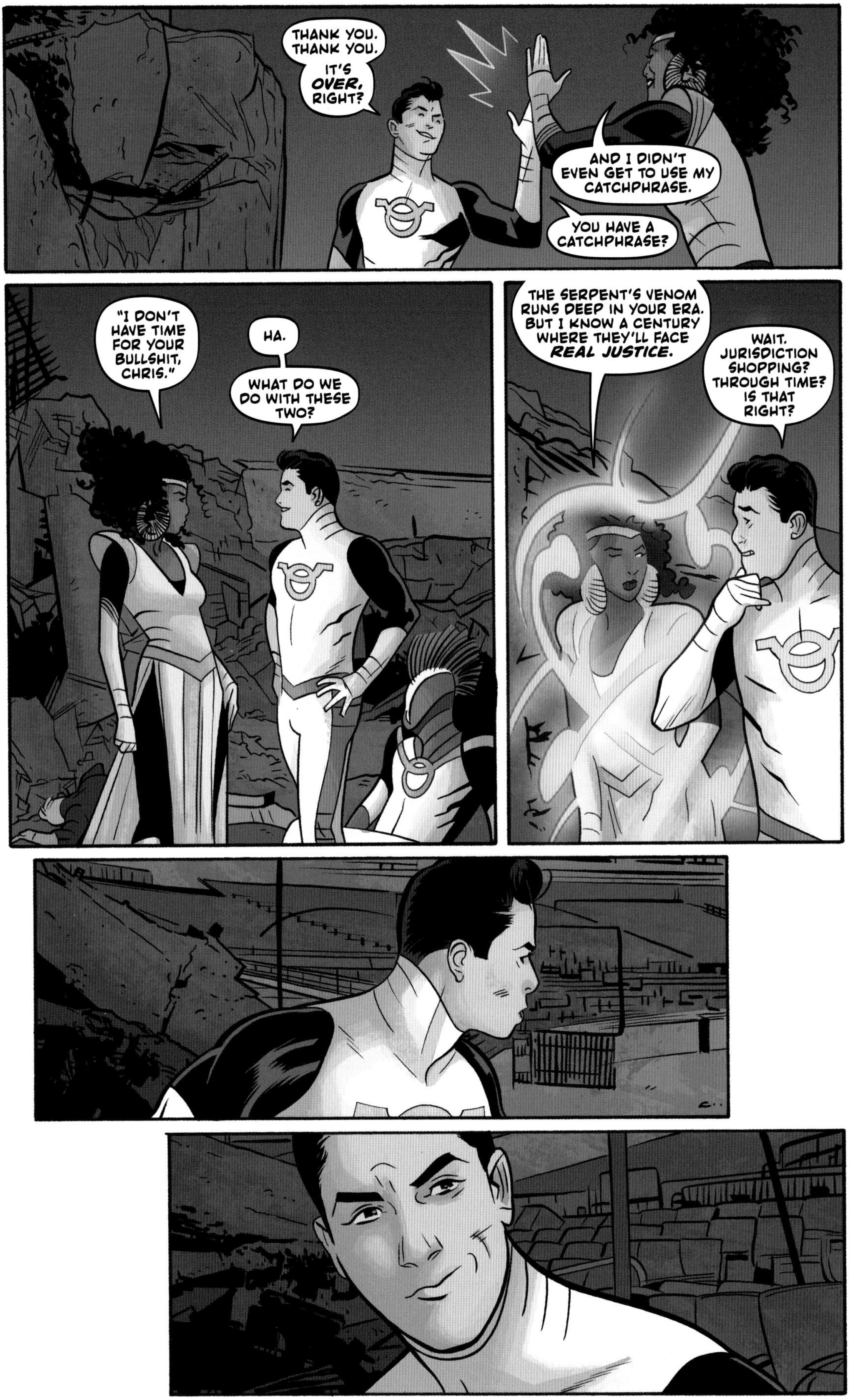
THANK YOU. THANK YOU.
IT'S *OVER*, RIGHT?
AND I DIDN'T EVEN GET TO USE MY CATCHPHRASE.
YOU HAVE A CATCHPHRASE?
"I DON'T HAVE TIME FOR YOUR BULLSHIT, CHRIS."
HA.
WHAT DO WE DO WITH THESE TWO?
THE SERPENT'S VENOM RUNS DEEP IN YOUR ERA. BUT I KNOW A CENTURY WHERE THEY'LL FACE *REAL JUSTICE*.
WAIT. JURISDICTION SHOPPING? THROUGH TIME? IS THAT RIGHT?

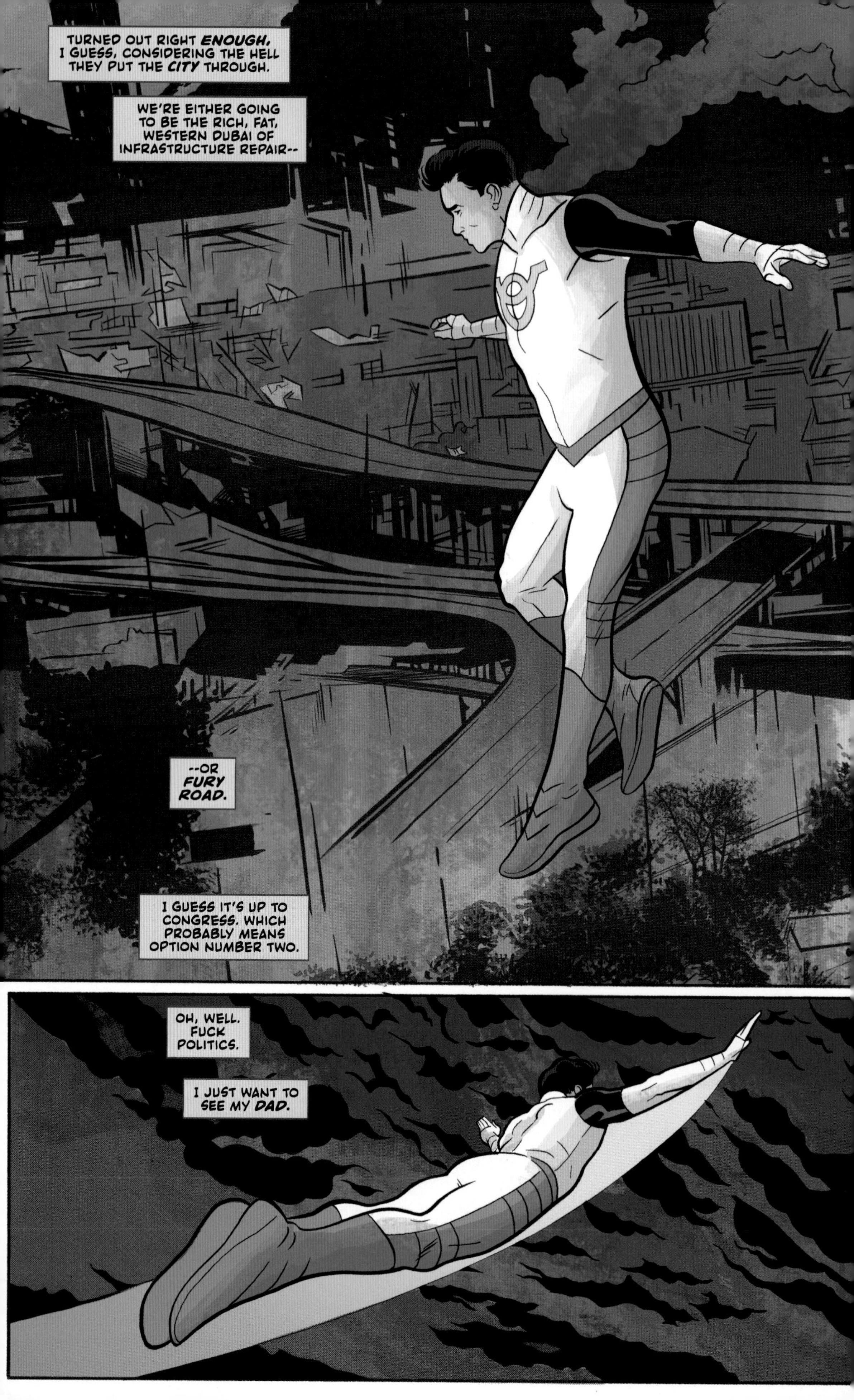
TURNED OUT RIGHT ENOUGH, I GUESS, CONSIDERING THE HELL THEY PUT THE CITY THROUGH.
WE'RE EITHER GOING TO BE THE RICH, FAT, WESTERN DUBAI OF INFRASTRUCTURE REPAIR--
--OR FURY ROAD.
I GUESS IT'S UP TO CONGRESS. WHICH PROBABLY MEANS OPTION NUMBER TWO.
OH, WELL. FUCK POLITICS.
I JUST WANT TO SEE MY DAD.

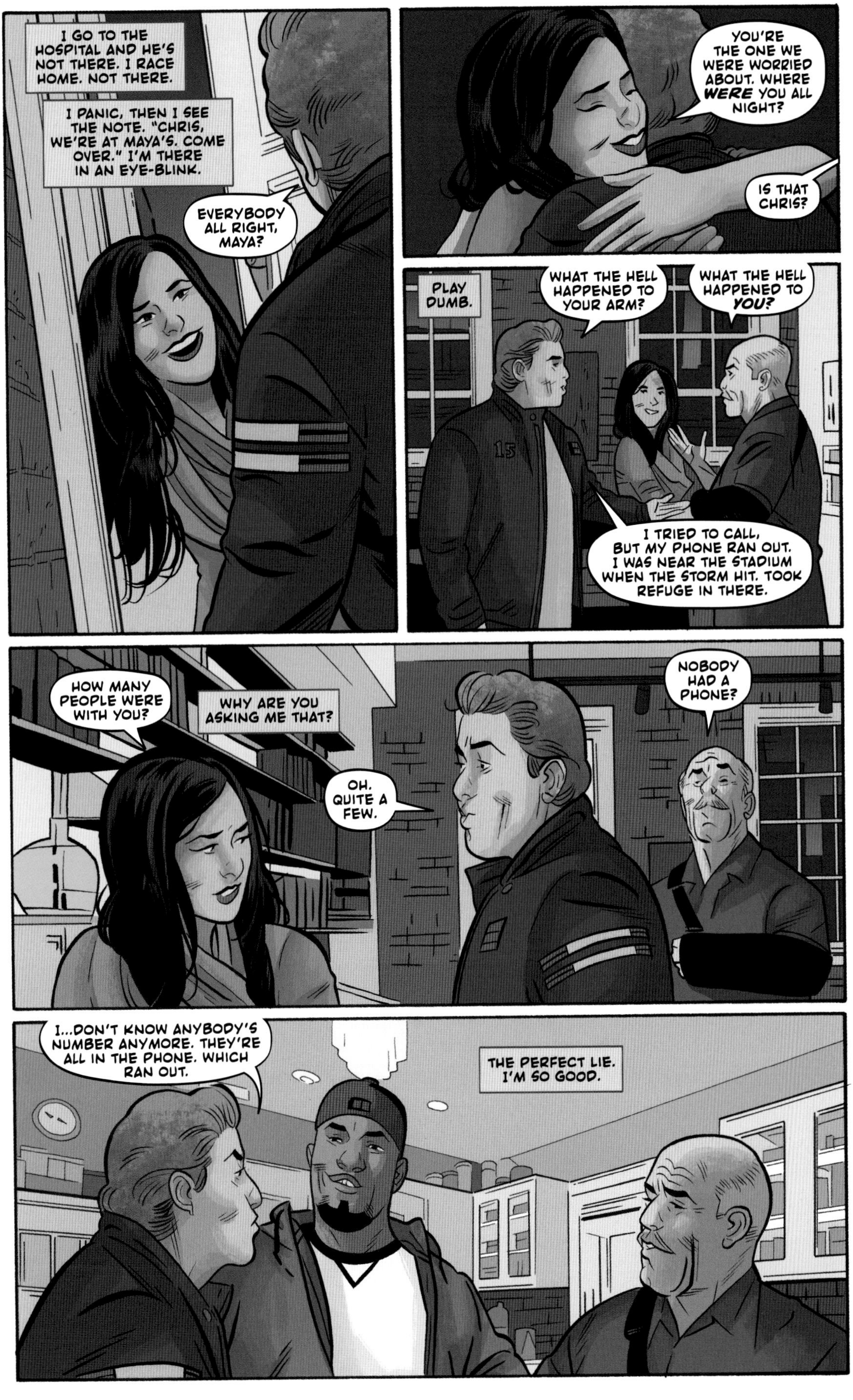

I GO TO THE HOSPITAL AND HE'S NOT THERE. I RACE HOME. NOT THERE.
I PANIC, THEN I SEE THE NOTE. "CHRIS, WE'RE AT MAYA'S. COME OVER." I'M THERE IN AN EYE-BLINK.
EVERYBODY ALL RIGHT, MAYA?
YOU'RE THE ONE WE WERE WORRIED ABOUT. WHERE *WERE* YOU ALL NIGHT?
IS THAT CHRIS?
PLAY DUMB.
WHAT THE HELL HAPPENED TO YOUR ARM?
WHAT THE HELL HAPPENED TO *YOU?*
I TRIED TO CALL, BUT MY PHONE RAN OUT. I WAS NEAR THE STADIUM WHEN THE STORM HIT. TOOK REFUGE IN THERE.
HOW MANY PEOPLE WERE WITH YOU?
WHY ARE YOU ASKING ME THAT?
OH. QUITE A FEW.
NOBODY HAD A PHONE?
I...DON'T KNOW ANYBODY'S NUMBER ANYMORE. THEY'RE ALL IN THE PHONE. WHICH RAN OUT.
THE PERFECT LIE. I'M SO GOOD.

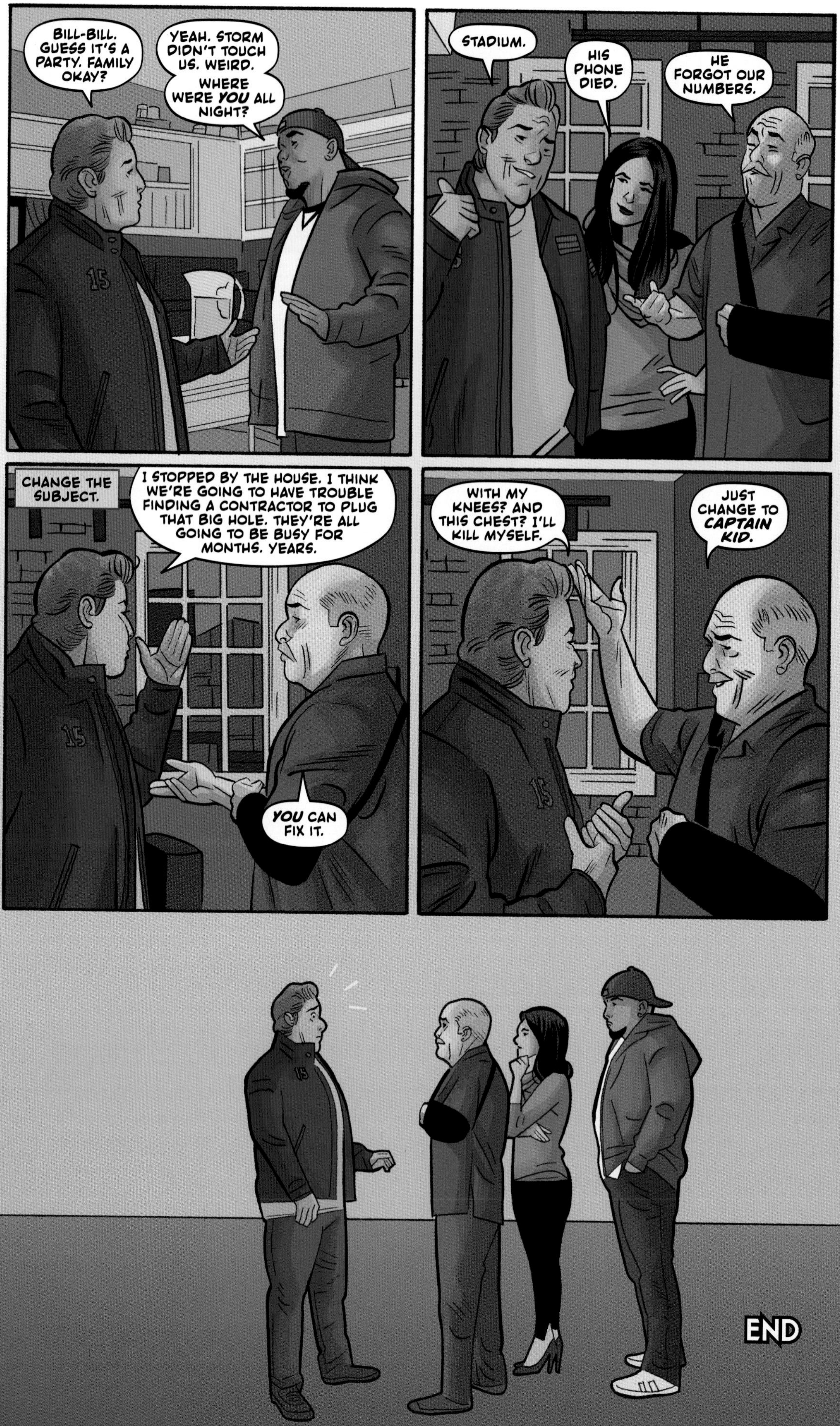
BILL-BILL. GUESS IT'S A PARTY. FAMILY OKAY?
YEAH. STORM DIDN'T TOUCH US. WEIRD.
WHERE WERE *YOU* ALL NIGHT?
STADIUM.
HIS PHONE DIED.
HE FORGOT OUR NUMBERS.
CHANGE THE SUBJECT.
I STOPPED BY THE HOUSE. I THINK WE'RE GOING TO HAVE TROUBLE FINDING A CONTRACTOR TO PLUG THAT BIG HOLE. THEY'RE ALL GOING TO BE BUSY FOR MONTHS. YEARS.
YOU CAN FIX IT.
WITH MY KNEES? AND THIS CHEST? I'LL KILL MYSELF.
JUST CHANGE TO *CAPTAIN KID.*
END

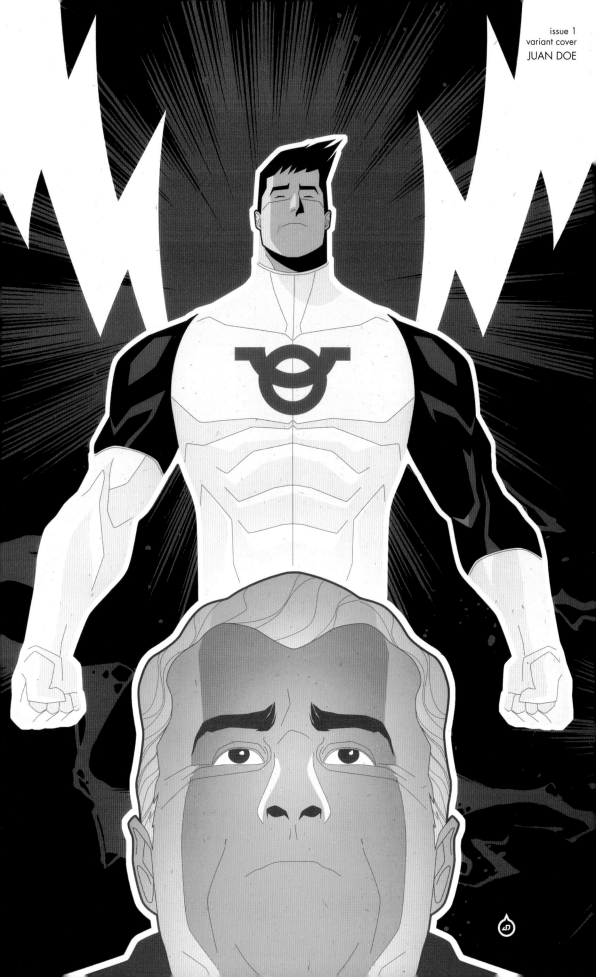

issue 1
variant cover
JUAN DOE

CHECK OUT THESE GREAT AFTERSHOCK
COLLECTIONS!

MARK WAID writer

@MarkWaid

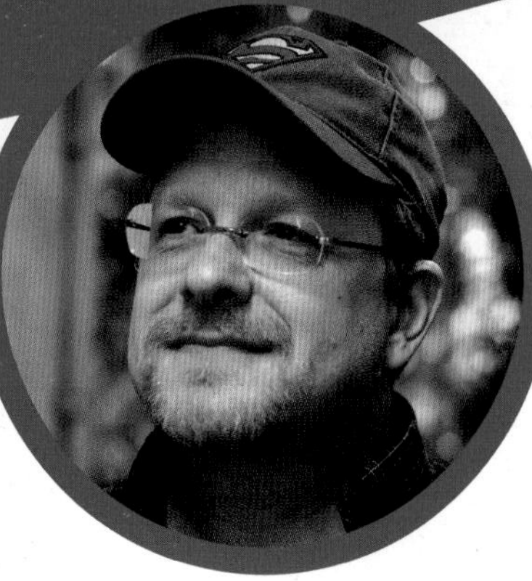

Mark Waid, a New York Times bestselling author, has worked for every major and minor publisher in comics during his thirty-year career. His best-known works include *Kingdom Come* (with artist Alex Ross), *Superman: Birthright*, his long runs on *Flash, Daredevil* and *Fantastic Four,* and his own series with co-creator Peter Krause, *Irredeemable,* currently under development as a feature film. Waid also runs his own digital publishing platform, Thrillbent.com, and co-owns a comics store (Aw Yeah Comics!) in Muncie, Indiana. When he's not trying to catch that long-overdue nap, you can find him on Twitter.

TOM PEYER writer

@TomPeyer

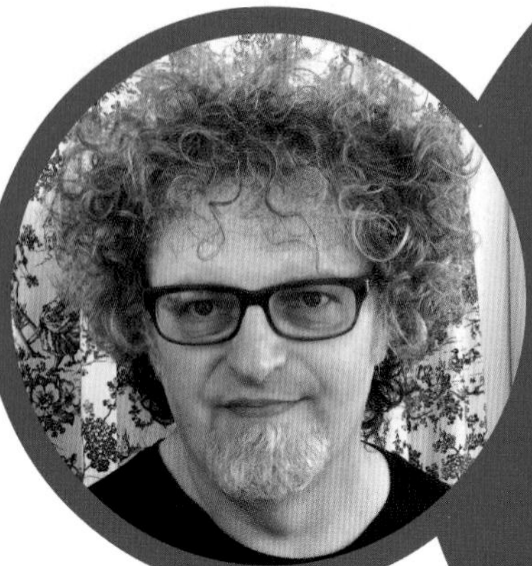

Tom has written stories for nearly every major comics character, but he's best known for his work on *Legion of Super-Heroes* and *Hourman.* He was a founding editor at DC/Vertigo, where he worked on *Doom Patrol, Hellblazer, Sandman* and many other titles. In recent years, he has written comics scripts for *Batman '66, The Atom* and *Twilight Zone.* He lives in Syracuse, NY.

WILFREDO TORRES artist

@mightyfineline

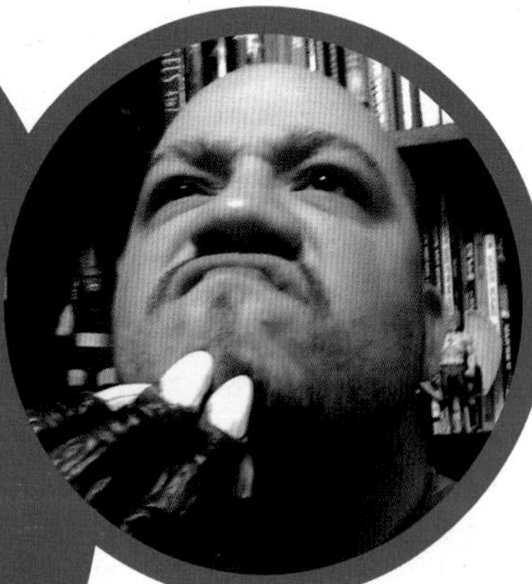

A self-taught artist, Wilfredo has been working professionally in the comic industry since 2007. He is best known for his work on Dynamite Entertainment's *The Shadow: Year One.* He has also worked on *Batman '66* (DC Comics), *Lobster Johnson: Prayer of Neferu* (Dark Horse Comics), *Quantum & Woody* (Valiant Entertainment) and most recently *Jupiter's Circle* (Millarworld/Image Comics).

KELLY FITZPATRICK colorist

@wastedwings

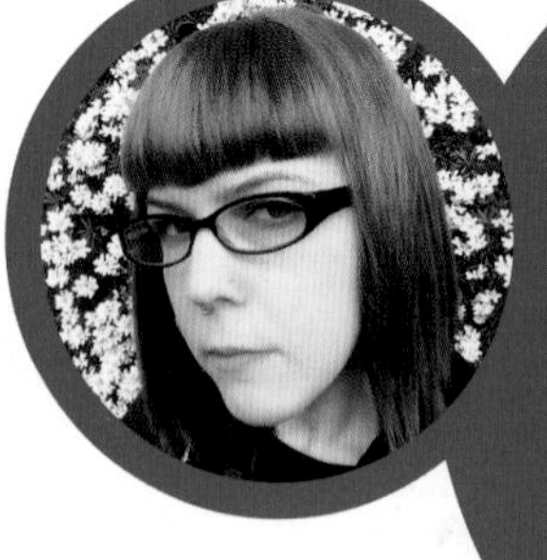

Kelly Fitzpatrick graduated with a BFA in Illustration/ minor in Photography and Digital Imaging from the Ringling College of Art and Design in Sarasota, FL in 2010. She started working in comics as a colorist assistant in 2013. Kelly has colored comics for companies such as Archie, Boom, Dark Horse, DC, Dynamite, IDW, Image, Oni, Stela, Valiant, etc. and is proud to be coloring now at AfterShock Comics!

A LARGER WORLD letterers

@A_Larger_World

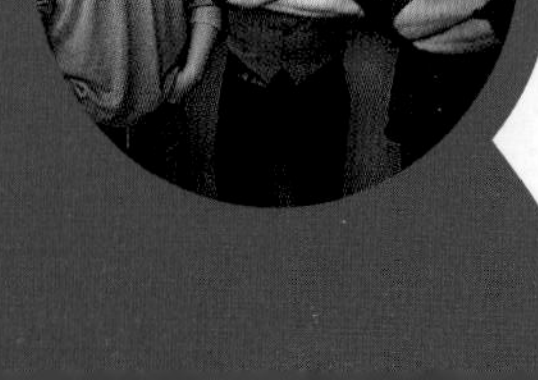

Troy Peteri, Dave Lanphear and Joshua Cozine are collectively known as A Larger World Studios. They've lettered everything from *The Avengers, Iron Man, Wolverine, Amazing Spider-Man* and *X-Men* to more recent titles like *The Spirit, Batman & Robin Eternal* and *Pacific Rim*. They can be reached at studio@largerworld.com for your lettering and design needs.